RECOVERY IN MENTAL ILLNESS

RECOVERY IN MENTAL ILLNESS

Broadening Our Understanding of Wellness

Edited by
**Ruth O. Ralph and
Patrick W. Corrigan**

American Psychological Association
Washington, DC

Published by
American Psychological Association
750 First Street, NE
Washington, DC 20002
www.apa.org

To order
APA Order Department
P.O. Box 92984
Washington, DC 20090-2984

Tel: (800) 374-2721; Direct: (202) 336-5510
Fax: (202) 336-5502; TDD/TTY: (202) 336-6123
Online: www.apa.org/books/
E-mail: order@apa.org

In the U.K., Europe, Africa, and the Middle East, copies may be ordered from
American Psychological Association
3 Henrietta Street
Covent Garden, London
WC2E 8LU England

Typeset in Goudy by Argosy, Waltham, MA

Printer: Victor Graphics, Inc., Baltimore, MD
Cover Designer: Aqueous Studio, Arlington, VA
Project Manager: Argosy, Waltham, MA

The opinions and statements published are the responsibility of the authors, and such opinions and statements do not necessarily represent the policies of the American Psychological Association.

Library of Congress Cataloging-in-Publication Data

Recovery in mental illness : broadening our understanding of wellness / edited by
   Ruth O. Ralph and Patrick W. Corrigan.
      p. cm.
   ISBN 1-59147-163-X
   1. Mentally ill—Rehabilitation. 2. Mental health. 3. Psychiatry—Research—
   Methodology. I. Ralph, Ruth O. II. Corrigan, Patrick W.

   RC439.5.R4228 2004
   616.89'1—dc22

                                                          2004003910

British Library Cataloguing-in-Publication Data

A CIP record is available from the British Library.

Printed in the United States of America
First Edition

To our fellow travelers in life who are recovered or in recovery.

CONTENTS

CONTRIBUTORS

Mary Jane Alexander, PhD, Center for the Study of Issues in Public Mental Health, Nathan Kline Institute, Orangeburg, NY

Mary Auslander, MSW, Center for the Study of Issues in Public Mental Health, Orangeburg, NY

Michael Boyle, MA, Fayette Companies, Peoria, IL

Joseph D. Calabrese, PhD Candidate, Committee on Human Development, University of Chicago, Chicago, IL

Patrick W. Corrigan, PsyD, Center for Psychiatric Rehabilitation, University of Chicago, Chicago, IL

Larry Davidson, PhD, School of Medicine and Institute for Social and Policy Studies, Yale University, New Haven, CT

Jeanne Dumont, PhD, Center for the Study of Issues in Public Mental Health, Orangeburg, NY

Alex Kopelowicz, MD, School of Medicine, University of California, Los Angeles

Robert P. Liberman, MD, Psychology Department, University of California, Los Angeles

David Loveland, PhD, Fayette Companies, Peoria, IL

Fred E. Markowitz, PhD, Department of Sociology, Northern Illinois University, Rockford

Kristina Muenzenmaier, MD, Department of Psychiatry, Albert Einstein College of Medicine, Bronx Psychiatric Center, New York

Maria O'Connell, PhD, Program for Recovery and Mental Health, Yale University, New Haven, CT

Ruth O. Ralph, PhD, Edmund S. Muskie School of Public Service, University of Southern Maine, Portland

Katie Weaver Randall, MA, University of Washington and Washington State Department of Social and Health Services, Mental Health Division, Olympia

Deborah A. Salem, PhD, Department of Psychology, Michigan State University, East Lansing

Stephanie Sangster, BA, Program for Recovery and Mental Health, Yale University, New Haven, CT

David Sells, PhD, Program for Recovery and Mental Health, Yale University, New Haven, CT

William White, MA, Chestnut Health Systems, Bloomington, IL

ACKNOWLEDGMENTS

This book could not have happened without inspiration, encouragement, and support from a variety of people. Consumer friends such as Ann Loder, Jeanne Dumont, Jean Campbell, Doug Dornan, Robert Lundin, Bonnie Schell, Yvette Sangster, and many others provided personal encouragement and support. Inspiration came from the writings and presentations of consumers who have lived recovery, such as Patricia Deegan, Dan Fisher, Judy Chamberlin, Sally Clay, and Ed Knight. Inspiration and encouragement also came from professionals who have advocated for and researched recovery such as Priscilla Ridgway, Steve Onken, Bill Anthony, and the authors of chapters in this book. Support—both personal and fiscal—came from Ron Manderscheid of the Center for Mental Health Services who provided opportunities for presentations, idea development, and writing.

Colleagues and friends at the Muskie School at the University of Southern Maine and the University of Chicago Center for Psychiatric Rehabilitation have been most supportive and proud of our work.

Encouragement and support also came from our families who believed in us and gave us the space and time to think and write and also discussed ideas and read papers. Ruth O. Ralph thanks her husband, Roger, her two sons and their wives, Tim and Monica, and Rob and Debby, and her extended family. Patrick W. Corrigan extends thanks to his wife, Georgeen, and his children, Abe and Liz.

I

OVERVIEW OF RECOVERY

1

INTRODUCTION: RECOVERY AS CONSUMER VISION AND RESEARCH PARADIGM

PATRICK W. CORRIGAN
AND RUTH O. RALPH

Recovery! This has been the clarion call shepherding radical change in the paradigms that explain mental health and mental health services during the past decade. Largely representing the intellectual product and lived experience of consumers, survivors, and ex-patients,[1] recovery champions a totally different picture of what it meant to be diagnosed with mental illness, especially a serious mental illness such as schizophrenia, major depression, or bipolar disorder. People with serious psychiatric disorders learned that, despite the symptoms and disabilities, mental illness need not irrevocably

---

[1]There is a debate among people with mental illness about the labels that should be used to refer to them. One preferred term is C/S/X: consumer (people who consume mental health services), survivor (people who have beaten their illness *and* the mental health system), and ex-patient, people who were, but no longer are, in need of services.

impede their life goals. Hope is a reality and psychological well-being is achievable.

With these kinds of messages, recovery signaled a monumental revolution in the mental health paradigm. Prior to this point, consumers had to foster ideas of hope and recovery and well-being in a mental health system that viewed serious psychiatric disorders as harbingers of doom. According to the old school, people with serious mental illness needed to accept that normal life was impossible, that dreams of independence were unattainable, and that long-term institutionalization was inescapable. Schizophrenia, in particular, was known as the kiss of death diagnosis with an essential treatment goal being the recognition of one's supreme limitations. In the face of such gloomy prognoses, notions of recovery seemed to be pipe dreams at best and just another delusional product of the illness.

As a result of this heritage, most psychologists, psychiatrists, and other mental health professionals were late arrivals to the idea of recovery. Prior to 1990, students of the major mental health disciplines learned that the serious mental illnesses were defined as poor prognoses with progressively downhill courses. Treatment was limited to custodial options. Hence, it is with uncertainty and trepidation that mental health professionals are learning to replace old notions that serious mental illness results in unconquerable disabilities with new ideas that all people can recover from mental illness.

Given this evolution, our book wishes to serve two masters in writing about recovery. First, it attempts to document the process by which consumers identified and came to fully understand recovery as a reality. Hence, some chapters in the book represent a consumer perspective on their community's experience with the phenomenon. Second, we write to professionals who seek to better understand recovery. What does it mean for their understanding of mental illness and for the services that are provided to people seeking recovery? Modern clinical practice is largely an evidence-based enterprise. Hence, answers to this question require a summary of the research. However, research of this topic seems to require more than traditional quantitative methodologies, as will be discussed repeatedly throughout the book.

The goal of this chapter is to briefly introduce the reader to what is meant by recovery. At this stage of our understanding, recovery comprises three related constructs:

1. *Recovery is a naturally occurring phenomenon.* Some people who meet diagnostic criteria for a serious mental illness are able to overcome their disabilities and fully enjoy a life in which their life goals are accomplished *without* any kind of treatment. Recovery for some is a spontaneously occurring event.
2. *As with other medical illnesses, people can recover from mental illness with proper treatment.* Others who do not enjoy spontaneous

recovery from mental illness are able to achieve a similar state of goal attainment and life satisfaction as the result of participating in a variety of services. These services may include psychopharmacological treatments as well as a variety of psychosocial interventions that have been demonstrated to lead to symptom reduction, disability resolution, ability to achieve life goals, and improved quality of life.

3. *Recovery reintroduces the idea of hope in understanding serious mental illness.* Recovery offers a beacon of light for people with serious mental illness. It means that even though a person is diagnosed with schizophrenia or other serious psychiatric disorder, his or her life need not be limited to institutions.

Each of these constructs is more thoroughly discussed later in this introductory chapter and developed more fully in one or more subsequent chapters of the book.

Note an interesting, as well as frustrating, result of the three different approaches to understanding recovery reviewed above. We are still without an answer to "Exactly what is meant by recovery?" In some ways, this uncertainty represents a split in the two ways in which recovery has been described: outcome versus process. Viewed as an outcome, recovery represents a change from a previously maladaptive state to a position of "normal" living. Note that change here is more than statistically significant improvement. Results of a clinical trial may be applauded if psychotic symptoms are reduced significantly after a trial of a new antipsychotic medication. Recovery as an outcome, however, means more than an improved state. It represents some kind of end point that approximates "normalcy." Although recovery does not necessarily mean being symptom free or without disability, descriptions of recovery as an outcome typically include accomplishing life goals in important life domains such as work and housing, as well as reporting both psychological well-being and improved quality of life. This kind of definition begs several questions that need to be addressed to come up with an understanding of recovery as outcome: How many goals must be achieved to be considered recovered? For that matter, how much life success is considered "normal"?

Many consumers find the definition of recovery as outcome to be unsatisfactory. It suggests an evaluative component; the patient is only a person if he or she meets some arbitrary and externally imposed criterion. As an alternative, this group proposes recovery as a process; namely, people who are concerned about their psychological well-being, struggling with their symptoms, and attempting their life goals are "in recovery" regardless of where they fall in terms of any outcome criteria. As a result, the process approach to recovery focuses less on measuring whether any change has occurred or end state has been achieved and instead concerns itself with indicators that represent the person is in recovery. Several important concepts in this area include the following:

- *Psychological well-being:* experiencing the present with both its satisfactions and its limitations as a personally meaningful and acceptable condition,
- *Hope:* looking toward the future with the promise of continued satisfaction and achievement despite the limitations that life may bring, and
- *Spirituality:* looking beyond the exigencies of the immediate world for inspiration and guidance.

Mental health professionals quickly realize that the concepts defining recovery as a process deal in ideas that are not grounded in typical theories of psychiatry and psychology.

RECOVERY AS A NATURALLY OCCURRING PHENOMENON

Emil Kraepelin (1913/1985), the father of modern psychopathology, first gave voice to the pessimistic ideas about serious mental illness that affected almost a century of subsequent ideas and services. According to Kraepelin, the prognosis of people diagnosed with schizophrenia is expected to be marked by a progressively degenerative, downhill course that is unresponsive to treatment. The etymology of Kraepelin's term for schizophrenia— *dementia praecox*—illustrates this point. Schizophrenia has all of the debilitating and unrelenting signs of dementia at a precocious age. This was the normal or naturally occurring result of having the disease. The psychiatric field endorsed this belief explicitly for more than 50 years. The degenerative downhill course was an explicit criterion in the first and second editions of the *Diagnostic and Statistical Manual of Mental Disorders* (DSM; American Psychiatric Association [APA], 1952, 1968) and was implied as a key criterion in *DSM–III* (APA, 1980). The implications are clear for those diagnosed with, as well as those who treated, the disorder. The outlook for people with schizophrenia was poor. Hence, patients, family members, and professionals needed to limit the possibilities and dreams for people diagnosed in the schizophrenia spectrum.

Consider how this prognostic paradigm should play out in long-term follow-up research. If Kraepelin were correct, following people diagnosed with schizophrenia at a young age for 20 or 30 years should yield the same end point; that is, they should be overwhelmed by psychotic symptoms, cognitively dysfunctional except for the most elementary tasks, and unable to maintain major roles in such important life domains as work, housing, and relationships. Researchers began just this line of research in the 1950s.

The chapter by Calabrese and Corrigan (chap. 3, this volume) more thoroughly reviews this line of research. Briefly, these studies identified adults who met the diagnostic criteria of the time for schizophrenia and who were relatively young (Johnstone, 1991). Researchers then repeated regular assessments to determine what became of these individuals. At the 20- and 30-year mark, they roughly found a rule of thirds (Harding, 1988). About one third of the sample seemed to have moved beyond the mental health system entirely and was pursuing life in what might be construed as "normal": competitive jobs, independent housing, and long-term relationships. About one third of the sample achieved a semblance of these goals with the support of a competent mental health system. About one third of the sample seemed to show a continued undulating course marked by periods of symptoms and significant disabilities interspersed with periods of relative remission. Note that only a third of this third (or one ninth of the entire sample) needed regular hospitalization to manage their illness. Hence, only about 10% of the group that Kraepelin predicted would end up demented actually showed any syndrome that approximated this end point.

The important group to focus on in terms of this definition of recovery is the first third, people who seemed to overcome their psychiatric illness without mental health services. This group suggests, contrary to fundamental principles of psychiatry, that a significant number of people with mental illness recover on their own. Put another way, the course of what has traditionally been considered an illness with a poor prognosis may include people who recover on their own. This conclusion is further supported by a separate body of research, nationwide epidemiological studies that have documented the prevalence of the major mental illnesses (Narrow, Rae, Robins, & Regier, 2002). One of the interesting findings in these analyses is the large number of people who meet diagnostic criteria for an illness such as schizophrenia but who never come to the attention of the mental health system (Wang, Demler, & Kessler, 2002). This finding may result from problems with the mental health system at the sociocultural level—either socioeconomic barriers that prevent distribution of ample services throughout the United States or stigma that dissuades potential patients from seeking services (Corrigan & Rusch, 2002). Alternatively, these findings may be explained by another conclusion: Many people who meet criteria for major mental illnesses are not sufficiently distressed to seek mental health services. Instead, they are able to cope with the difficulties using their existing skills and resources. Put another way, they achieve life goals, psychological well-being, and an improved quality of life naturally. Research has yet to specify the numbers within the population who fall into this category. Nevertheless, it is apparent that a large number of people seem to "recover" from mental illness without any intervention.

Note that another third of the samples in the long-term follow-up studies seemed to reach recovery after participating in mental health services (Harding, 1988). For some researchers, this frames recovery by understanding serious psychiatric disorder as a medical illness. Namely, careful diagnosis of the breadth and depth of a disorder, and corresponding prescription of treatments and services that target identified symptoms and disabilities, will produce recovery. The reader should note that we do not use "the medical model" in a pejorative sense here. Although others have written extensively about the injustices that have resulted from a medical perspective on mental illness (Chodoff, 2002; Svensson, 1995), we recognize that treating the illness in a medical sense has led to significant benefits for a segment of the population. Chapter 5, by Liberman and Kopelowicz, addresses this point in a comprehensive manner; their chapter is notable for attempting to define criteria that indicate a specific outcome or end point as recovery. We also acknowledge that the medical model has its limits in serving people with mental illness and in understanding the process of recovery. Several other chapters in the book (including the one authored by Davidson) review this point in depth.

Briefly, the point is that, like other medical illnesses, participation in aggressive treatment can lead to symptom remission, achievement of goals, and psychological well-being, all markers of recovery. Concurrent with the movement toward recognizing recovery during the past decade has been a call for evidenced-based treatment that is especially relevant to this medical model of recovery (Drake, Goldman, et al., 2001; Torrey et al., 2001). Namely, clinical and services researchers have asserted that the body of interventions made available for people with serious mental illness should be limited to those that have survived rigorous empirical testing. A list of services that consensus groups have identified as evidence-based includes the following:

- Assertive community treatment (Phillips et al., 2001),
- Family psychoeducation (Dixon et al., 2001),
- Illness self-management skills (Mueser et al., 2002),
- Integrated treatments for mental illness and substance abuse (Drake et al., 2001),
- Supported employment (Bond et al., 2001), and
- Targeted psychopharmacology (Mellman et al., 2001).

Evidence-based approaches yield both benefits and limitations. In terms of advantages, a focus on evidence-based approaches ensures that consumers will be involved only in services that have been shown to be effective. This is reassuring to all stakeholders who have witnessed a mental health system that has pursued treatments in the past that have not only been ineffective (e.g., psychoanalytic therapy for schizophrenia), but have also yielded unintended, but nevertheless egregious, effects (e.g., insulin shock therapy). Hence, a list of evidence-based treatments is an invaluable tool for the public mental health system. Facing ever-restricted budgets that fail to sufficiently fund the mental health service needs, public administrators can now decide to invest their resources in proven services (Goldman et al., 2001).

Disadvantages of evidence-based approaches have been cited. Some advocates have noted that the criteria for identifying a service as effective and worthwhile—an empirical evidence base—reflect the priorities of the research community, but not necessarily the community of consumers, survivors, and ex-patients (Fisher & Ahern, 2002; Frese, Stanley, Kress, & Vogel-Scibilia, 2001). In particular, empirical research does not necessarily include the kinds of epistemologies that led to the development of such important ideas of the consumer movement as empowerment and recovery (Corrigan, 2002; Van Tosh, Ralph, & Campbell, 2000). Moreover, empirical research approaches do not easily crosswalk with issues related to spirituality (Plante & Sherman, 2001), a construct that has a central role in many consumer conceptions of recovery. Finally, the excitement about evidence-based initiatives puts several possible intervention programs that may be effective candidates for treating people with mental illness into limbo. A prominent example here is the consumer-operated services, including support groups, drop-in centers, and education programs, that were developed by people with mental illness for people with mental illness (Davidson et al., 1999; Solomon & Draine, 2001). Although both consumer and mental health advocates have endorsed this approach as a fruitful avenue for meeting some of the needs of people with serious psychiatric disorders (Mueser et al., 2002), research meeting consensus standards for evidence-based practices is lacking. Hence, consumer-operated services do not make it onto the evidence-based practices list, thereby excluding what a sizable proportion of the consumer community believes to be an effective approach to issues related to recovery. Moreover, some investigators question whether typical outcome research strategies that govern assessment of clinical interventions such as the randomized trial are appropriate for research on consumer-operated services (Corrigan & Salzer, 2003; Humphreys & Rappaport, 1994).

The sometimes tenuous balance between the costs and benefits of an evidence-based approach needs to be worked out in additional intellectual enterprises that include empirical research. However, the moral is still apparent. A sizable portion of the mental health community that includes both providers and consumers view mental illness as a medical disorder and recovery as the outcome of effective treatment. This view defines the parameters that govern the second definition of recovery.

RECOVERY AS PROCESS

One of the unintended consequences of Kraepelin's views about serious mental illness was to remove hope from the prognosis of people with schizophrenia. One of the purposes of recovery as a movement that emerged from consumers, survivors, and ex-patients was to reinject hope into the lives of people diagnosed with these disorders. As a result, recovery from this perspective is less concerned about outcomes—whether the person achieves some kind of symptom- and disability-free end point—and more concerned about processes. What actions and activities foster an environment where a person's search for a meaningful life can be supported? As indicated earlier, several chapters in the book review this point in depth; see those by Ralph and by Davidson. Our goal here is to briefly introduce the reader to the spirit of recovery as a process.

An important bit of evidence that consumers, survivors, and ex-patients frequently call on to understand and embrace important constructs like recovery comes to us through the wisdoms of leaders in the consumer movement. Consider these:

> Recovery is a process, a way of life, an attitude, and a way of approaching the day's challenges. It is not a perfectly linear process. At times, our course is erratic and we falter, slide back, regroup, and start again. . . . The need is to meet the challenge of the disability and to re-establish a new and valued sense of integrity and purpose within and beyond the limits of the disability; the aspiration is to live, work, and love in a community in which one makes a significant contribution. (Deegan, 1988, p. 15)

> One of the elements that makes recovery possible is the regaining of one's belief in oneself. (Chamberlin, 1997, p. 9)

> Having some hope is crucial to recovery; none of us would strive if we believed it a futile effort. . . . I believe that if we confront our illnesses with courage and struggle with our symptoms persistently, we can overcome our handicaps to live independently, learn skills, and contribute to society, the society that has traditionally abandoned us. (Leete, 1988, p. 52)

> To return renewed with an enriched perspective of the human condition is the major benefit of recovery. To return at peace, with yourself, your experience, your world, and your God, is the major joy of recovery. (Granger, 1994, p. 10)

Note a common element in these statements: inspiration. For many people who write about this process, recovery is a personally meaningful goal rather than an abstract construct worthy of study.

An important construct in recovery as a process is psychological well-being. Rather than being symptom free and without disabilities, recovery here is more concerned with a sense of meaning in life and personal comfort. Intellectual work in this area has focused on such important ideas as validation of personhood, recognition of common humanity, and tolerance for individual differences (Campbell, 1992; Campbell & Schraiber, 1989). Note that although these are important concepts in the study of human development, these constructs have been largely absent from psychiatry.

An essential element of recovery as a process is empowerment. People must have the power to act on their decisions to produce an optimistic future that reflects their personal goals. Research has shown empowerment to be a complex phenomenon that includes a sense of personal control over one's environment and a feeling of agency in one's world (Rogers, Chamberlin, Ellison, & Crean, 1997; Segal, Silverman, & Temkin, 1995). Studies have also indicated that these forms of empowerment are highly correlated with measures of recovery that reflect process (Corrigan, Giffort, Rashid, Leary, & Okeke, 1999; Corrigan, Salzer, Ralph, Sangster, & Keck, in press). These points are developed more fully in later chapters of the book. We wish only to highlight the intimate role of empowerment in understanding recovery.

Although recovery as process deals in issues of purpose and vision, this perspective does not mean that assertions like those above escape research evaluation. Ralph (2000) reviewed more than a dozen studies that have examined some component of the process involved in recovery. Two points are important here. First, consumers and others who embrace recovery as a process still recognize the value of empirical research of this construct. Only with these kinds of analyses can we separate validated aspects of the processes from biased perceptions. Second, investigations of recovery as process offer some significant methodological problems. Note, however, that our presentation of the other two definitions of recovery also highlighted methodological conundrums in studying these concepts. We do not believe that the presence of barriers in using more traditional research methods highlights a failure of the theory as much as a challenge for researchers to develop strategies for testing this theory.

HOW DIFFERENT MODELS OF RECOVERY PLAY OUT

The theoretical distinctions among the three paradigms of recovery are more apparent when placed in the real world. Consider how different stakeholder groups gravitate to each model. Family groups and most mental health providers frequently define recovery as an outcome. Important to them is the idea that their patient or family member "gets better"; that they somehow overcome the symptoms and disabilities that trouble them and society so much (Lefley, 1997). Consumer, survivor, and ex-patient groups are more likely to embrace recovery as a naturally occurring phenomenon or as process (Ralph, 2000). They have frequently experienced the outcome desires of seemingly well-intentioned family members and service providers as imposed on them, not relevant to their experience, and sometimes harmful. Consumer groups are troubled by how mental illness and its treatment system are a tremendous burden—burden in the sense of lost hope and stolen goals—which they seek to overcome.

These differences are tangible when viewing varying perspectives on treatment and services. Consider programs of assertive community training (PACT) as an example of this distinction. Most provider and family groups have endorsed this as an essential mechanism for the recovery of people with the most serious of disabilities (Mueser, Bond, Drake, & Resnick, 1998; Phillips et al., 2001). The PACT team helps people with mental illness overcome the kinds of disabilities that result in their hospitalization. In addition, regular and aggressive services assist the person to remain independent in his or her community. Consumer, survivor, and ex-patient groups, however, are sensitive to the loss of empowerment in some versions of PACT. Control over individually relevant goals may be lost in such programs. As a result, an alternative to PACT called *personal assistance in community existence* (PACE) has been proposed as a way to assist people in recovering from mental illness that is based on self-determination, respect, and noncoercion, all concepts that are central to viewing recovery as a process (Fisher & Ahern, 2000). An even more emotionally loaded example is mandated treatments such as outpatient commitment. Family groups and providers are often in strong disagreement with consumer and survivor groups on this issue. If recovery from medical illness—where all symptoms are remitted and disabilities resolved—is the goal, it makes sense to mandate services for those individuals who are not currently capable of recognizing what will "cure" them (Torrey & Zdanowicz, 2001). Conversely, coercing or in some other way requiring people to participate in treatment is antithetical to notions of empowerment and goal setting. Many consumer, survivor, and ex-patient groups are vociferous opponents of mandated services.

Clearly, these models are diverse, potent, and effective in the real world. More and more, the vision of recovery is being embraced by all facets of the mental health community. In a recent example, President George W. Bush's National New Freedom Commission on Mental Health featured a recovery-based continuum of care as fundamental for the new generations of system's development (http://www.mentalhealthcommission.gov/reports/reports.htm). Our goal in the remainder of the book is to more fully develop how the diversity and effectiveness of different models of recovery play out in accomplishing this vision.

AN ORGANIZED SYNOPSIS OF THE BOOK'S CHAPTERS

Thus far, we have alluded to the relevance of other chapters for answering the overall question "What is recovery?" We provide a more organized discussion of the book's chapters here. Through the individual chapters of the book, we attempt to provide a comprehensive overview of recovery by weaving the strongly considered views of some consumer investigators with the dispassionate view of mental health researchers. The first group brings to the book a combination of intellectual knowledge of and lived experience with recovery. The second group attacks questions about recovery with the methodological rigor with which all concepts about human behavior need to be broached. By the way, research in our book is meant in the broadest tradition of social science. It not only includes the internally valid approaches of psychologists, but also methods more common in sociology that represent externally valid concerns. Moreover, research includes not only quantitative approaches, but also the rich field of qualitative methods, including concerns voiced by ethnographers and phenomenologists. This mix of research approaches makes for difficult bedfellows at times. Of course, the tension from a variety of perspectives for investigating social phenomena is not unique to questions of recovery. We hope that some of this tension is evident in the diverse perspectives of the authors of chapters within this book.

Note that this book is divided into three parts. Part I provides an overview and combines this introductory chapter with a review by David Loveland and colleagues that examines the question of what it means to "investigate" the concept of recovery. Part II comprises five chapters that offer models representing one or more of the three perspectives on recovery. Joseph Calabrese and Patrick Corrigan summarize the long-term follow-up research that produced the idea that recovery is a naturally occurring phenomenon in chapter 3. Fred Markowitz provides the sociologist's perspective on recovery, including a review of some of his own research, in chapter 4. Robert Liberman and Alex Kopelowicz review their extensive series of investigations on defining criteria that describe recovery as outcome in chapter 5.

When the surgeon general prepared his first report on mental health published in 1999, he convened a panel of consumers to provide feedback on various components including recovery. A key action resulting from this was development of a Recovery Advisory Group that, over several months of teleconference discussions, developed a model of recovery. Ruth Ralph, who chaired this committee, reviews their conclusions in chapter 6. Larry Davidson, a champion of phenomenological perspectives, and colleagues apply that method to recovery in chapter 7.

Notions of illness and recovery are crafted by the culture in which the person is immersed. The Western mental health system has been dominated by the medical model for understanding psychiatric illness. Recovery may be better understood when it is framed in terms of a diverse set of perspectives, both Western and international. Part III targets this goal.

Katie Weaver Randall and Deborah Salem summarize the relationship between recovery in mutual-help groups in chapter 8. In chapter 9, Mary Jane Alexander and colleagues shed light on recovery by reviewing the perspective as it is understood in terms of trauma. In chapter 10, William White, Michael Boyle, and David Loveland attempt to bridge recovery as discussed in the substance abuse community with ways it is understood in mental health.

UNLIKELY BEDFELLOWS

One of the many goals of this introduction was to highlight the diverse perspectives on recovery from mental illness. In the process, we hoped to show that producing a single definition of recovery may be an insurmountable task. Previous writings on the topic have chosen to handle this challenge by ignoring the diversity of perspectives and limiting their definition to a natural phenomenon, outcome, or process. As a result, authors end up describing recovery in a manner that seems unrecognizable to a significant set of readers. If nothing else, our goal was to highlight the complexity of the phenomenon. The authors on the subsequent pages of this book are some of the national leaders in this endeavor. We hope their thoughts enhance the reader's perceptions.

REFERENCES

American Psychiatric Association. (1952). *Diagnostic and statistical manual of mental disorders* (1st ed.). Washington, DC: Author.

American Psychiatric Association. (1968). *Diagnostic and statistical manual of mental disorders* (2nd ed.). Washington, DC: Author.

American Psychiatric Association. (1980). *Diagnostic and statistical manual of mental disorders* (3rd ed.). Washington, DC: Author.

Bond, G. R., Becker, D. R., Drake, R. E., Rapp, C. A., Meisler, N., Lehman, A. F., et al. (2001). Implementing supported employment as an evidence-based practice. *Psychiatric Services, 52,* 313–322.

Campbell, J. (1992). The Well-Being Project: Mental health clients speak for themselves. In *Third Annual Conference Proceedings on State Mental Health Agency Research* (p. 16). Alexandria, VA: NASMHPD Research Institute.

Campbell, J., & Schraiber, R. (1989). *The Well-Being Project: Mental health clients speak for themselves.* Sacramento, CA: California Department of Mental Health.

Chamberlin, J. (1997). Confessions of a non-compliant patient. *National Empowerment Center Newsletter, 122*. Lawrence, MA: National Empowerment Center.

Chodoff, P. (2002). The medicalization of the human condition. *Psychiatric Services, 53*, 627–628.

Corrigan, P. W. (2002). Empowerment and serious mental illness: Treatment partnerships and community opportunities. *Psychiatric Quarterly, 73*, 217–228.

Corrigan, P. W., Giffort, D., Rashid, F., Leary, M., & Okeke, I. (1999). Recovery as a psychological construct. *Community Mental Health Journal, 35*, 231–239.

Corrigan, P. W., & Rusch, N. (2002). Mental illness stereotypes and service use: Do people avoid treatment because of stigma? *Psychiatric Rehabilitation Skills, 6*, 312–334.

Corrigan, P. W., & Salzer, M. (2003). The conflict between random assignment and treatment choice: Implications for internal validity. *Evaluation and Program Planning, 26*, 109–111.

Corrigan, P. W., Salzer, M., Ralph, R., Sangster, Y., & Keck, L. (in press). Examining the factor structure of the Recovery Assessment Scale. Manuscript submitted for publication.

Davidson, L., Chinman, M., Kloos, B., Weingarten, R., Stayner, D., & Tebes, J. K. (1999). Peer support among individuals with severe mental illness: A review of the evidence. *Clinical Psychology-Science & Practice, 6*, 165–187.

Deegan, P. E. (1988). Recovery: The lived experience of rehabilitation. *Psychosocial Rehabilitation Journal, 11*, 11–19.

Dixon, L., McFarlane, W. R., Lefley, H., Lucksted, A., Cohen, M., Falloon, I., et al. (2001). Evidence-based practices for services to families of people with psychiatric disabilities. *Psychiatric Services, 52*, 903–910.

Drake, R. E., Essock, S. M., Shaner, A., Carey, K. B., Minkoff, K., Kola, L., et al. (2001). Implementing dual diagnosis services for clients with severe mental illness. *Psychiatric Services, 52*, 469–476.

Drake, R. E., Goldman, H. E., Leff, H. S., Lehman, A. F., Dixon, L., Mueser, K. T., & Torrey, W. C. (2001). Implementing evidence-based practices in routine mental health service settings. *Psychiatric Services, 52*, 179–182.

Fisher, D. B., & Ahern, L. (2000). Personal assistance in community existence (PACE): An alternative to PACT. *Ethical Human Sciences & Services, 2*, 87–92.

Fisher, D. B., & Ahern, L. (2002). Evidenced-based practices and recovery. *Psychiatric Services, 53*, 632–633.

Frese, F. J., Stanley, J., Kress, K., & Vogel-Scibilia, S. (2001). Integrating evidence-based practices and the recovery model. *Psychiatric Services, 52*, 1462–1468.

Goldman, H. H., Ganju, V., Drake, R. E., Gorman, P., Hogan, M., Hyde, P. S., & Morgan, O. (2001). Policy implications for implementing evidence-based practices. *Psychiatric Services, 52*, 1591–1597.

Granger, D. A. (1994). Recovery from mental illness: A first person perspective of an emerging paradigm. In *Recovery: The new force in mental health* (p. 10). Columbus, OH: Ohio Department of Mental Health.

Harding, C. M. (1988). Course types in schizophrenia: An analysis of European and American studies. *Schizophrenia Bulletin, 14*, 633–643.

Humphreys, K., & Rappaport, J. (1994). Researching self-help/mutual aid groups and organizations: Many roads, one journey. *Applied & Preventive Psychology, 3*, 217–231.

Johnstone, E. C. (Ed). (1991). Disabilities and circumstances of schizophrenic patients: A follow-up study. *British Journal of Psychiatry, 159*(Suppl. 3), 46.

Kraepelin, E. (1985). *Lectures on clinical psychiatry.* Birmingham, AL: Classics of Medicine Library. (Original work published 1913)

Leete, E. (1988). A consumer perspective on psychosocial treatment. *Psychosocial Rehabilitation Journal, 12*, 45–52.

Lefley, H. P. (1997). The consumer recovery vision: Will it alleviate family burden? *American Journal of Orthopsychiatry, 67*, 210–219.

Mellman, T. A., Miller, A. L., Weissman, E. M., Crismon, M. L., Essock, S. M., & Marder, S. R. (2001). Evidence-based pharmacologic treatment for people with severe mental illness: A focus on guidelines and algorithms. *Psychiatric Services, 52*, 619–625.

Mueser, K. T., Bond, G. R., Drake, R. E., & Resnick, S. G. (1998). Models of community care for severe mental illness: A review of research on case management. *Schizophrenia Bulletin, 24*, 37–74.

Mueser, K. T., Corrigan, P. W., Hilton, D. W., Tanzman, B., Schaub, A., Gingerich, S., et al. (2002). Illness management and recovery: A review of the research. *Psychiatric Services, 53*, 1272–1284.

Narrow, W. E., Rae, D. S., Robins, L. N., & Regier, D. A. (2002). Revised prevalence based estimates of mental disorders in the United States: Using a clinical significance criterion to reconcile 2 surveys' estimates. *Archives of General Psychiatry, 59*, 115–123.

Phillips, S. D., Burns, B. J., Edgar, E. R., Mueser, K. T., Linkins, K. W., Rosenheck, R. A., et al. (2001). Moving assertive community treatment into standard practice. *Psychiatric Services, 52*, 771–779.

Plante, T. G., & Sherman, A. C. (2001). Research on faith and health: New approaches to old questions. In T. G. Plante & A. C. Sherman (Eds.), *Faith and health: Psychological perspectives.* New York: Guilford Press.

Ralph, R. (2000). Recovery. *Psychiatric Rehabilitation Skills, 4*, 480–517.

Rogers, E. S., Chamberlin, J., Ellison, M. L., & Crean, T. (1997). A consumer-constructed scale to measure empowerment among users of mental health services. *Psychiatric Services, 48*, 1042–1047.

Segal, S. P., Silverman, C., & Temkin, T. (1995). Measuring empowerment in client-run self-help agencies. *Community Mental Health Journal, 31*, 215–227.

Solomon, P., & Draine, J. (2001). The state of knowledge of the effectiveness of consumer provided services. *Psychiatric Rehabilitation Journal, 25*, 20–27.

Svensson, T. (1995). *On the notion of mental illness: Problematizing the medical-model conception of certain abnormal behaviour and mental afflictions*. Brookfield, VT: Avebury.

Torrey, E. F., & Zdanowicz, M. (2001). Outpatient commitment: What, why, and for whom. *Psychiatric Services, 52*, 337–341.

Torrey, W. C., Drake, R. E., Dixon, L., Burns, B. J., Flynn, L., Rush, A. J., et al. (2001). Implementing evidence-based practices for persons with severe mental illnesses. *Psychiatric Services, 52*, 45–50.

Van Tosh, L., Ralph R. O., & Campbell, J. (2000). The rise of consumerism. *Psychiatric Rehabilitation Skills, 4*, 383–409.

Wang, P. S., Demler, O., & Kessler, R. C. (2002). Adequacy of treatment for serious mental illness in the United States. *American Journal of Public Health, 92*, 92–98.

2

RESEARCH METHODS FOR EXPLORING AND ASSESSING RECOVERY

DAVID LOVELAND, KATIE WEAVER RANDALL,
AND PATRICK W. CORRIGAN

The purpose of this chapter is to examine the methodological issues involved in researching the phenomenon of recovery from mental illness. Because of the nascent stage of research on this evolving phenomenon, information regarding useful strategies and methodologies for investigating recovery is limited (Corrigan, Giffort, Rashid, Leary, & Okeke, 1999; Harding, Brooks, Ashikaga, Strauss, & Breier, 1987; Morse, 1997; Ralph, 2000). Therefore, this chapter focuses on what research strategies have been used to study recovery, their strengths and weaknesses, the ideological and epistemological issues that need to be considered when using certain strategies, and some suggestions for future research.

Although a primary purpose of this book is to begin to create a knowledge base for understanding recovery, there is no consensus on how recovery should be defined (e.g., as a process or an end state) or how it should be measured. This lack of an agreed-on conceptual model or paradigm presents problems for researchers who are looking for guidance on how to measure people's recovery from mental illness. Despite the absence of an explicit conceptual definition of recovery from mental illness, researchers are influenced by implicit assumptions regarding the investigation of this or any other human phenomenon. It is these implicit assumptions, which stem from theoretical paradigms and specific epistemologies, that have traditionally guided the selection of methodologies and research designs in the mental health field and which, in turn, predetermine the scope of the inquiry (Caplan & Nelson, 1973; Kingry-Westergaard & Kelly, 1990).

Before delving into a discussion of methodologies and research designs for measuring recovery, we need to examine the underlying epistemological assumptions that researchers investigating mental illness possess regarding the acquisition of knowledge and consequently how these assumptions influence the questions asked, how people are viewed and treated in the research process, and what is considered valuable (i.e., legitimate) information.

RELATIONSHIP BETWEEN EPISTEMOLOGY AND METHODOLOGY

The selection of a method or a combination of methods to examine the process of recovery, or any other human phenomenon, is determined by multiple factors, such as the researcher's bias and epistemological views, theoretical formulations and definitions of phenomena, and the basic questions that research is intended to answer, which are related to the first two factors. This section addresses the first issue of epistemology, and the following section deals with the second issue of definition and theoretical formulations.

Many methods are available for collecting data in research, each having advantages and disadvantages. No one method or collection of methods is better suited than others for all research (Shadish, 1990). The appropriateness of any method is based on the goals of the research (Cronbach, 1982). Conversely, the selection of a particular methodology will determine what data can be collected and, subsequently, what questions can be answered by the research. Furthermore, what is considered valuable or relevant data also influences the selection of research methods, which, in turn, influences what is collected. What is considered to be valuable data is influenced by one's epistemological assumptions about what constitutes knowledge and how it can be observed and measured (Guba & Lincoln, 1989).

Epistemology focuses on how knowledge is generated and viewed and beliefs about reality or the "truth." In psychology, psychiatry, and related fields, researchers have been influenced primarily by one of two epistemological perspectives: positivism or constructivism. Table 2.1 displays the major distinctions between these two ways of knowing.

Historically, the dominant epistemological perspective that has guided research in psychology and related mental health fields has been termed the positivist, conventional, or scientific model (Guba & Lincoln, 1989; Manicas & Secord, 1983). The positivist epistemology promotes a hypothetico-

TABLE 2.1
Comparison of Positivism and Constructivism

Issue	Positivism	Constructivism
Purpose of research	Explanation; prediction and control	Understanding; reconstruction
Nature of knowledge	Single truth, established through empirical research	Knowledge is constructed through consensus
Values	Excluded—influence denied	Included—value driven
Types of data	Quantitative data	Qualitative data
Types of analysis	Deductive hypotheses testing, statistical analyses	Inductive analysis, thematic content analysis
Perspective	Objective	Subjective
Style of data collection	Distant, aloof, assumed to be unbiased	Close to the phenomenon of study, interacting with people, acknowledge biases
Assumptions of behavior	Linear, sequential modeling, and interactions	Systems perspective and dynamic transactions between people and context
Style of change	Beginning and end states, pre–post focus	Dynamic and ongoing change
Style of research	Fixed, controlled designs	Emergent, flexible designs

Note. From Guba and Lincoln (1994) and Patton (1997).

deductive methodology consisting of quantitative measures, experimental designs, and statistical analyses; it emphasizes maintaining prediction and control over contextual factors (Patton, 1997; Riger, 1990). The positivist paradigm posits that the observer can and should remain distant and detached in order to objectively record phenomena as they occur. Moreover, researchers are expected to remain value free and unbiased toward the phenomena or group being studied (Guba & Lincoln, 1994). Within a positivist framework, there is a single, measurable truth that can be generalized across people, contexts, and situations.

A second epistemological perspective that has been gaining support in psychology and related fields is called the constructivist view of human behavior (Kingry-Westergaard & Kelly, 1990; Strauss, 1992). The constructivist view asserts that there are multiple, socially constructed realities and that "truth" is based on consensus among perspectives rather than on immutable laws of nature. This assertion is central to the constructivist perspective because it reflects the belief that laws or truth may change over time and across different contexts. In the constructivist paradigm, the roles of researcher and participant are replaced by a collaborative relationship that leads to the generation of research questions, research design, and methods of inquiry. Researchers in this paradigm are driven by strong values and an awareness, indeed a desire, that people will experience positive change through their involvement in the research process (Rappaport, 1990). The constructivist paradigm promotes a hermeneutical–dialectical methodology consisting of qualitative data and naturalistic inquiry; it emphasizes the dynamic, nonlinear movement of human behavior, transactions between people and society, and reiteration of information leading to a joint construction of meaning and definition (Guba & Lincoln, 1994).

These descriptions of positivism and constructivism represent absolute or polarized perspectives of knowledge generation, but probably do not reflect actual practice. In reality, whether researchers endorse the positivist or constructivist perspective, they are usually concerned about similar issues, such as reliability and meaningfulness of the data, validity and generalization of the findings, and overall quality and rigor of the research. Nonetheless, the purpose of delineating these two perspectives illustrates how they can implicitly or explicitly influence the research process. The epistemological view one adopts, as well as the theoretical model that is used to guide the research (discussed in the next section), influences the selection of particular research questions, designs, methodologies, and procedures for analyzing data. In other words, epistemology and the selection of methodologies for data collection are interrelated aspects of any research endeavor, whether the researcher is aware of it or not.

In practice, most researchers implicitly use a positivist or conventional perspective, but even for those who are guided by a constructivist perspective, the underlying epistemological perspective that guides researchers has implications for how the research is carried out, what phenomenon can be investigated, and the type of knowledge generated. For instance, certain tacit assumptions and common practices reflect the positivist or the constructivist view of knowledge. A sample of these common practices and assumptions regarding the investigation of recovery are listed in Table 2.2.

Before suggesting whether these assumptions and practices are appropriate for the investigation of recovery from mental illness or which epistemological view is more useful, it is helpful to understand how recovery is being conceptualized and how it is being applied, which can help guide the selection of an appropriate research paradigm, study design, and measurement tools.

RELATIONSHIP BETWEEN DEFINITIONS OF RECOVERY AND METHODOLOGY

The concept of recovery from mental illness is not new to the mental health field. However, how recovery has been defined, beliefs about whether recovery from serious mental illness is possible, and where the definition of

TABLE 2.2
Relationship Between Epistemology and Research Practices

	Common Practices	Benefits	Limitations
	Reducing recovery to measurable components	Can more easily compare recovery stages within people over time and across people	Cannot examine the individual process of recovery
	Creating relatively stable constructs of recovery (i.e., a single, consistent reality of recovery)	Can be used to develop reliable, standardized measures of recovery and is useful for quantitative methods of research	Cannot examine the potential dynamic and transforming nature of recovery within people over time
Positivistic View of Recovery	Creating surveys and other "reliable" and "valid" measures of recovery (using the classic measurement definitions of reliability and validity; see, for example, Nunnally and Bernstein (1994)	Objective measures that can be used to examine the efficacy and effectiveness of clinical and nonclinical interventions to enhance the recovery process; useful and inexpensive for program evaluations	Reduces the dynamic, individualized nature of the recovery process into static, general measures and, thus, it may be unrealistic to assume that measures are objective
	Measuring recovery outcomes in short periods of time (e.g., less than 2 years)	Lower research costs; more information can be generated in shorter periods of time	May truncate the actual recovery process
	Viewing change in terms of linear movement	Lends itself to established general linear models for statistical analyses	Cannot detect nonlinear, reciprocal, nested, or dynamic trends
	Adopting a value-free stance toward participants and the phenomenon under investigation	Impartial and unbiased; useful for multisite studies and the assessment of program fidelity	Unrealistic expectation, disempowering practice for research participants, and potentially misleading

(continues)

	Common Practices	Benefits	Limitations
Constructivist View of Recovery	Measuring recovery as a dynamic, multidimensional, and interrelated phenomenon	Captures the unfolding, individualized process as well as the comprehensive nature of the process	Difficult to measure or compare across people and difficult to use for evaluation of programs or other structured interventions
	Uncovering aspects or components of the recovery process through qualitative interviews	Highly individualized; can capture context; useful for exploratory research	Difficult to replicate the findings, thus, limiting the ability to use multiple sites or replication studies and is resource intensive
	Measuring recovery as an ongoing process with no end state	Captures the lifelong, fluid process of recovery; useful for measuring changes in peoples' psychological, spiritual, and interpersonal domains over time	Difficult to translate into meaningful, short-term benchmarks that could be used for evaluating the efficacy of interventions
	Viewing change in terms of nonlinear, reciprocal transactions that are nested within context	Can be used to evaluate the transactions between people and their environment in the process of recovery; incorporates context into the evaluation process	Difficult to measure and statistically analyze and more resources are needed to measure multiple levels of analyses and more frequent time points
	Adopting a collaborative, valued model with research participants	Empowering process that allows knowledge to evolve over time and acknowledges the influence of researchers on the recovery process	Alters the research process and outcomes across sites; resource intensive and usually time consuming

recovery have been coming from have changed during the past 200 years. Until recently, the definition of recovery was restricted by the medical model and was usually defined as the complete remission of symptoms. Dr. Benjamin Rush's book *Medical Inquiries and Observations Upon the Diseases of the Mind* (1812), in which he argued that mental illness was curable through medical treatment, had a profound impact on the concept of mental illness and recovery and established, by default, the biomedical paradigm as the guiding framework for defining and treating mental illness in the United States (Deutsch, 1949). The biomedical model of mental illness, which Rush helped establish in the early 1800s, provides theoretical justification for relying on professional and researcher-generated definitions of recovery and for using specific methodologies.

Early use of the term *recovery* was ascribed to hospital superintendents who were reporting treatment outcomes of people admitted and discharged from their asylums (Bockoven, 1972). Data collection consisted of simple counts, compiled from hospital records, of people who were discharged as either recovered or improved. Their definition of recovery usually consisted of elimination of observed symptoms, at least during the hospital stay. Using these methods, Worcester State Hospital—the first state-operated psychiatric asylum in the United States—reported annual recovery rates of approximately 70% from 1833 to 1852 (Bockoven, 1972; Deutsch, 1949). These recovery rates were inflated by excluding those individuals who were admitted but never discharged and not controlling for the large number of people who were cycling back through the hospitals. The failure to account for the cycling of many patients ended in 1887 with the publication of Dr. Pliny Earle's book *The Curability of Insanity* (1885/1994), in which he exposed the invalid statistical procedures used for computing recovery rates. Earle's recalculated recovery rates were at or below 30% annually for most of the major asylums of the 19th century. Although the term *recovery* was still used to describe discharges, Earle's report led to the immutable beliefs, fortified by Emil Kraepelin's research on dementia praecox at the turn of the century (Alexander & Selesnick, 1966), that serious forms of mental illness were almost always incurable, usually led to progressive deterioration, and were unresponsive to treatment.

Beliefs about the possibility of recovery changed in the first half of the 20th century when somatic interventions, such as shock therapies (e.g., insulin, Metrazol, and electric shock treatment [ECT]), psychosurgery, and early psychopharmacology were used (Grob, 1994; Pressman, 1998). The hope of curing mental illness through somatic interventions reintroduced what Pressman (1998) termed the "revived cult of curability" (p. 159). Again, the term *recovery* used during this period was based on the medical model and consisted of the elimination of symptoms caused by mental illness. This definition of recovery did not necessarily include a return to normal functioning in society, which partially explains why psychosurgery and shock therapies were initially considered to be effective (Pressman, 1998; Valenstein, 1986). Consistent with the medical model, the physician or mental health professional, rather than people who were diagnosed with a mental illness, defined recovery (Grob, 1994; Pressman, 1998). As a result, the methods used to evaluate these interventions focused on observed behaviors, as viewed and interpreted by physicians and other clinicians. People diagnosed with mental illness were rarely given the opportunity to voice what outcomes were of importance to them or their experience of recovery.

Because of limitations of the biomedical model at explaining the onset, treatment, and potential recovery from mental illness, an expanded model was introduced in the late 1970s that incorporated the dynamic interactions among biological, psychological, and environmental or socio-political factors that influence the labeling, diagnosing, treatment, and course of any nonacute illness (Engel, 1977; Kiesler, 2000; Smith & Nicassio, 1995). This biopsychosocial model of mental illness indicated that people are not diagnosed with a mental illness nor do they recover from it in a biological vacuum, but rather that interpersonal, contextual, sociopolitical, and socioeconomic factors influence the interpretation, onset, and course of mental illness (Kiesler, 2000). This paradigm of illness (e.g., see Engel, 1977) suggests that methods used in researching the course and recovery process from mental illness need to capture the multidimensional and transactional nature of the process, such as measuring changes in biological (e.g., symptoms of the mental illness, genetic influence), psychological (e.g., interpersonal coping skills, resilience, cognitive stages of change), environmental (e.g., access to effective psychosocial rehabilitation programs and supportive social networks), and sociopolitical factors (e.g., impact of stigma from the community, attributes of the treatment system, and the impact of consumer advocacy) over time.

The biopsychosocial paradigm of mental illness has gained acceptance among mental health researchers (Department of Health and Human Services [DHHS], 1999; Kiesler, 2000). However, it has proved more difficult to examine as a heuristic than the biomedical model and, therefore, has been minimally tested as a paradigm for assessing the process of recovery. Several long-term longitudinal studies and evaluations of clinical interventions (discussed later) have incorporated multidimensional measurement protocols to capture changes in peoples' lives beyond the reduction of symptoms, such as employment, independent living, and quality of life, but only a few studies were found that attempted to examine the transactional relationship among these domains (e.g., Strauss, Hafez, Lieberman, & Harding, 1985). A detailed discussion of these studies is presented in the next section.

A third, more recent model of recovery has been introduced through the rise of the consumer advocacy movement in the United States. As consumers of mental health services have gained more voice around issues that impact their lives, a new understanding of recovery has emerged based on their lived experience with a psychiatric disability (Deegan, 1988). This understanding of recovery was introduced in the 1970s with the rise of the consumer/survivor/ex-patient (C/S/X) movement (Chamberlin, 1990; Frese & Davis, 1997; Kaufmann, 1999) and is the only one of the three paradigms discussed in this chapter that is not based on a disease model framework. This view has emanated from individuals who were living with and trying to recover from mental illness and the iatrogenic effects of institutional and other medically based treatment interventions (Chamberlin, 1978; Frese, 1998; Mead & Copeland, 2000).

Several theories and models of recovery from mental illness have been derived from the perspective of those who are experiencing it (e.g., Davidson & Strauss, 1992; Morse, 1997; Ralph, 2000; Strauss & Carpenter, 1981; Weaver Randall, 2000; Young & Ensing, 1999). Some common themes that emerge from all of these theoretical formulations of recovery include: People play an active role in their recovery process; recovery is a nonlinear, ongoing process—people do not move through the recovery process in a predetermined, orderly manner; hope is an essential ingredient; meaning and purpose in life are necessary; and relapse is part of the process and not a failure. In all of these models, recovery is defined in terms of continual growth, increased control over one's life, and either a redefining or reestablishing of a sense of self in the recovery process. This new understanding of recovery in terms of a highly individualized process, rather than as a universally defined end state, requires methods of research that can capture or, at least, more accurately assess the dynamic and varied nature of this phenomenon.

All three of these paradigms of recovery from mental illness provide researchers with a framework, tools, and assumptions regarding the investigation of recovery. Consequently, the selection of research methods available to researchers in the investigation of this or any other phenomenon is influenced by the parameters of the research paradigm. The selection and range of research methods available and, thus, the questions that can be asked and answered are predetermined by the theoretical paradigm overtly chosen or tacitly accepted by researchers (Kuhn, 1996). In the following section, we review the methods that have been used to investigate the phenomenon of recovery from mental illness and the theoretical paradigms supported by these methods.

RESEARCH ON RECOVERY: METHODS OF INQUIRY

For the purpose of presentation, research methods have been grouped into five categories: (a) naturalistic-longitudinal studies, (b) cross-cultural studies, (c) personal accounts and stories, (d) qualitative/phenomenological investigations, and (e) experimental and quasi-experimental designs. Although separated into discrete categories for this discussion, in practice, most researchers use a combination of methods in the same study.

Naturalistic-Longitudinal Studies

Longitudinal studies are ideal for understanding the ongoing, dynamic nature of the recovery process. As a result, many studies that have examined the concept of recovery have used some type of naturalistic-longitudinal design. The term *naturalistic* refers to the absence of any interventions used by the researchers during the study. The purpose of this method of data collection is to examine the natural course of peoples' psychiatric disabilities over time and what happens to those people as a result of their disabilities. This method of data collection can support both positivist and constructivist research models. In fact, all three theoretical paradigms discussed in this chapter include the provision that recovery is a long-term process, requiring an extended period of time to examine.

An effective longitudinal study involves extensive planning and resources. Five key components should be considered when developing a longitudinal design:

1. *Time:* How much time is needed to observe significant changes in people related to different domains of recovery? Also, is there an expected end state or ceiling of recovery and, if so, is there enough time built into the study to observe it?
2. *Sampling:* What is the most effective way of achieving a representative sample of people with psychiatric disabilities living in the community? The researcher needs to consider how people are included in the study. Are people selected on the basis of convenience, such as at discharge from a hospital? Are people selected on the basis of specific criteria, such as diagnostic category, ethnicity, or age or will the sample include all potential individuals with a psychiatric disability living in the community? In addition, at what point in the recovery or disease process will people be selected for participation (e.g., early onset, first acute phase, late onset, or post acute phase)?
3. *Number and frequency of observations:* How often should people be interviewed or assessed during the study? In theory, the frequency and number of follow-up points are based on the expected rate of change in certain domains of recovery, but in reality they may be determined by the resources available to the researcher.
4. *Tracking procedures:* How will people be tracked during the course of the study? To avoid attrition of study participants, it is critical to develop an effective plan for keeping track of people over time.

5. *Data collection:* What types of data will be collected (e.g., open-ended interviews from participants, clinical scales, indicators of employment, housing, or hospitalization rates) and from what sources (e.g., participants' self-reporting or family, or clinical observations)? In addition, what, if any, community or sociopolitical variables will be collected and how?

Variations among any one of these five components will have a significant impact on research findings across studies. The structure and design of a longitudinal study will predetermine what can be measured and what is observed. Nearly all longitudinal studies have used the biomedical definition of recovery, although most also included social indicators, such as employment and social functioning. Researchers viewed recovery, or the lack thereof, in terms of end states, which occurred after a period of time had elapsed (e.g., Bleuler, 1978; Harrow, Sands, Silverstein, & Goldberg, 1997; Mason, Harrison, Glazebrook, Croudace, & Medley, 1996). Several researchers referred to this phenomenon as a plateau, wherein the illness ran its course to an end state (Carpenter & Strauss, 1991; Ciompi, 1980; Harrison, Croudace, Mason, Glazebrook, & Medley, 1996), and that, as a result of this "predictable" course, researchers could determine within 2 to 5 years the final outcome of an individual's recovery state (i.e., fully recovered, partially recovered, no change, or progressive deterioration; e.g., Carpenter & Strauss, 1991; Harrison et al., 1996; Harrow et al., 1997; Mojtabai et al., 2001). Perhaps the biological dimension of mental illness can be described in terms of a beginning and end state; however, this end state does not reflect the psychological and interpersonal changes that make up other aspects of the recovery process, such as peoples' ability to manage their symptoms, their redefinition of self, and their discoveries of a new sense of meaning and purpose. The only way these other dimensions of the recovery process can be examined is by measuring them in the study.

An ongoing problem with most of the longitudinal studies on recovery published to date is that variations in methodology across studies have at least partially influenced divergent research findings. For example, longitudinal studies of individuals diagnosed with a mental illness have varied in duration from 2 years (Strauss et al., 1985) to 36.9 years (Ciompi, 1980); the number of follow-up interviews from two (Ciompi, 1980) to seven (Strauss et al., 1985); the selection of participants from individuals with early onset of disability and first admission to a psychiatric hospital or outpatient clinic (Jablensky et al., 1992) to individuals with an extended duration of disability and long-term hospitalization (Chittick, Brooks, Irons, & Deane, 1961); in data collection methods from prospective tracking (Mason et al., 1996; World Health Organization [WHO], 1979) to retrospective chart reviews (Ciompi, 1980; DeSisto, Harding, McCormick, Ashikaga, & Brooks, 1995); in location from Vermont (Chittick et al., 1961), Iowa (Tsuang, Woolson,

& Fleming, 1979), and Washington, DC (Carpenter & Strauss, 1991), to Zurich, Switzerland (Blueler, 1978), and Nottingham, England (Mason et al., 1996); in time periods from the early 1900s in Europe, to the mid-1990s in the United States; and in the definition and measurement of recovery from being able to return to society and work (Ciompi, 1980) to the elimination of symptoms (i.e., full remission of symptoms; Harrow et al., 1997).

This heterogeneity in methods and research designs has created a problem for cross-study comparisons as well as contradictions in research findings (Davidson & McGlashan, 1997; Moller & Von Zerssen, 1995). For instance, as Harding and Zahniser (1994) argued, the duration of the study has a profound impact on peoples' outcomes. If recovery from mental illness is a long-term process, the duration of the study will impact the outcome regarding the proportion of people that has achieved it at any given time point. Consider these examples:

- Harrow et al. (1997) reported that 30% of their sample (22/ 79) had achieved complete remission of symptoms at the 7.5- year follow-up (third follow-up) and that only 5% ($n = 2$) had achieved consistent remission of symptoms at all three time points. Mason et al. (1996) reported that 44% of their sample had recovered or had only mild impairments at the 13-year follow-up.
- Bleuler (1978) reported that 20% of the individuals in his sample had fully recovered and that an additional 33% showed significant improvement after approximately 20 years from admission into the study, and that 96% of his entire sample achieved an end state (either recovered, improved, unchanged, or deteriorated) within 15 years.
- Harding et al. (1987) reported that between 50% and 66% of their sample had achieved either full recovery or significant improvement on multiple domains within 20 to 25 years after admission into their study.

The differences in duration, as well as other methodological components, provide a challenge in discerning whether the divergent research findings of the studies noted above are artifacts of differences in populations, sampled at different time points and in different locations; measures of recovery; or the duration of each study. Are the divergent research findings between Harrow et al. (1997) and Harding et al.'s (1987) studies due to differences in duration, with the latter study using a follow-up time frame that was three times the duration of the former, in location, or in the initial sample of participants?

In addition, what impact did the historical time frame have on recovery outcomes? For instance, Ciompi's (1980) sample was selected around the turn of the century in Switzerland, Blueler's (1978) sample was selected during World War II in Switzerland, Harding et al.'s (1987) sample was selected between 1955 and 1965 in Vermont, and Harrow et al.'s (1997) sample was selected in the late 1970s. Warner (1994) argued that differences in recovery rates over the course of the 20th century and across different countries could be attributed to sociopolitical and economical forces that were occurring during different time frames, for example, the Depression and post–World War II. This is not to suggest that these factors can be controlled, but that it is difficult to discern epoch effects across studies.

Moreover, diagnostic and classification procedures have changed substantially over the course of many of these studies, thus complicating cross-study comparisons. The first edition of the *Diagnostic and Statistical Manual of Mental Disorders* (*DSM–I*) was published in 1952 and the fourth edition was published in 1994 (*DSM–IV*; American Psychiatric Association, 1994). Each new edition contained changes and other modifications to the classification of all psychiatric disorders. This problem of changes in diagnostic criteria is inherent in long-term studies and cannot be avoided. To better account for these inevitable changes over time, it is practical to gather extensive information regarding diagnosis, such as through the application of the structured diagnostic interview and by reassessing people at each time point.

Another problem that is at least partially related to the duration of the study is sample attrition. Several longitudinal studies suffered from high attrition rates due to death, people being lost to follow-up, or individuals refusing to participate (e.g., 82% [Ciompi, 1980], 37% [Bleuler, 1978], 32% [Harding et al., 1987]). High attrition of research participants is a problem in any study, but is particularly problematic for longitudinal studies of 10 or more years because of the potential confounding effect of death rates that could be inversely related to recovery rates: Those individuals who experienced a deteriorating condition as a result of their mental illness died earlier than those individuals who progressively improved (i.e., recovered) over time. The impact of attrition can be reduced by using improved tracking procedures and by adding additional follow-up time points, which reduces the duration between follow-up time points and makes it more likely that participants will be successfully tracked over time. Also, several long-term studies of 15 or more years used collateral information (e.g., interviews with family members) to ascertain the cause of death and assess peoples' level of psychiatric impairment just prior to death. This collateral information can help researchers understand if participants' deaths were related to their psychiatric disability, but nevertheless, collateral information cannot completely replace interviews with participants.

Another problem is that nearly all longitudinal studies selected participants from either psychiatric hospitals or outpatient mental health programs. This technique has an obvious bias toward selecting individuals who were in need of intensive psychiatric services or were placed in these types of settings as a result of sociological circumstances (e.g., being indigent, the availability of psychiatric hospitals, or state laws supporting involuntary hospitalization). By selection, those individuals who had a psychiatric disability but did not require hospitalization or were diverted into another institutional system, such as the correctional or addiction treatment systems, were excluded from the research. This exclusion of individuals who either experienced natural recovery—recovered outside the realm of the mental health treatment system—or entered another system of care may have had an impact on the research findings.

Before making generalizations across all individuals who are diagnosed with a mental illness, it seems important to understand what the recovery trajectories of these excluded individuals look like and if they are different than those of people who experienced at least one psychiatric hospitalization. Furthermore, with improvements in peoples' legal rights and consumer advocacy, the advent of modern psychosocial rehabilitative services, supported employment, education, and housing programs, advances in psychopharmacology, and the rise of managed care and the subsequent reduction of hospital beds across the United States, it is likely that a substantial portion of individuals who have a psychiatric disability will not require or receive treatment in a psychiatric hospital or even an outpatient community mental health program. How will these individuals be selected in future longitudinal studies? Moreover, what effect will this group have on rates of recovery? Without the iatrogenic effects of forced or involuntary institutionalization (e.g., see Goffman, 1961) influencing the process of recovery for some people, what will their course of recovery look like, and will it be different than that reported by Harding and colleagues (1987) and others?

Other individuals with psychiatric disabilities who have frequently been excluded from longitudinal research are those who have a co-occurring substance use disorder (e.g., Carpenter & Strauss, 1991; DeSisto et al., 1995; Strauss et al., 1985). Again this selection bias may have an impact on research findings. Epidemiological research indicates that as many as 50% of all individuals with psychiatric disabilities have some type of co-occurring substance use disorder (Regier et al., 1990). By excluding this population, researchers limit the generalizability of their findings across all individuals who have psychiatric disabilities. Those studies that were able to track individuals with dual diagnoses (i.e., the existence of co-occurring disorders) usually found poorer long-term outcomes (Davidson & McGlashan, 1997), Many of these problems can be linked to how sampling of the cohort was accomplished in longitudinal studies. Use of a representative sample of individuals with psychiatric disabilities that is reflective of the general population in the community rather than a more narrow treatment (i.e., hospital-based) population can minimize the potential confounding impact of sample bias. Future research endeavors should expand sampling procedures to include people with psychiatric disabilities who have entered other systems of care, such as the criminal justice, addiction treatment, public welfare, and primary medical systems and self-help organizations.

Cross-Cultural Studies

Cross-cultural studies on recovery from mental illness are longitudinal studies that compare the incidence and long-term outcome of serious mental illnesses (e.g., schizophrenia, bipolar disorder, and major depression) among developed (e.g., United States and England) and developing countries (e.g., Nigeria and India).

Most of the cross-cultural studies on mental illness that have been implemented over the past 30 years were products of WHO's multicountry International Pilot Study of Schizophrenia (IPSS) and the Determinants of Outcome of Severe Mental Disorders (DOSMeD; Jablensky et al., 1992; Sartorius, Gulbinat, Harrison, Laska, & Siegel, 1996; WHO, 1973, 1979). Several of the United States and European sites of both studies were noted earlier (e.g., Carpenter & Strauss, 1991; Mason et al., 1996). A third ongoing WHO study is a long-term follow-up of individuals who participated in the IPSS or the DOSMeD studies: the International Study of Schizophrenia (ISoS; Sartorius et al., 1996). The purpose of the third WHO study was to examine the recovery process 15 to 25 years from onset of the illness. All three of the WHO studies were naturalistic-longitudinal studies that included multiple developed and developing countries; thus, most of the issues noted above also apply to this category of methodology.

An invaluable contribution of cross-cultural studies is the comparison and contrast among cultures and how these cultural differences can influence both the incidence of mental illness and peoples' recovery processes. Another benefit of the three WHO studies is that each multisite study was initiated at the same time thus, eliminating the impact of different historical time frames (i.e., the effects of different epochs). Moreover, the second and third WHO studies used standard protocols across all sites, thereby reducing the confounding impact of varying follow-up time points, diagnostic criteria, and measures of recovery. Nonetheless, the first two WHO studies still suffered from variations in sampling procedures and attrition across sites.

In cross-cultural studies it is important to assess those social and cultural factors that may help or hinder the recovery process. For instance, Lin and Kleinman (1988) noted that it was easier for individuals with schizophrenia to return to work in developing countries than in industrialized societies. They speculated that this might be a result of how work is structured in traditional communal settings found in developing countries and specifically that they may support inclusion of all residents, regardless of disability. Considering that employment can be viewed as both a rehabilitative tool and a proxy indicator of social adjustment, cultural differences in employment and what is defined as a job should be assessed prior to cross-country comparisons.

Unfortunately, sociocultural factors like these were not specifically assessed in the WHO study. Instead, the study was assumed, by default, to have influenced the divergent outcomes across countries (Sartorius, Jablensky, & Shapiro, 1978). Attempts were made to rectify this in the second WHO study, but research findings have yet to fully explain the consistent differences between Western and non-Western countries (Jablensky, 1989; Sartorius et al., 1996). Although it seemed logical to assume that sociocultural variables influenced the process of recovery, given the consistent differences found between developed and developing countries, both WHO initiatives provided only minimal insight into what aspects of non-Western cultures facilitate recovery from mental illness and why the rates of recovery are better in undeveloped countries.

Future cross-cultural studies can be enhanced by combining qualitative methods of data collection with the standardized, quantitative methods such as those used in the second and third WHO studies. Qualitative methods (described next) can help delineate aspects of different cultures that appear to influence the recovery process. Culturally linked factors that may help explain differential recovery rates include independent versus interdependent social structures, religious and medical practices, levels and types of environmental stress (e.g., industrialization, war, famine, and poverty), cultural acceptance of alcohol and other drugs, levels of tolerance for deviant behaviors, levels of social support, interpretations of mental illness, types of kinship networks, opportunities for social reintegration and normalized work roles, and sociopolitical and economical factors (Egeland, Hostetter, & Eshleman, 1983; Leff, 1988; Lefley, 1999; Lin & Kleinman, 1988; Warner, 1994). This list provides a sample of community or country level variables that could be assessed through the development of structured measures, qualitative techniques, anthropological examinations, or sociological analyses.

Personal Accounts and Stories

Personal accounts, narratives, and stories provide a third frequently used method of understanding the process of recovery (e.g., *Schizophrenia Bulletin*; Spaniol, Gagne, & Koehler, 1997). Personal narratives and stories of recovery are autobiographical accounts of peoples' experiences with a mental illness and how they experience recovery. By design, this type of method for collecting data reflects the C/S/X conceptualization of recovery and a constructivist view of knowledge.

This method has generated a wealth of information on mental illness and recovery. For instance, researchers have become more aware of factors that contribute to the recovery process, such as feelings of hope and empowerment (Deegan, 1988; Houghton, 1982), people who experience natural recovery (i.e., recovery outside of the mental health system) or successfully used nonbiomedical interventions (Deegan, 1990; Mead & Copeland, 2000), and the iatrogenic effects of treatment (Chamberlin, 1978; Fisher, 1994). Personal stories have provided researchers with insights into how people have managed their mental illness, what is considered to be important to people in the process of recovery, the understanding of recovery as an ongoing process and not an end state, and a new way to understand recovery that is based on lived experiences (Ridgway, 2001). This information can help researchers when developing future projects that use understandings of recovery based on lived experiences. In addition, personal accounts are retrospective and often span 30 to 40 years, providing readers with one continuous story that usually includes critical junctures, events, and factors that contributed to the recovery process.

A disadvantage of using unstructured personal accounts to examine trends in recovery is the possible omission of critical factors and events that may have contributed to the recovery process and, conversely, the selective recollection of events. In addition, the lack of consistency in themes and terminology among storytellers limits comparisons across stories and can lead to misinterpretation of meaning. Moreover, although the reporting of personal accounts is a common and valuable technique for disseminating information on how people can recover and manage their mental illness, these stories do not lend themselves to the structure of formalized research endeavors and, thus, may be of limited utility in prospective projects. Finally, published accounts of recovery from mental illness may represent a biased selection of remarkable individuals who are not reflective of the general population of individuals with psychiatric disabilities (Ridgway, 2001).

Qualitative-Phenomenological Methods

Using qualitative methods to examine the process of recovery can overcome the limitations of personal accounts and stories, such as the potential for misinterpretation, the omission of critical information, and sample bias, while still optimizing the person's perspective. Moreover, qualitative methods are well suited for early exploration of concepts and ideas of recovery that can then be used to develop a conceptual model. As described by Maton (1990), "Qualitative methodology grapples with understanding phenomena by focusing on their human meaning and by interpreting human experience in context" (p. 153). Like personal narratives, qualitative-phenomenological methods for collecting data reflect the C/S/X conceptualization of recovery and a constructivist view of knowledge because they emphasize knowledge from the participant's perspective or the perspective of the person experiencing the phenomenon.

Qualitative-phenomenological methods consist of a variety of techniques designed to capture first-person subjective experiences with the goal of discovering the meaning of a phenomenon or experience within a particular social context (Holstein & Gubrium, 1995; Schwandt, 1994). These techniques include nonparticipant and participant observations; archival retrieval and analysis of documentation (e.g., reexamining personal narratives; Ridgway, 2001), focus groups, and semistructured interviewing of key informants (Caudle, 1994; Maton, 1990; Onken, Dumont, Ridgway, Dornan, & Ralph, 2002). In all of these techniques, the observer or interviewer plays a key role in interpreting and making sense of the data provided by participants.

Unlike more traditional, positivistic research methods, some qualitative methods emphasize the interaction between the interviewer (i.e., researcher) and interviewee (e.g., consumers of mental health services) and an overt acknowledgment of shared values. A common qualitative method that reflects this style of knowledge generation and has been used to examine first-person accounts of recovery is referred to as grounded theory analysis (Glaser & Strauss, 1967). In this form of analysis, questions are usually presented in an open-ended format and are used to provide opportunities for further exploration. This collaborative process of interpretation and reinterpretation of information can require several interviews with one participant. Despite the open nature of the questions, most qualitative methods provide substantial structure, which, as noted previously, allows the researcher to clarify the meaning of the participant's experience and to compare these experiences across participants. Several computer software programs are available that can aid in the process of content analyzing interviews and documentation (e.g., NU*DIST, Ethnograph, and Atlas).

Several researchers have used qualitative methods in combination with quantitative methods of data collection. In the Yale Longitudinal Study of Prolonged Psychiatric Disorders, Strauss and colleagues (1985) used a combination of open-ended questions and structured surveys to explore peoples' social functioning and symptoms as they evolved across a variety of contexts during a 3-year period (Davidson & Strauss, 1992; Strauss et al., 1985). A unique component of this study was an intensive bimonthly follow-up for the first year and then yearly follow-ups after that. The open-ended questions focused on individuals' experiences within different situations, such as work, family, and the community, and how they interacted in these situations over time. Their research also revealed the nonlinear course of recovery using multiple time points within the first year of the study (Strauss et al., 1985). A noteworthy aspect of this study is the amount of information that was generated in only 3 years of follow-up for 66 individuals who had experienced psychiatric hospitalizations.

Using a similar semistructured interview format with a cross-sectional sample of individuals with a psychiatric disability, Sullivan (1994) was able to extrapolate numerous factors related to peoples' success in managing and recovering from mental illness. The semistructured format revealed factors that had rarely been addressed in previous studies on recovery, such as peoples' successful attempts at self-monitoring and self-managing of their symptoms and the power of spirituality. Sullivan's findings as well as those discussed by Strauss and colleagues (1985) reveal the benefits of using qualitative methods of data collection in research on recovery. An advantage of this group of methods is their ability to richly depict the experiences of people and to identify complex, dynamic interactions between people and their environments (Maton, 1990). In addition, as shown by Strauss and colleagues, qualitative methods can be used to enhance and explain quantitative results, a process referred to as *triangulation*.

Finally, Onken et al. (2002) demonstrated the benefits of using focus groups to examine the process of recovery for a cross section of 115 consumer/survivor participants across 10 groups in nine states. In addition to interviewing a large sample of participants in a multisite study, other advantages of the methodology used in the study were the collection of data on peoples' interactions with their environments (e.g., family and the community) and with mental health services providers and how factors within their environment and the treatment system can either support or hinder the recovery process.

A limitation of qualitative methodology is the time required to collect and interpret the information (e.g., see the Onken et al., 2002, study for a detailed discussion of this issue). Multiple raters are needed to collect and validate the interpretations of the responses. Consequently, research personnel require more training to use qualitative methods than they would if they were using closed-ended and other structured, quantitative formats for data collection. In addition, by design, qualitative research is rarely used to replicate the findings of another qualitative study (Morse, 1997), which limits the pool of studies in any one area of inquiry.

Another problem that is not limited to qualitative methods is the determination of rigor, integrity, or the overall quality of the research. Using classical measurement theory vernacular, this refers to assessing the reliability and validity of the research. These classical measurement terms, however, may not be applicable or accurate for assessing qualitative methods. In place of classical measurement theory criteria, Lincoln and Guba (1985, 1986) developed criteria of trustworthiness for qualitative methods, which includes (a) credibility, (b) transferability, (c) dependability, and (d) confirmability. Credibility is defined as the match between the participants' realities and the realities represented in the research conclusions. Transferability ensures that the conclusions drawn from a study are only transferred to other appropriate contexts. The third and fourth criteria of trustworthiness are dependability and confirmability. These criteria can be addressed by keeping a detailed record of all of the empirical data and all of the data analysis techniques and decisions that were used in a study.

Either classical measurement theory or qualitative definitions of rigor refer to the researcher's capacity to assess the consistency and accuracy of their data in terms of interpretations, associations, and conclusions. Researchers who use either set of tools are concerned with the same issues of quality and rigor in their research. Human error in terms of personal biases, leading questions, mistakes in recording of data, and misinterpretation of data are just a few of the problems that can undermine the credibility and trustworthiness of the findings in qualitative research. In addition, other universal problems of research that were noted previously, such as sampling bias, can also influence qualitative research findings. Although several techniques can be used to enhance the credibility and trustworthiness of the findings (discussed next), these techniques require extensive resources in terms of additional coders and time for reanalyzing information and retesting hypotheses.

Despite these limitations, qualitative methods are invaluable tools in the investigation of the recovery process. Because qualitative methods are not widely used by researchers in the mental health field and are measured by a different set of criteria of quality and rigor compared to the more widely used and accepted quantitative methods, such as experimental designs (discussed next), we have provided a list of recommendations noted by Caudle (1994) for effectively using qualitative methods for research:

- *Implement preresearch (preparation)*: Good qualitative research requires extensive preparation and a thorough understanding of the people and context within which the research will take place. Part of this preparation involves selecting the most appropriate method or combination of qualitative methods for the research.
- *Structure data collection:* A data collection plan should be developed that will capture the most relevant data. This plan is developed during the preparation stage and involves preinterviews and preobservations of people and settings. This plan includes techniques for maintaining accuracy in coding of field notes, documenting steps for interviewing participants, and procedures for recording and storing interview data.
- *Use purposeful sampling:* A component of the data collection plan is the type of sampling that will be used. To maximize credibility, it is useful to use either purposeful or probability sampling procedures to limit sample bias.
- *Organize an evaluation team:* Another technique to enhance credibility and reduce human error is to use a team of researchers, preferably from different disciplines. Multidisciplinary teams can enhance reliability by providing multiple observers/interviewers and interpreters of data while also providing different perspectives when content analyzing the data.
- *Use triangulation techniques:* Triangulation of data is the combining of different methods and different sources of data to compare trends, congruencies, and inconsistencies in the data. Triangulation can help researchers test particular hypotheses by combining

qualitative results with quantitative data, such as indicators of employment or housing, or with other types of qualitative data, such as feedback from family members. Triangulation of data can be viewed as a form of concurrent or social validity.

- *Consider rival explanations:* A practical technique for reducing bias in interpretation of findings is by overtly testing alternative or rival hypotheses with the same data set. A benefit of organizing a multidisciplinary team is the access to different perspectives on human behavior. Credibility of findings is enhanced when researchers from different disciplines arrive at the same conclusions.
- *Build in replication:* An extremely useful technique is replicating the findings of the primary group (e.g., people or documents) on a second set of observations/interviews. The logic is similar to replicating the findings of a factor or cluster analysis. The research team uses the replication sample to reconfirm the findings of the first sample
- *Provide detailed documentation:* Provide detailed documentation on all phases of the study. This documentation can help guide other researchers who want to replicate the steps of the study, including the process and hypotheses used to content analyze the data.
- *Provide opportunities for feedback:* Provide feedback to participants and other key stakeholders to corroborate the findings. Include participants and other key stakeholders in the process of interpreting the findings. Another related technique is to bring in a peer researcher (i.e., someone who is knowledgeable about what is being evaluated) in a "devil's advocate" role to examine the findings.

All of these techniques can help improve the credibility of the data, neutrality (i.e., objectivity), and trustworthiness of the findings. Because of limitations in resources, it may not be possible to use all of the techniques recommended by Caudle (1994); nonetheless, it is suggested that the research team use as many of these procedures as possible when using qualitative methods for data collection.

Experimental and Quasi-Experimental Designs

Experimental designs and other related methods of established social science research, such as randomized clinical trails (RCTs), are not considered as tools for evaluating the process of recovery per se, but rather for evaluating the efficacy and real-world effectiveness of interventions that can contribute to the recovery process. This collection of quantitative tools can be used to evaluate and compare the efficacy of different biomedical (e.g., psychopharmacology), cognitive–behavioral (e.g., cognitive–behavioral therapy [CBT] and other illness management techniques), or psychosocial (e.g., supported employment and education) interventions that can foster the process of recovery (Liberman, Kopelowicz, Ventura, & Gutkind, 2002). A large array of methods fall into this category that range from highly controlled, completely randomized designs for efficacy research (e.g., double-blind, pharmacological studies) to quasi or nonrandomized control group designs that are used in applied, community settings with preexisting treatment conditions (Campbell & Stanley, 1963; Keppel, 1991; Kirk, 1995). These quantitative methods of research reflect a positivist epistemology and are essential methodological tools for examining biomedical and psychosocial interventions. Because the literature on experimental and quasi-experimental designs is vast (e.g., the preceding references and Sage Publications' *Quantitative Applications in the Social Sciences*, volumes 1–110), only a few points related to the investigation of recovery from a mental illness are discussed here.

Experimental designs, such as RCTs, are used to support a theoretical model and, as is true of all the methods reviewed in this chapter, should not be used as a substitute for program theory. Theory-driven program evaluations link the processes of treatment to expected outcomes (Chen & Rossi, 1983, 1987). The purposes of using a theoretical model as a framework for evaluating the efficacy and effectiveness of an intervention are to both create a logical link between processes and outcomes and to predict any unintended or iatrogenic consequences of the intervention that could occur. If an intervention, such as a psychosocial rehabilitation program or a CBT program, is believed to impact the recovery process, a logical link between these interventions and some aspect(s) of recovery needs to be established before implementing a clinical trial. Liberman and colleagues (2002) suggest using a spectrum of operational definitions of recovery in controlled research to examine the program's impact on multiple dimensions, such as symptomatology, vocational functioning, independent living, and social relationships (this is discussed in more detail in the next section).

A theory-driven model of program evaluation also asserts that multiple stakeholders, who are impacted by the research, should be involved in all stages of the research (Chen, 1990; Patton, 1997). This would suggest that if an intervention is believed to impact the recovery process, those individuals who are trying to recover from psychiatric disabilities should be involved in the evaluation process, including developing the intervention. Another related issue that will need to be considered when using an experimental design is the potential conflict between random assignment and aspects of the recovery process, such as consumer choice and self-determination. It is possible that the process itself of randomly assigning potential participants to various treatment conditions could lead to treatment dropout and research attrition. Again, using a theory-driven program evaluation should illuminate this potential methodological confound prior to implementing the research.

Most theoretical models of recovery discussed previously include the assessment of context, that is, environmental factors and the transactions between people and these factors, in the recovery process. This would suggest that clinical trials, such as examining different types of pharmacotherapy, should include an assessment of contextual factors that can influence treatment outcomes. In other words, even in efficacy research, treatment outcomes are influenced by contextual variables, regardless of the type of mental health intervention under examination. Several researchers have noted, for example, that adherence to prescribed medications is influenced by five interrelated factors: (a) consumer characteristics, for example motivation for treatment, presence of a substance use disorder; (b) provider characteristics, for example, receptiveness, style of service delivery; (c) medication characteristics, for example, side effect profiles; (d) system characteristics, for example, access to insurance and medication costs, social stigma associated with certain medications; and (e) environmental factors, for example, family support, access to transportation (Dunbar-Jacob, Burke, & Puczynski, 1995; Fenton, Blyler, & Heinssen, 1997; Kihlstrom, 1998; Talbott, Bachrach, & Ross, 1986).

A related issue is examining treatment dropouts and how these departures may be related to the intervention. As was noted for longitudinal studies, high treatment dropout numbers can limit the generalizability of results, but, unlike naturalistic studies, treatment dropouts from a structured intervention are influenced, at least partially, by an interaction between participants and the intervention. High dropout rates are an indication that the intervention may be ineffective for those who left the program or treatment. For example, Whitehorn, Brown, Richard, Rui, and Kopala (2002) excluded participants in their analyses who either did not adhere to their pharmacological intervention for first episodes of psychosis or left the program for other reasons (e.g., moved out of the area). This was purposeful because the authors wanted to examine the 1-year recovery rates for those individuals who adhered to the medication regimen. The authors do not provide exact numbers for those individuals who were excluded from the analyses, but half the original sample was not included in the two time points. The results indicated that two thirds of the remaining sample met their criteria for symptom remission and recovery in two other domains at 6 and 12 months. Although this figure may be accurate for those who adhered to the regimen, it may overestimate the recovery rates for all individuals who initially enrolled in the intervention. Contrasting this view, it is also possible that those individuals who dropped out of the program, moved out of the area, or did not adhere fully to the protocol displayed similar or even better outcomes at 6 and 12 months. These alternative outcomes were not examined in the manuscript.

High dropout rates have also been found with other interventions that are believed to contribute to the process of recovery. Recent reviews of illness management techniques for individuals with a serious mental illness (SMI), such as schizophrenia, bipolar, and major depression, have indicated that several, highly structured cognitive–behavioral, behavior-based, and psychosocial-educational interventions were effective at helping individuals learn how to proactively manage the symptoms of their illness (Garety, Fowler, & Kuipers, 2000; Gould, Mueser, Bolton, Mays, & Goff, 2001; Mueser et al., 2002). Nonetheless, many researchers who found significant results in support of their illness management intervention reported low recruitment rates (e.g., Atkinson, Coia, Gilmour, & Harper, 1996; Boczkowski, Zeichner, & DeSanto, 1985; Kelly & Scott, 1990; Perry, Tarrier, Moriss, McCarthy, & Kate, 1999) and either high research and treatment attrition (from both the treatment and control groups) or that individuals were unable to proceed through the intervention because of problems associated with their psychiatric illnesses or their lives (Atkinson et al., 1996; Garland & Moorhead, 2001; Hogarty et al., 1997; Hornung, Feldmann, Klingberg, Buchkremer, & Reker, 1999; Kelly & Scott, 1990; Kemp, Kirov, Everitt, Hayward, & David, 1998). Moreover, post hoc analyses revealed that attrition was not random in many of these studies, but was instead related to individuals' symptoms or level of functioning at baseline or an interaction between participants and the treatment condition.

In addition, several researchers also excluded individuals who had an active substance use disorder (addiction or abuse; e.g., Azrin & Teichner, 1998; Hogarty et al., 1997; Hornung et al., 1999; Lam et al., 2000; Perry et al., 1999; Schaub, Behrendt, Brenner, Mueser, & Liberman, 1998) or severe, active psychiatric symptoms (Hornung et al., 1999; Lam et al., 2000; Schaub et al., 1998) from their research on illness management interventions. Although the exclusion of individuals with co-occurring disorders is common in clinical trials research (although not all studies excluded them), such a practice limits the generalizability of the findings for community mental health programs and may, again, provide overestimates of recovery rates related to these types of interventions.

It may be impractical to assume that any one intervention can keep people engaged in professionalized programs and, therefore, a certain amount of treatment attrition will need to be accepted; nevertheless, researchers should build into the research design a set of procedures for interviewing individuals who chose to leave an intervention. A better understanding of why some people leave treatment will help researchers and service providers improve on their interventions. In addition, to control for inflation or other types of errors in recovery rates becuase of dropouts, researchers should report a second set of analyses that includes the entire baseline sample: a technique referred to as *intent-to-treat*.

Summary of Methods Used in Research

Multiple methods are available for acquiring knowledge about peoples' recovery processes from their mental illnesses and although we cannot offer any one method or collection of methods that is superior over others, we do recommend that researchers examine their own assumptions regarding the phenomenon of recovery and how the use of certain tools and methods can influence what can and cannot be explored. Stated another way, it is important to examine what the goals of a study are before selecting the methods of research to achieve them.

A related research issue is selecting the tools, surveys, and indicators that will be used to measure recovery in the study. The next section provides a discussion on the types of measures and indicators that can be used to assess recovery from a mental illness (process or end state) and what issues need to be considered when selecting one or several measures for the study.

MEASURING RECOVERY: QUANTIFIABLE TOOLS FOR ASSESSING PROCESS AND OUTCOMES

Quantifiable measures of recovery have been used in nearly all of the studies referenced in this chapter and, with few exceptions, consist of scales or indicators that are fairly reliable and produce either a rank or interval scale score or a simple numerical count (e.g., number of days employed full-time or days hospitalized). Quantifiable measures of recovery tend to reflect a positivist view of knowledge that assumes that components of human behavior, such as the recovery process, can be accurately measured at a point in time with a standardized instrument. Measures of recovery have been developed to assess or quantify components of the traditional biomedical and more recent C/S/X conceptualizations of recovery. Two groups of quantifiable measures are used in recovery-based research: (a) surveys and other scales and (b) societal indicators of recovery. In addition, a third category of quantifiable measures—context and fidelity measures—that have yet to be applied or even developed is discussed at the end of this section.

Surveys and Other Scales

Surveys and other scales can be categorized into direct measures of recovery and its related dimensions, such as the Recovery Assessment Scale (Corrigan et al., 1999), Consumer Empowerment Scale (Rogers, Chamberlin, Ellison, & Crean, 1997), or the Hope Scale (Snyder et al., 1991), and indirect, negative, or clinical measures of recovery that assess the absence of symptoms, such as the Global Assessment Scale (GAS; Endicott, Spitzer,

Fleiss, & Cohen, 1976) and the Disability Assessment Scale (DAS) developed for the two WHO cross-cultural studies discussed previously (Satorius et al., 1996). By design, these two categories reflect the type of format that is typically used in collecting data—self-report (direct indicators of recovery) and clinical observations and assessments (clinical or indirect indicators of recovery)—and the definition of recovery—multidimensional process (direct indicators of recovery) and unidimensional, biomedical end state (clinical or negative indicators of recovery). Clinical or negative indicators have been used throughout the history of mental health research and in nearly all the studies reviewed in this chapter. Direct indicators that measure positive dimensions of recovery, however, have only been developed in the past 15 years (Ralph, Kidder, & Phillips, 2000) and have yet to be used extensively in mental health research. The purpose of either group of measures is to quantify interpersonal, psychological, or behavioral dimensions of a person's life at a point in time.

A primary benefit of using these measures, assuming that they are both reliable and valid indicators of the phenomena being assessed, is the capacity to assess differences across individuals at one time point or change within individuals over time. Another benefit, which is reflected in their common usage in research, is that standardized measures are usually easy to administer and score, associated with low cost as compared to qualitative methods of data collection, and provide audiences (e.g., researchers, funders, service providers, families, and consumers) with information that is universally understood.

A limitation of direct measures of recovery is that most, such as Rogers et al.'s (1997) Consumer Empowerment Scale or Corrigan et al.'s (1999) Recovery Assessment Scale, have been minimally examined through empirical research and, as a result, have not been established as being either reliable or valid indicators of recovery from a mental illness. A recently concluded 4-year, multisite study on consumer-operated services funded by the Substance Abuse and Mental Health Service Administration will provide useful psychometric information on numerous direct indicators of recovery (Consumer-Operated Services Program, 2002). A limitation of clinical or indirect indicators of recovery is the assumption that the absence of symptoms represents the presence of recovery or vice versa. Is it reasonable to assume that recovery is the absence of symptoms and that the presence of symptoms indicates poor recovery or not recovered? A related limitation of all measures and surveys is the assumption that aspects of the dynamic, complex, transactional, and highly individualized process of recovery can be meaningfully quantified or measured at any one point in time. As noted, although several measures have been developed to assess the C/S/X model of recovery, it could be argued that by design, none of these measures can accurately assess it and that only through a constructivist view of knowledge can we assess the recovery process in a meaningful way.

Societal Indicators

The second group of quantifiable measures is comprised of societal indicators, such as employment, hospitalization, and housing stability or the obtainment of independent housing. This group of indicators reflects common social standards of functioning. Similar to direct and indirect measures of recovery, societal indicators can be viewed as direct indicators of recovery, such as being employed at least part-time or living independently in the community, or as indirect or negative indicators of recovery, such as the reduction or elimination of hospitalizations or incarcerations over a period of time. Historically, the gold standard of psychiatric stability has been assessed through the number of days hospitalized and frequency of rehospitalizations. Hospitalization has been used in all longitudinal studies and most cross-sectional studies of recovery from mental illness. As a result of a significant and ongoing decline in public psychiatric hospital beds during the past 30 years and private psychiatric hospital beds in the past 8 years in the United States (DHHS, 1999; Manderscheid et al., 2001) and improvements in psychosocial rehabilitation and psychopharmacology over the same period of time, hospitalization may no longer reflect a common or inevitable outcome for most individuals with a psychiatric disability. In addition, like clinical measures of recovery, using an indirect indicator of recovery, such as the absence of hospitalization, can be a tenuous position, albeit commonly used, as an outcome indicator that is only minimally related to individual variables (Moller & Von Zerssen, 1995).

A benefit of using societal indicators of recovery is that they can provide objective measures of recovery that are easily understood by funders, legislative personnel, and the general public. In addition, a subtle benefit of using societal indicators is the natural link between people with psychiatric disabilities and the community. Societal indicators assess how well individuals are adapting to life in the community. A limitation of most direct and indirect indicators is a lack of capacity to detect incremental or minor changes. For example, the obtainment of a competitive job is often the final stage of a recovering person's process toward acquiring employment, which may take several years to complete. Unfortunately, most employment indicators lack the capacity to detect growth toward the goal until a competitive job has been acquired. Another limitation is that most indicators reflect commonly held social norms and expectations that may not incorporate the entire range of options available to people (e.g., under-the-table jobs) or an individual's choice.

Measures of Context and Program Fidelity

Another area that has yet to be developed is the application of measures or tools for assessing environmental factors that can impact peoples' recovery processes. Several researchers have suggested that the mental health system needs to be assessed for its hindrances as well as its promotion of recovery-based services (Anthony, 1993, 2000; Jacobson & Curtis, 2000; Marsh, Koeske, Onken et al., 2002; Schmidt, Martz, & Redpath, 1997). We are unaware of any established tools to accomplish this task, but several are being developed, such as the second edition of the Mental Health Statistics Improvement Project's (MHSIP's) Consumer Survey (2003). The technology for measuring aspects of the environment has been developed in other areas, such as Moos's (1976, 1987, 1988) social climate scales for measuring the perceived treatment environment of participants in psychiatric wards, addiction treatment programs, and school settings; Toro, Rappaport, and Seidman's (1987) Group Environment Scale (modified from Moos's work) that was used to examine differences between consumer-driven, mutual-help organizations and professionally driven support groups for people with mental illnesses; and Barker's (1968) elaborate behavior settings model for measuring various observable aspects and interactions of the environment that can influence human behavior.

Another related issue is the measurement of fidelity to the recovery model. Assessment of fidelity involves determining if an intervention, program, agency, or system has been implemented as planned (King, Morris, & Fitz-Gibbon, 1987; McGrew, Bond, Dietzen, & Salyers, 1994; Yeaton & Sechrest, 1981). Again, although several elements have been noted that are believed to be indicative of a recovery-based program or system, no functional and reliable tools are available for assessing the integrity of programs, agencies, or systems of care. Examples of tools that have been used for assessing the fidelity of various psychosocial programs include the Dartmouth Assertive Community Treatment Scale (DACTS; Teague, Bond, & Drake, 1998), the Strengths-Based Fidelity Measure (Marty, Rapp, & Carlson, 2001), and several psychosocial rehabilitation and clubhouse measures (see review by Bond et al., 2000).

Summary of Measures and Surveys

The selection of process and outcome measures for research is based on a theoretical model, the goals of the study, the needs of stakeholders involved in the study, and the definition of recovery. No one measure or group of measures or indicators is better suited than others. The appropriateness of each measure will be based on the goals of the study and the definition of recovery that is used. It is always practical to use a variety of measures and indicators that assess multiple domains of recovery and represent multiple sources of data, such as the research participant (i.e., self-report, direct indicators of recovery), family members, service providers (i.e., clinical indicators of recovery), and societal indicators. Consensus exists for using a multidimensional outcome model of recovery that can capture several aspects of the process (Liberman et al., 2002; Noordsy et al., 2002; Ralph, 2000).

PLANNING A RESEARCH PROJECT ON RECOVERY FROM MENTAL ILLNESS

This selective review of research on recovery from mental illness indicates that multiple methods have been used to acquire knowledge on this topic and that no one method is without its limitations or weaknesses. The application of any research method will be based on multiple factors associated with the goals of the research team and the present state of knowledge. Shadish (1990, p. 18) provided four questions that researchers should answer prior to implementing projects for community research. These questions have been adapted to the recovery theme of this book:

1. What is the implicit theory of recovery from mental illness?
2. How could the resulting research be useful in helping people recover from mental illness?
3. What values are implicated in the theory?
4. What approach to knowledge construction will be used; that is, what are the epistemological assumptions built into the conceptualization of recovery?

These four questions illustrate the interdependence of theory and research methodology. Research methods should be derived from the theoretical framework of recovery. To this end, it is essential that the theory of recovery chosen by the research team be explicitly examined prior to developing a research project. Support is growing for a transactional, multidimensional, process-oriented, and nonlinear conceptual model of recovery, which was briefly mentioned in this chapter and is described in detail in several chapters of this book. This newer, consumer–survivor conceptualization will require an alternative set of rules, tools, and epistemological assumptions that is compatible with the expansive, fluid, and dynamic structure of the process of recovering from a mental illness. Several suggestions are provided here to address the complex methodological issues that will arise in this area of inquiry.

Collaborative Research

Research on recovery from mental illness should be done in collaboration with people who have been diagnosed with mental illness. This is compatible with the C/S/X movement, which has made the declaration of "nothing about me, without me." Rappaport (1990), quoting from Sarason (1972), argued that the collaborative component of research should "begin before the beginning" (p. 56). The beginning is before the questions about recovery are asked, which of course precedes the development of a project. Guided by this view, researchers need to develop community-based partnerships prior to even posing the research questions. In fact, research planning is born out of these partnerships. Nelson and colleagues (Nelson, Ochocka, Griffin, & Lord, 1998; Ochocka, Janzen, & Nelson, 2002) have demonstrated the effectiveness of creating research and planning partnerships with consumers of several community mental health agencies in Ontario, Canada. From these experiences, they have outlined four components of the collaboration process that are needed to maximize the potential benefits for all participants (Nelson, Prilleltensky, & MacGillivary, 2001):

- *Build relationships and trust among research participants:* The first step in any collaborative project between researchers and oppressed groups, such as consumers of mental health services, is the development of trusting, caring, and respectful relationships among all participants of the research team. This is a time-intensive endeavor, but critical and worthwhile for sustaining long-term relationships among researchers and consumers. During the development phase of the partnerships, values are shared and a common agenda is developed.

- *Establish norms, ground rules, and procedures:* It is helpful to establish roles and norms for all participants on the research team. This is especially helpful to empower individuals with psychiatric disabilities who are unsure of their roles on the team and it also provides guidance to all team members.

- *Share power and resources:* Probably the most difficult task for researchers who are collaborating with oppressed groups is to relinquish their roles as the sole experts of the research project. To do this, researchers must share their power (i.e., expert status) and resources with other participants on the team. To ensure a truly collaborative process, oppressed groups must be given equal weight in decision making and voting.

- *Challenge ourselves:* To sustain trusting, reciprocating relationships with oppressed groups, researchers will need to remain open to the process of collaboration. Participatory research with oppressed groups will usually be an unfamiliar and often uncomfortable process for researchers. The process will challenge the way researchers have been trained to perform research in the community; therefore, it is important that they remain open to the experience and willing to challenge their own preconceptions of "good" science and who they are as people.

These recommendations are made to preserve the meaning of recovery for those who defined it and to ensure that the research process does not undermine some of the processes that are thought to be connected to recovery, such as self-determination, while exploring the process. An important issue for researchers to consider is how to examine the phenomenon of recovery without diluting or diminishing its value and meaning to those who strive to achieve it every day. The method of study not only changes our understanding of a particular phenomenon, it changes the people who participated in the research (Rappaport, 1990). To this end, research can either hinder or help people in their process of recovery. The task of the research team is to implement a research endeavor that is meaningful and can enhance our knowledge about the process of recovery while empowering those who participate in the project (Fetterman, 2000; Rappaport, 1990).

Recovery as a Process and as an Outcome

Spaniol and Koehler (1998) offer a definition of recovery that encompasses recovery as a process, an outcome, and a vision. As a process, recovery is a common human phenomenon that we all experience at some point after injury, illness, loss, or trauma. The process includes healing physically and emotionally; adjusting one's attitudes, feelings, perceptions, beliefs, roles, and goals in life; and engaging in a process of self-discovery, self-renewal, and transformation. Recovery as a process also involves creating a new personal vision for oneself. As an outcome, recovery is engaging in work, having friends, and living in a place of one's own choosing. This is the aspect of recovery most often embraced by researchers and professionals. Other researchers have also supported this dynamic interpretation of recovery (e.g., Liberman et al., 2002; Noordsy et al., 2002). In terms of research design, Spaniol and Koehler's (1998) definition suggests that a combination of measures and methodologies should be used to capture both processes and potential outcomes over time.

Combining Qualitative and Quantitative Methods

Several researchers have demonstrated the value of combining qualitative and quantitative methods to examine the process of recovery (Davidson & Strauss, 1992; Strauss et al., 1985). Both methods address different issues and answer different questions (Patton, 1997). By combining methods, researchers avoid limiting the types of questions that can be asked. Moreover, a combination of qualitative and quantitative methods of data collection can overcome the inherent limitations of each one (Patton, 1997).

Assess Factors at Multiple Levels

A person's recovery from mental illness is considered to be an interactive process that involves transactions between the person and his or her immediate support system, the treatment system, the community, and sociopolitical and cultural variables (Onken et al., 2002). To better understand and explain the recovery process, these micro- and macro-level factors need to be assessed. To better understand the recovery process and what factors can help or hinder it, researchers will need to devise methods for measuring these nonbiological factors.

REFERENCES

Alexander, F., & Selesnick, S. (1966). *The history of psychiatry: An evaluation of psychiatric thought and practice from prehistoric times to the present.* New York: Harper & Row.

American Psychiatric Association. (1994). *Diagnostic and statistical manual of mental disorders* (4th ed.). Washington, DC: Author.

Anthony, W. (1993). Recovery from mental illness: The guiding vision of the mental health service system in the 1990s. *Psychosocial Rehabilitation Journal, 16,* 11–23.

Anthony, W. (2000). A recovery oriented service system: Setting some system level standards. *Psychiatric Rehabilitation Journal, 24,* 159–168.

Atkinson, J. M., Coia, D. A., Gilmour, W. H., & Harper, J. P. (1996). The impact of education groups for people with schizophrenia on social functioning and quality of life. *British Journal of Psychiatry, 168,* 199–204.

Azrin, N. H., & Teichner, G. (1998). Evaluation of an instructional program for improving medication compliance for chronically mentally ill outpatients. *Behavior Research and Therapy, 36,* 849–861.

Barker, R. G. (1968). *Ecological psychology: Concepts and methods for studying the environment of human behavior.* Stanford, CA: Stanford University Press.

Bleuler, M. (1978). *The schizophrenic disorders: Long-term patient and family studies.* New Haven, CT: Yale University Press.

Bockoven, J. (1972). *Moral treatment in community mental health.* New York: Springer Publishing Company.

Boczkowski, J. A., Zeichner, A., & DeSanto, N. (1985). Neuroleptic compliance among chronic schizophrenic outpatients: An intervention outcome report. *Journal of Consulting and Clinical Psychology, 53,* 666–671.

Bond, G., Williams, J., Evans, L., Salyers, M., Kim, H.W., & Sharpe, H. (2000). *Psychiatric rehabilitation fidelity toolkit.* Cambridge, MA: Evaluation Center at the Human Services Research Institute.

Campbell, D., & Stanley, J. (1963). *Experimental and quasi-experimental designs for research.* Boston: Houghton Mifflin.

Caplan, N., & Nelson, S. D. (1973). On being useful: The nature and consequences of psychological research on social problems. *American Psychologist, 28,* 199–211.

Carpenter, W. S., & Strauss, J. S. (1991). The prediction of outcome in schizophrenia IV: Eleven year follow-up of the Washington IPSS cohort. *Journal of Nervous and Mental Disease, 179,* 517–525.

Caudle, S. L. (1994). Using qualitative approaches. In J. S. Wholey, H. P. Hatry, & D. E. Newcomer (Eds.), *Handbook of practical program evaluation* (pp. 69–95). San Francisco: Jossey-Bass.

Chamberlin, J. (1978). *On our own: Patient controlled alternatives to the mental health system*. New York: McGraw-Hill.

Chamberlin, J. (1990). The ex-patients' movement: Where we've been and where we're going. *Journal of Mind and Behavior, 11*, 323–336.

Chen, H. (1990). *Theory-driven evaluations*. Newbury Park, CA: Sage.

Chen, H., & Rossi, P. H. (1983). Evaluating with sense. *Evaluation Review, 7*, 283–302.

Chen, H., & Rossi, P. H. (1987). The theory-driven approach to validity. *Evaluation and Program Planning, 10*, 95–103.

Chittick, R. A., Brooks, G. W., Irons, F. S., & Deane, W. N. (1961). *The Vermont story: Rehabilitation of chronic schizophrenic patients*. Burlington, VT: Queen City Printers.

Ciompi, L. (1980). The natural history of schizophrenia in the long term. *British Journal of Psychiatry, 136*, 413–420.

Consumer-Operated Services Program. (2002). Retrieved from http://www.cstprogram.org/cosp/index.html

Corrigan, P. W., Giffort, D., Rashid, F., Leary, M., & Okeke, I. (1999). Recovery as a psychological construct. *Community Mental Health Journal, 35*, 231–239.

Cronbach, L. J. (1982). *Designing evaluations of educational and social programs*. San Francisco: Jossey-Bass.

Davidson, L., & McGlashan, T. H. (1997). The varied outcomes of schizophrenia. *Canadian Journal of Psychiatry, 42*, 34–43.

Davidson, L., & Strauss, J. S. (1992). Sense of self in recovery from severe mental illness. *British Journal of Medical Psychology, 65*, 131–145.

Deegan, P. (1988). Recovery: The lived experience of rehabilitation. *Psychosocial Rehabilitation Journal, 11*, 11–19.

Deegan, P. (1990). Spirit breaking: When the helping professions hurt. *Humanistic Psychologist, 18*, 301–313.

Department of Health and Human Services. (1999). *Mental health: A report of the surgeon general*. Rockville, MD: U.S. Department of Health and Human Services.

DeSisto, M. J., Harding, C. M., McCormick, R. V., Ashikaga, T., & Brooks, G. W. (1995). The Maine and Vermont three-decade studies of serious mental illness. *British Journal of Psychiatry, 167*, 331–342.

Deutsch, A. (1949). *The mentally ill in America* (2nd ed.). New York: Columbia University Press.

Dunbar-Jacob, J., Burke, L. E., & Puczynski, S. (1995). Clinical assessment and management of adherence to medical regimens. In P. M. Nicassio & T. W. Smith (Eds.), *Managing chronic illness: A biopsychosocial perspective* (pp. 313–350). Washington, DC: American Psychological Association.

Earle, P. (1994). The curability of insanity: A statistical study. *American Journal of Psychiatry, 151*(Sesquicentennial Supplement), 113–124. (Original work published 1885)

Egeland, J. A., Hostetter, A., & Eshleman, S. K. (1983). Amish study III: The impact of cultural factors in the diagnosis of bipolar illness. *American Journal of Psychiatry, 140,* 67–71.

Endicott, J., Spitzer, R. L., Fleiss, J. L., & Cohen, J. (1976). The global assessment scale: A procedure for measuring overall severity of psychiatric disturbance. *Archives of General Psychiatry, 33,* 766–771.

Engel, G. L. (1977). The need for a new medical model: A challenge to biomedicine. *Science, 196,* 129–136.

Fenton, W. S., Blyler, C. R., & Heinssen, R. K. (1997). Determinants of medication compliance in schizophrenia: Empirical and clinical findings. *Schizophrenia Bulletin, 23,* 637–651.

Fetterman, D. (2000). *Foundations of empowerment evaluation.* Newbury Park, CA: Sage.

Fisher, D. (1994). Hope, humanity, and value in recovery from psychiatric disability. *The Journal, 5,* 13–15.

Frese, F. (1998). Advocacy, recovery, and the challenges of consumerism for schizophrenia. *Psychiatric Clinics of North America, 21,* 233–249.

Frese, F. J., & Davis, W. W. (1997). The consumer-survivor movement, recovery, and consumer professionals. *Professional Psychology: Research and Practice, 28,* 243–245.

Garety, P. A., Fowler, D., & Kuipers, E. (2000). Cognitive–behavioral therapy for medication-resistant symptoms. *Schizophrenia Bulletin, 26,* 73–86.

Garland, J., & Moorhead, S. (2001). A pilot study of cognitive therapy in bipolar disorders. *Psychological Medicine, 31,* 459–467.

Glaser, B. G., & Strauss, J. S. (1967). *The discovery of grounded theory.* Chicago: Aldine.

Goffman, E. (1961). *Asylums: Essays on the social situation of mental patients and other inmates.* New York: Anchor Press.

Gould, R. A., Mueser, K. T., Bolton, E., Mays, V., & Goff, D. (2001). Cognitive therapy for psychosis in schizophrenia: An effect size analysis. *Schizophrenia Research, 48,* 335–342.

Greenley, J. R., Greenberg, J. S., & Brown, R. (1997). Measuring quality of life: A new and practical Survey Instrument. *Social Work, 42,* 244–254.

Grob, G. N. (1994). *The mad among us: A history of the care of America's mentally ill.* New York: Free Press.

Guba, E. G., & Lincoln, Y. S. (1985). *Naturalistic inquiry.* Newbury Park, CA: Sage.

Guba, E. G., & Lincoln, Y. S. (1989). *Fourth generation evaluation.* Newbury Park, CA: Sage.

Guba, E. G., & Lincoln, Y. S. (1994). Competing paradigms in qualitative research. In N. K. Denzin & Y. S. Lincoln (Eds.), *Handbook of qualitative research* (pp. 105–117). Newbury Park, CA: Sage.

Harding, C. M., Brooks, G., Ashikaga, T., Strauss, J., & Breier, A. (1987). The Vermont longitudinal study of persons with severe mental illness, I: Methodology, study sample, and overall status 32 years later. *American Journal of Psychiatry, 144,* 718–726.

Harding, C. M., & Zahniser, J. H. (1994). Empirical correction of seven myths about schizophrenia with implications for treatment. *Acta Psychiatrica Scandinavica, Supplementum, 90,* 140–146.

Harrison, G., Croudace, T., Mason, P., Glazebrook, C., & Medley, I. (1996). Predicting the long-term outcome of schizophrenia. *Psychological Medicine, 26,* 697–706.

Harrow, M., Sands, J. R., Silverstein, M. L., & Goldberg, J. F. (1997). Course and outcome for schizophrenia versus other psychotic patients: A longitudinal study. *Schizophrenia Bulletin, 23,* 287–303.

Hogarty, G. E., Kornblith, S. J., Greenwald, D., DiBarry, A. L., Cooley, S., Ulrich, R. F., et al. (1997). Three-year trials of personal therapy among schizophrenic patients living with or independent of family, I: Description of study and effects on relapse rates. *American Journal of Psychiatry, 154,* 1504–1513.

Holstein, J. A., & Gubrium, J. F. (1995). *The active interview.* Newbury Park: Sage.

Hornung, W. P., Feldmann, R., Klingberg, S., Buchkremer, G., & Reker, T. (1999). Long-term effects of a psychoeducational psychotherapeutic intervention for schizophrenic outpatients and their key-persons—Results of a five-year follow-up. *European Archives Psychiatry Clinical Neuroscience, 249,* 162–167.

Houghton, J. F. (1982). First person account: Maintaining mental health in a turbulent world. *Schizophrenia Bulletin, 8,* 548–553.

Jablensky, A. (1989). Epidemiology and cross-cultural aspects of schizophrenia. *Psychiatric Annals, 19,* 516–524.

Jablensky, A., Sartorius, N., Ernberg, G., Anker, M., Korten, A., Cooper, J. E., et al. (1992). Schizophrenia: Manifestations, incidence and course in different cultures A World Health Organization ten-country study. *Psychological Medicine, 20*(Monograph Supplement), 92–94.

Jacobson, N., & Curtis, L. (2000). Recovery as a policy in mental health services: Strategies emerging from the states. *Psychiatric Rehabilitation Journal, 23,* 333–341.

Karp, D. (1996). *Speaking of sadness.* New York: Oxford.

Kaufmann, C. (1999). An introduction to the mental health consumer movement. In A. Horwitz & T. Scheid (Eds.), *A handbook for the study of mental health: Social contexts, theories, and systems* (pp. 493–507). Cambridge, London: Cambridge University Press.

Kelly, G. R., & Scott, J. E. (1990). Medication compliance and health education among outpatients with chronic mental disorders. *Medical Care, 28,* 1181–1197.

Kemp, R., Kirov, G., Everitt, B., Hayward, P., & David, A. (1998). Randomized controlled trial of compliance therapy: 18-month follow-up. *British Journal of Psychiatry, 172,* 413–419.

Keppel, G. (1991). *Design and analysis: A researcher's handbook* (3rd ed.). Englewood Cliffs, NJ: Prentice Hall.

Kiesler, D. (2000). *Beyond the disease model of mental disorders.* Westport, CT: Praeger Publishers.

Kihlstrom, L. C. (1998). Managed care and medication compliance: Implications for chronic depression. *Journal of Behavioral Health Services and Research, 25*, 367–376.

King, J. A., Morris, L. L., & Fitz-Gibbon, C. T. (1987). *How to assess program implementation.* Newbury Park, CA: Sage.

Kingry-Westergaard, C., & Kelly, J. (1990). A contextualist epistemology for ecological research. In P. Tolan, C. Keys, F. Chertok, & L. Jason (Eds.), *Researching community psychology: Issues of theory and methods* (pp. 23–31). Washington, DC: American Psychological Association.

Kirk, R. E. (1995). *Experimental design: Procedures for the behavioral sciences* (3rd ed.). Pacific Grove, CA: Brooks/Cole.

Kuhn, T. S. (1996). *The structure of scientific revolutions* (3rd ed.). Chicago: University of Chicago Press.

Lam, D. H., Bright, J., Jones, S., Hayward, P., Schuck, N., Chisholm, D., & Sham, P. (2000). Cognitive therapy for bipolar illness—A pilot study of relapse prevention. *Cognitive Therapy and Research, 24*, 503–520.

Leff, J. (1988). *Psychiatry around the globe: A transcultural view* (2nd ed.). London: Gaskell.

Lefley, H. P. (1999). Mental health systems in cross-cultural context. In A. Horwitz & T. Scheid (Eds.), *A handbook for the study of mental health: social contexts, theories, and systems* (pp. 566–585). Cambridge, London: Cambridge University Press.

Liberman, R. P., Kopelowicz, A., Ventura, J., & Gutkind, D. (2002). Operational criteria and factors related to recovery from schizophrenia. *International Review of Psychiatry, 14*, 256–272.

Lin, K. M., & Kleinman, A. M. (1988). Psychopathology and clinical course of schizophrenia: A cross-cultural perspective. *Schizophrenia Bulletin, 14*, 555–567.

Lincoln, Y. S., & Guba, E. G. (1985). Naturalistic inquiry. Newbury Park, CA: Sage.

Lincoln, Y. S., & Guba, E. G. (1986). But is it rigorous? Trustworthiness and authenticity in naturalistic evaluation. In D. D. Williams (Ed.), *Naturalistic evaluation. New Directions for Program Evaluation* (Vol. 30, pp. 73–84). San Francisco: Jossey-Bass.

Link, B. G., Cullen, F. T. (1990). The labeling theory of mental disorder: A review of the evidence. In J. R. Greeley (Ed.) *Research in community and mental health* (Vol. 6, pp. 202–233). Greenwhich, CT: JAI Press.

Manderscheid, R. W., Atay, J. E., Hernandez-Cartagena, M. R., Edmond, Y., Male, A., Parker, A., et al. (2001). Highlights of organized mental health services in 1998 and major national and state trends. In R. W. Manderscheid & M. J. Henderson (Eds.), *Mental health, United States, 2000* (DHHS Pub No. SMA 01-3537, pp. 135–171). Washington, DC: U.S. Government Printing Office.

Manicas, P. T., & Secord, P. F. (1983). Implications for psychology of the new philosophy of science. *American Psychologist, 38,* 399–413.

Marsh, D. T., Koeske, R. D., Schmidt, P. A., Martz, D. P., & Redpath, W. B. (1997). A person-driven system: Implications for theory, research, and practice. In L. Spaniol, C. Gagne, & M. Koehler (Eds.), *Psychological and social psychiatric disability* (pp. 358–369). Boston: Center for Psychiatric Rehabilitation.

Marty, D., Rapp, C., & Carlson, L. (2001). The experts speak: The critical ingredients of strengths model of case management. *Psychiatric Rehabilitation Journal, 24,* 214–221.

Mason, P., Harrison, G., Glazebrook, C., Croudace, T., & Medley, I. (1996). The course of schizophrenia over 13 years: A report from the international study on schizophrenia (ISoS) coordinated by the World Health Organization. *British Journal of Psychiatry, 169,* 580–586.

Maton, K. I. (1990). Toward the use of qualitative methodology in community psychology research. In P. Tolan, C. Keys, F. Chertok, & L. Jason (Eds.), *Researching community psychology: Issues of theory and methods* (pp. 153–156). Washington, DC: American Psychological Association.

Matt, G., & Dean, A. (1993). Social support from friends and psychological distress among elderly persons: Moderator effects of age. *Journal of Health and Social Behavior, 34,* 187–200.

McGrew, J., Bond, G., Dietzen, L., & Salyers, M. (1994). Measuring the fidelity of implementation of a mental health program model. *Journal of Consulting and Clinical Psychology, 62,* 670–678.

Mead, S., & Copeland, M. E. (2000). What recovery means to us: Consumers' perspectives. *Community Mental Health Journal, 36,* 315–328.

Mental Health Statistics Improvement Project. (2003). Retrieved from http://www.mhsip.org

Mojtabai, R., Varma, V. K., Malhotra, S., Mattoo, S. K., Misra, A. K., Wig, N. N., et al. (2001). Mortality and long-term course in schizophrenia with a poor 2-year course: A study in a developing country. *British Journal of Psychiatry, 178,* 71–75.

Moller, H. J., & Von Zerssen, D. (1995). Course and outcome of schizophrenia. In S. R. Hirsch & D. R. Weinberger (Eds.), *Schizophrenia* (pp. 106–127). Oxford, UK: Blackwell Science.

Moos, R. H. (1976). *The human context: Environmental determinants of behavior.* New York: Wiley.

Moos, R. H. (1987). Person-environment congruence in work, school, and health care settings. *Journal of Vocational Behavior, 31,* 231–247.

Moos, R. H. (1988). Assessing the program environment: Implications for program evaluation and design. In K. J. Conrad & C. Roberts-Gray (Eds), *Evaluating program environments, New directions for program evaluation, No. 40: The Jossey-Bass higher education and social and behavioral sciences series* (pp. 7–23). San Francisco: Jossey-Bass.

Morse, J. (1997). Responding to threats to integrity of self. *Advances in Nursing Science, 19*(4), 21–36.

Mueser, K. T., Corrigan, P. W., Hilton, D. W., Tanzman, B., Schaub, A., Gingerich, S., et al. (2002). Illness management and recovery: A review of the research. *Psychiatric Services, 53,* 1272–1284.

Nelson, G., Ochocka, J., Griffin, K., & Lord, J. (1998). "Nothing about me, without me": Participatory action research with self-help/mutual aid organizations for psychiatric consumer/survivors. *American Journal of Community Psychology, 26,* 881–912.

Nelson, G., Prilleltensky, I., & MacGillivary, H. (2001). Building value-based partnerships: Toward solidarity with oppressed groups. *American Journal of Community Psychology, 29,* 649–677.

Noordsy, D., Torrey, Mueser, K., Mead, S., O'Keefe, & Fox, L. (2002). Recovery from severe mental illness: An intrapersonal and functional outcome definition. *International Review of Psychiatry, 14,* 318–326.

Nunnally, J. C., & Bernstein, I. H. (1994). *Psychometric theory* (3rd ed.). New York: McGraw-Hill.

Ochocka, J., Janzen, R., & Nelson, G. (2002). Sharing power and knowledge: Professional and mental health consumer/survivor researchers working together in a participatory action research project. *Psychiatric Rehabilitation Journal, 25,* 379–387.

Onken, S. J., Dumont, J. M., Ridgway, P., Dornan, D. H., & Ralph, R. (2002). *Mental health recovery: What helps and what hinders?* (National Technical Assistance Center for State Mental Health Planning, National Association of State Mental Health Program Directors). Retrieved September 10, 2003, from http://www.nasmhpd.org/ntac/reports/MHSIPReport.pdf

Patton, M. Q. (1997). *Utilization-focused evaluation: The new century text* (3rd ed.). Thousand Oaks, CA: Sage.

Perrucci, R., & Targ, D. B. (1982). Network structure and reactions to primary deviance of mental patients. *Journal of Health and Social Behavior, 23,* 2–17.

Perry, A., Tarrier, N., Moriss, R., McCarthy, E., & Kate, L. (1999). Randomised controlled trial of efficacy of teaching patients with bipolar disorder to identify early symptoms of relapse and obtain treatment. *British Medical Journal, 318,* 149–153.

Pressman, J. (1998). *Last resort: Psychosurgery and the limits of medicine.* Cambridge, England: Cambridge University Press.

Ralph, R. O. (2000). Recovery. *Psychiatric Rehabilitation Skills, 4,* 480–517.

Ralph. R. O., Kidder, K., & Phillips, D. (2000). *Can we measure recovery? A compendium of recovery and recovery-related instruments.* Cambridge, MA: Evaluation Center at the Health Services Research Institute.

Rappaport, J. (1990). Defining excellence criteria in community research. In P. Tolan, C. Keys, F. Chertok, & L. Jason (Eds.), *Researching community psychology: Issues of theory and methods* (pp. 51–63). Washington, DC: American Psychological Association.

Regier, D., Farmer, M., Rae, D., Locke, B., Keith, S., Judd, L., & Goodwin, F. (1990). Comorbidity of mental disorders with alcohol and other drug abuse. *Journal of the American Medical Association, 264,* 2511–2518.

Ridgway, P. (2001). Restoring psychiatric disability: Learning from first person recovery narratives. *Psychiatric Rehabilitation Journal, 24,* 335–343.

Riger, S. (1990). Ways of knowing and organizational approaches to community research. In P. Tolan, C. Keys, F. Chertok, & L. Jason (Eds.), *Researching community psychology: Issues of theory and methods* (pp. 42–50). Washington, DC: American Psychological Association.

Rogers, E. S., Chamberlin, J., Ellison, M. L., & Crean, T. (1997). A consumer-constructed scale to measure empowerment among users of mental health services. *Psychiatric Services, 48,* 1042–1047.

Ross, C. (2000). Neighborhood disadvantage and adult depression. *Journal of Health and Social Behavior, 41,* 177–187.

Rush, B. (1812). *Medical inquiries and observations upon the diseases of the mind.* Philadelphia: Kimber and Richardson.

Sarason, S. B. (1972). *The creation of setting and the future societies.* San Francisco: Jossey-Bass.

Sartorius, N., Gulbinat, W., Harrison, G., Laska, E., & Siegel, C. (1996). Long-term follow-up of schizophrenia in 16 countries: A description of the International Study of Schizophrenia conducted by the World Health Organization. *Social Psychiatry and Psychiatric Epidemiology, 31,* 249–258.

Sartorius, N., Jablensky, A., & Shapiro, R. (1978). Cross-cultural differences in the short-term prognosis of schizophrenia psychoses. *Schizophrenia Bulletin, 4,* 102–113.

Schaub, A., Behrendt, B., Brenner, H. D., Mueser, K. T., & Liberman, R. P. (1998). Training schizophrenia patients to manage their symptoms: Predictors of treatment response to the German version of the Symptom Management Module. *Schizophrenia Research, 31,* 121–130.

Schizophrenia Bulletin. This is the journal of the National Institute of Mental Health (NIMH). The journal has been publishing the First Person Account series since the late 1980s. Washington, DC: Superintendent of Documents, Government Printing Office.

Schwandt, T. (1994). Constructivist, interpretivist approaches to human inquiry. In N. K. Denzin & Y. Lincoln (Eds.), *Handbook of qualitative research* (pp. 118–137). Thousand Oaks, CA: Sage.

Shadish, W. R. (1990). Defining excellence criteria in community research. In P. Tolan, C. Keys, F. Chertok, & L. Jason (Eds.), *Researching community psychology: Issues of theory and methods* (pp. 9–22). Washington, DC: American Psychological Association.

Silver, E. (2000). Race, neighborhood disadvantage, and violence among persons with mental disorders: The importance of contextual measurement. *Law and Human Behavior, 24,* 449–456.

Smith, T. W., & Nicassio, P. M. (1995). Psychological practice: Clinical application of the biopsychosocial model. In P. M. Nicassio & T. W. Smith (Eds.), *Managing chronic illness: A biopsychosocial perspective* (pp. 1–32). Washington, DC: American Psychological Association.

Snyder, C. R., Harris, C., Anderson, J. R., Holleran, S. A., Irving, L. M., Sigmon, S. T., et al. (1991). The will and the ways: Development and validation of an individual-differences measure of hope. *Journal of Personality and Social Psychology, 60,* 570–585.

Spaniol, L., Gagne, C., & Koehler, M. (1997). *Psychological and social aspects of psychiatric disability.* Boston: Center for Psychiatric Rehabilitation.

Spaniol, L., & Koehler, M. (1998). *The experience of recovery.* Boston: Boston University, Center for Psychiatric Rehabilitation.

Srole, L., Langner, S., Michael, T., Kirkpatrick, P., Opler, M. K., & Rennie, T. A. C. (1962). *The Midtown Manhattan Study.* New York: McGraw-Hill.

Strauss, J. S. (1992). The person-key to understanding mental illness: Towards a new dynamic psychiatry, III. *British Journal of Psychiatry, 161*(Suppl. 18), 19–26.

Strauss, J. S., & Carpenter, W. T., Jr. (1981). *Schizophrenia.* New York: Plenum Press.

Strauss, J. S., Hafez, H., Lieberman, P., & Harding, C. M. (1985). The course of psychiatric disorder, III: Longitudinal principles. *American Journal of Psychiatry, 142,* 289–296.

Sullivan, W. (1994). A long and winding road: The process of recovery from severe mental illness. *Innovations in Research, 3*(3), 19–27.

Talbott, J. A., Bachrach, L., & Ross, L. (1986). Noncompliance and mental health systems. *Psychiatric Annals, 16,* 596–599.

Teague, G., Bond, G., & Drake, R. (1998). Program fidelity in assertive community treatment: Development and use of a measure. *American Journal of Orthopsychiatry, 68,* 216–232.

Toro, P., Rappaport, J., & Seidman, E. (1987). Social climate comparison of mutual help and psychotherapy groups. *Journal of Consulting and Clinical Psychology, 56,* 631–632.

Townsend, J. M. & Rakfeldt, J. (1985). Hospitalization and first contact mental patients: Stigma and changes in self-concept. In J. R. Greenley (Ed.), *Research in community and mental health* (Vol. 5, pp. 269–302). Greenwich, CT: JAI Press.

Tsuang, M. T., Woolson, R. F., & Fleming, J. A. (1979). Long-term outcome of major psychoses, I: Schizophrenia and affective disorders compared with psychiatrically symptom-free surgical conditions. *Archives of General Psychiatry, 36,* 1295–1301.

Valenstein, E. S. (1986). *Great and desperate cures: The rise and decline of psychosurgery and other radical treatments for mental illness.* New York: Basic Books.

Warner, R. (1994). *Recovery from schizophrenia: Psychiatry and the political economy* (2nd ed.). London: Routledge.

Weaver Randall, K. (2000). *Understanding recovery from schizophrenia in a mutual-help setting.* Unpublished master's thesis, Michigan State University.

Whitehorn, D., Brown, J., Richard, J., Rui, Q., & Kopala, L. (2002). Multiple dimensions of recovery in early psychosis. *International Review of Psychiatry, 14,* 273–283.

World Health Organization. (1973). *Report of the International Pilot Study of Schizophrenia* (Vol. 1). Geneva, Switzerland: World Health Organization Press.

World Health Organization. (1979). *Schizophrenia. An international follow-up study.* Chichester, UK: Wiley.

Yeaton, W., & Sechrest, L. (1981). Critical dimensions in the choice and maintenance of successful treatments: Strength, integrity, and effectiveness. *Journal of Consulting and Clinical Psychology, 49,* 156–167.

Young, S. L., & Ensing, D. S. (1999). Exploring recovery from the perspective of people with psychiatric disabilities. *Psychiatric Rehabilitation Journal, 22,* 219–231.

II

MODELS OF RECOVERY

3

BEYOND DEMENTIA PRAECOX: FINDINGS FROM LONG-TERM FOLLOW-UP STUDIES OF SCHIZOPHRENIA

JOSEPH D. CALABRESE
AND PATRICK W. CORRIGAN

With his characterization of schizophrenia as *dementia praecox* (an early-onset form of dementia), Emil Kraepelin (1902), the father of modern psychiatric nosology, set a pessimistic tone for understandings of the course and outcome of schizophrenia for the century to follow. The term *dementia praecox* implies a progressively degenerative course, leading the individual from initial onset toward increasing impairment in social and cognitive functioning. Kraepelin arrived at this diagnostic construct through a categorical division of severe mental illness into conditions with a good prognosis (manic depression) or a poor prognosis (dementia praecox). Those classified in the latter group were doomed to a symptom-ridden, disability-dominated future. However, several lines of research have arisen to challenge these views.

In this chapter we review the long-term follow-up studies that have tested Kraepelin's assumptions about the course and outcome of schizophrenia. These studies provide support for a more positive prognosis than is typically assumed for people with this illness. In reviewing these findings, we discuss criteria for recovery, contrasting symptom-based criteria and criteria based on functionality. We also discuss the effect of diverse diagnostic criteria on the research findings and the question of whether medications and rehabilitative treatment play a significant role in recovery or whether recovery occurs spontaneously regardless of treatment. Finally, we argue for a greater understanding of the role of sociocultural factors as they influence the course and outcome of schizophrenia.

ONWARD FROM KRAEPELIN

Eugen Bleuler (1911) renamed Kraepelin's dementia praecox as a "group of schizophrenias," giving greater emphasis to the heterogeneity of the diagnostic category and shifting the focus from the course of the disorder to its symptomatology. Bleuler's new term literally means a "splitting in the mind" and is derived from his view that the disorder reflects a loss of integration between mental functions, especially emotional and cognitive functions. However, Bleuler's view of the prognosis of people diagnosed with the disorder ultimately left Kraepelin's theory of an unrelenting downward course unchanged.

Today, many still share the pessimistic views of schizophrenia held by Kraepelin and E. Bleuler. This has not only reinforced a view of schizophrenia as a catastrophe for people who have the illness, it has also limited treatment options. If schizophrenia is seen as a lost cause, clinicians are likely to limit their time and effort on these cases, leaving people with schizophrenia with the lowest common denominator of treatment (Liberman, Kopelowicz, Ventura, & Gutkind, 2002). If schizophrenia is seen in the same way by the people who have it, they will not be encouraged to work toward recovery, but will instead feel stigmatized and afraid. A pessimistic view of the disorder may thus become a self-fulfilling prophecy for many.

The lasting influence of Kraepelin's emphasis on progressively deteriorating course as a diagnostic feature can be seen in the diagnostic criteria set forth by the American Psychiatric Association's *Diagnostic and Statistical Manuals* (DSM). Beginning in 1952, the American Psychiatric Association (APA) has included in its description of schizophrenia statements that reflect the expectation of many mental health professionals that the disease's course will include a progressive increase in symptom severity (APA, 1952). Echoing Kraepelin, the authors of *DSM–III* (APA, 1980) added that remission of symptoms or return to premorbid functioning is so rare that it would likely result in the clinician questioning the original diagnosis. Even in the recent *DSM–IV* (APA, 1994), authors stated that for those diagnosed with this disorder, a return to premorbid functioning "is probably not common" (p. 232).

Long-term follow-up research, however, beginning with a study by Eugen Bleuler's son Manfred, has challenged the diagnostic legacy of Kraepelin and his followers. These studies present evidence that suggests heterogeneity in the outcomes of schizophrenia, with significant improvement or recovery typically occurring in more than half of the participants (Bleuler, 1968, 1978; Ciompi, 1980; DeSisto, Harding, McCormick, Ashikaga, & Brooks, 1995; Harding, Brooks, Ashikaga, Strauss, & Breier, 1987; Huber, Gross, Schuttler, & Linz, 1980). Given these findings, it has been suggested that the dementia praecox view may have been an artifact of "the clinician's illusion," in which clinicians view their patients who are the most severely ill as typical of the illness when they are not (Cromwell, 1993; Harding, Zubin, & Strauss, 1987). Both Kraepelin and E. Bleuler worked exclusively with patients with chronic schizophrenia who remained in contact with their hospitals; this, no doubt, biased their views on the prognosis of schizophrenia. As Manfred Bleuler himself wrote, Eugen Bleuler visited his former patients at the psychiatric clinic of Rheinau each summer and was depressed to note that those people with schizophrenia who greeted him appeared to have deteriorated. However, "E. Bleuler did not know how many improved patients were out for their Sunday walks during his visits, and certainly not how many had been released and were living at home, recovered" (Bleuler, 1978). In addition, it is possible that Kraepelin's sample included people with organic disorders such as tertiary syphilis for which diagnostic tests were not yet available (Davidson & Bagley, 1969; Harding, Zubin, & Strauss, 1992). It was left for Manfred Bleuler to initiate follow-up studies on people who were no longer in touch with the hospital, many of whom had gone on to recover from their illness. Note that in addition to the clinician's illusion, an epoch effect is likely at play. Some part of the findings of improved outcomes over time is likely a result of the historical development of new psychopharmacological and therapeutic/rehabilitative treatments.

In addition to these long-term studies, investigations of schizophrenia outside industrialized Europe and North America also support the view that the course of the illness is much more heterogeneous than was once thought. The World Health Organization (WHO) has completed the most important of these studies, beginning with the 9-country International Pilot Study of Schizophrenia (WHO, 1973, 1979), and continuing through the 10-country Determinants of Outcome Study (Jablensky, Sartorius, Ernberg, Ankar, Korten, et al., 1992) and the International Study of Schizophrenia (Harrison, et al., 2001; Sartorius, Gulbinat, Harrison, Laska, & Siegel, 1996), a study that unites the cross-cultural and long-term research literature. All of these studies had the same startling and controversial finding. The course and outcome of schizophrenia were better for people in developing societies than they were for people in developed societies. Though the categorical distinction between developing and developed societies is too simplistic to capture the complexity of world cultures, these findings from the WHO studies strongly suggest that we must view schizophrenia in its various sociocultural contexts.

THE LONG-TERM FOLLOW-UP STUDIES OF SCHIZOPHRENIA

We were able to identify 10 long-term follow-up studies of schizophrenia that had average follow-up periods of 15 years or more. In this section, we briefly summarize the findings of each study and the various criteria for improvement and recovery used in each.

The Burgholzli Hospital Study (Switzerland)

In the first of the long-term follow-up studies, Manfred Bleuler (1978), who succeeded his father as director of the Burgholzli clinic in Zurich, Switzerland, followed a cohort of 208 patients for an average of 23 years. This cohort included both first admissions and readmissions to the hospital during 1942 and 1943. Bleuler's diagnostic criteria emphasized psychotic symptoms and excluded people who had never had a severe psychotic episode. Outcome assessment was based on clinical interviews conducted by Manfred Bleuler and was based on end-state criteria he defined as stable functioning for at least 5 years prior to assessment. According to these criteria, 53% of research participants overall and 66% of the first-admission group were judged to have recovered or significantly improved. Twenty-three percent of the first-admission group and 20% of all research participants were considered to have fully recovered.

The Iowa 500 Study (United States)

The Iowa 500 study (Tsuang & Winokur, 1975) assessed 186 people with schizophrenia for an average of 35 years. One important aspect of this study was the inclusion of individuals with a diagnosis of affective disorder, as well as a control group of 160 surgical patients. People with mental illness were selected on the basis of operationalized criteria (Feighner, et al., 1972) that required 6 months of illness without prominent affective symptoms; presence of delusions, hallucinations, or disorganized communication; and presence of various psychosocial status factors. Outcome was assessed by rating marital, residential, occupational, and psychiatric status on a three-point scale representing good, fair, or poor outcome in each area. Compared to people from other psychiatric groups in the study (i.e., people diagnosed with affective and schizoaffective disorders), those diagnosed with schizophrenia were reported to have not fared as well. However, 46% of the participants diagnosed with schizophrenia had either improved or recovered.

The Bonn Hospital Study (Germany)

The Bonn Hospital study (Huber et al., 1980; Huber, Gross, & Schuttler, 1975) followed 502 people with schizophrenia for an average of 22.4 years. Follow-up exams, which focused on psychopathology and social functioning, indicated that 22% of research participants had complete psychopathological remission, 43% had noncharacteristic types of remission, and 35% experienced characteristic schizophrenia residual syndromes. *Noncharacteristic remission* was described as involving nonpsychotic symptomatology such as cognitive disturbances, lack of energy, sleep disturbances, and hypersensitivity (a more favorable outcome than characteristic schizophrenia residual syndromes such as persisting psychosis). Thus, 65% had a more favorable outcome than would have been expected with schizophrenia. With regard to social functioning, 56% of all participants were judged to have "socially recovered," which was defined as full-time employment. At the last follow-up, 86.7% were living at home and 13.3% were permanently hospitalized.

The Lausanne Study (Switzerland)

The Lausanne study (Ciompi, 1980; Ciompi & Mueller, 1976) reported the longest term follow-up of the major long-term studies. In this study, 289 research participants (92 men and 197 women with an average age of 75) were followed for an average of 37 years and up to a total of 64 years. The criterion for inclusion of research participants in the study was a clinical diagnosis of schizophrenia at first hospitalization. Diagnostic criteria at the Lausanne hospital initially followed Kraepelin's standards and later those of E. Bleuler and M. Bleuler. Outcome was measured using M. Bleuler's (1978) 5-year end-state criteria. The results indicated that 27% reached a stabilized 5-year end state of "recovery," 22% reached an end state described as "mild," 24% were "moderately severe," and 18% were "severe" (Ciompi, 1980). Nearly half of the interview participants (47%) had been hospitalized only once during their lives. However, 14% of probrands remained hospitalized "almost constantly" (i.e., for 80% to 100% of the observation period), indicating that many people with schizophrenia remained chronically disabled.

The Chestnut Lodge Study (United States)

In the Chestnut Lodge Study (McGlashan, 1984a, 1984b), 446 (72%) of the people treated between 1950 and 1975 at Chestnut Lodge, a private psychiatric hospital in Rockville, Maryland, were followed for an average of 15 years. This site specialized in psychotherapy-oriented long-term residential treatment. Psychopharmacological medication was not a standard element of treatment until the late 1960s. Research participants in this study were described as chronic and largely treatment resistant. These participants were rediagnosed using current operational criteria, including *DSM–III*. Multiple outcome criteria (hospitalization, employment, social activity, and psychopathology) were combined into a global assessment in an effort to achieve a comprehensive picture of outcome. The ratings were on a five-point scale with the following rather restrictive definition of normality: "Take as 'normal' someone fully employed, experiencing no symptoms or need for treatment, and engaged meaningfully in family and social relationships" (McGlashan, 1984b, p. 587). This study found that two thirds (64%) of people with schizophrenia were chronically ill or marginally functional at follow-up and one third (36%) were recovered or functioning adequately. The author points out that recoveries included people who had been "the most chronic and 'hopeless' cases in the hospital" (p. 600).

The Japanese Long-Term Study (Japan)

This study took place at Gumma University Hospital in Japan (Ogawa et al., 1987). Follow-up evaluations were conducted for 105 people with diagnoses of schizophrenia who had been discharged between 1958 and 1962. Follow-up periods were 21 to 27 years. Results on psychopathological outcomes indicated that 31% were "recovered," 46% improved, and 23% unimproved. Results on social outcome indicated that 47% were fully or partially self-supportive (i.e., were productive, had a home, and were often married) and 31% were hospitalized. Early stages of illness course were typically found to fluctuate with regard to social functioning, whereas later stages stabilized to either a stable, self-supportive state or a chronic, institutionalized state.

The Vermont Longitudinal Research Project (United States)

The Vermont Longitudinal Research Project (Harding, et al., 1987) was a study of 269 people who were followed for an average of 32 years. At the time of selection for the study, the cohort had been ill for an average of 16 years, totally disabled for 10 years, and hospitalized on the back wards of the Vermont State Hospital for 6 years. This study is also unique in that the patients participated in an innovative rehabilitation program and were released with community supports already in place.

Participants were rediagnosed using *DSM–III* criteria. At follow-up, one half to two thirds of all participants (including both living and deceased participants) were considered to have improved or recovered. Of the living participants who met *DSM–III* schizophrenia criteria, 68% did not display further signs or symptoms of schizophrenia at follow-up. Almost one half (45%) of participants displayed no psychiatric symptoms at all. More than two thirds (68%) of participants were rated as having good functioning on the Global Assessment Scale, which provides a global measure combining psychological and social functioning.

The Maine–Vermont Comparison Study (United States)

The Maine–Vermont Comparison Study (DeSisto et al., 1995) used a group-matching design, comparing the outcomes of 269 people with schizophrenia in Maine with the outcomes of the 269 research participants in the Vermont Longitudinal Study. The average length of follow-up was 32 years for the Vermont participants and 36 years for the Maine participants. The Vermont participants participated in a model rehabilitation program organized around the goal of self-sufficiency, immediate residential and vocational placements in the community, and long-term continuity of care. The Maine group received standard inpatient treatment and aftercare. Results showed that the Vermont participants alive at follow-up ($n = 180$) were more productive ($P < 0.0009$) and had fewer symptoms ($P < 0.002$), better community adjustment ($P < 0.001$), and global functioning ($P < 0.0001$) than Maine participants ($n = 119$). Roughly one half (49%) of the Maine participants were rated as having good functioning on the Global Assessment Scale, the main global measure used for both the Maine and Vermont studies. The authors suggest that the model rehabilitation program utilized in the Vermont study, which gave Vermont participants an earlier opportunity to adapt to life in the community, may explain the better outcomes for these participants.

The Cologne Long-Term Study (Germany)

The Cologne Long-Term Study (Marneros, Deister, Rohde, Steinmeyer, & Junemann, 1989; Steinmeyer, Marneros, Deister, Rohde, & Junemann, 1989) followed 148 people with DSM–III schizophrenia and 101 people with schizoaffective disorder for an average of 25 years. Outcome was established using the Global Assessment Scale, the Disability Assessment Schedule, the Psychological Impairment Rating Schedule, and the global categorization of psychopathological outcome used by Huber and colleagues (1975, 1980), which divided participants into full remission, noncharacteristic remission, and characteristic schizophrenia deficiency syndrome. On the Global Assessment Scale, 30.5% were found to have moderate, slight, or no difficulties. On the Disability Assessment Schedule, 36% of those with schizophrenia achieved good to excellent adjustment. Of people with schizophrenia, 6.8% had full psychopathological remission and 51.4% had noncharacteristic residua. Thus, 58.2% had a more favorable outcome than would have been expected with schizophrenia. Comparing their findings to the more favorable outcomes described by Huber et al. (1975, 1980), the authors suggested that the Cologne modified DSM–III criteria are narrower than Huber's, and the narrower the criteria for schizophrenia, the less favorable the outcomes will be.

The World Health Organization International Study of Schizophrenia

The WHO International Study of Schizophrenia is a long-term follow-up study of 14 culturally diverse, treated incidence cohorts and 4 prevalence cohorts totaling 1,633 people diagnosed with schizophrenia and other psychotic illnesses. Global outcomes at 15 and 25 years were judged favorable for more than half of all people followed. This study found that 56% of the entire incidence cohort and 60% of the prevalence cohort were rated "recovered" using a four-point scale based on Bleuler's criteria applied to the past month only. This global assessment took into account all information related to course, symptoms, and functioning. Nearly half had not experienced psychotic episodes in the past 2 years (Harrison et al., 2001). Those participants with a specific diagnosis of schizophrenia had slightly lower recovery rates (48% for the incidence cohort and 53% for the prevalence), though these are still close to 50%.

The authors suggested, however, that a stricter operationalization of recovery may be more meaningful. If recovery is operationalized as a Bleuler rating of "recovered" and a Global Assessment of Functioning (GAF) disability rating greater than 60, then only 37% of people with schizophrenia can be considered recovered. The authors also cautioned that these figures are based on the living cohort of participants and that many cases lost to follow-up may have fallen into poor outcome categories. However, the authors cite a study by Drake, Levine, and Laska (2001) that found the biasing effects of basing analysis on the living cohort alone were negligible. This study reported striking heterogeneity across the different dimensions of outcome. This is illustrated by the finding that 20% or more of the cohort managed to sustain employment despite persisting symptoms or disability.

The short-term course of psychosis, specifically the percentage of time spent experiencing psychotic symptoms in the 2 years following onset, was the best predictor of all long-term outcome measures. Interestingly, however, this study found that 15.7% of people with schizophrenia in the incident cohort and 18.4% in the prevalence cohort showed late improvements, rating "recovered" at long-term follow-up after a period of continuous symptoms. Living in certain sociocultural contexts also appears to have had a significant role in determining both symptoms and social disability. Certain research locations were associated with improved chances of recovery, even for participants with unfavorable early-illness courses. The authors state that the precise nature of these setting- or culture-specific effects "remains to be unravelled" (Harrison et al., 2001, p. 515). A comprehensive report of the findings, including more information on cross-cultural findings, had not yet been published at the time of this review (Hopper, Harrison, Janca, & Sartorius, in press).

Table 3.1 summarizes the findings of improvement or recovery in the long-term studies reviewed in this chapter and lists the criteria used by each study to determine outcome. In this table, noncharacteristic remissions without psychosis (as described in the Bonn and Cologne studies) were counted as improvements. Each of these studies found that, rather than having a progressively deteriorating course, schizophrenia has a heterogeneous range of courses from severe cases requiring repeated or continuous hospitalization to cases in which a single illness episode is followed by complete remission of symptoms. The findings reported in these studies as a whole indicate that roughly half of the participants recovered or significantly improved over the long-term, suggesting that remission or recovery is much more common than originally thought.

Diagnostic Criteria and Sample Characteristics

Cultural differences in diagnostic criteria for schizophrenia complicate the findings of these studies and lead some scholars to discount them, arguing that the resulting samples studied are so different that they cannot be meaningfully compared. In discussing these differences, Angst (1998) points out that the Swiss and German criteria of M. Bleuler, Ciompi and Muller, and Huber are broad and inclusive, including conditions that in other classificatory systems would be called affective psychoses, reactive psychoses, and schizophreniform psychoses. In contrast to the Swiss and German criteria, Scandinavian diagnostic approaches separate "true schizophrenia" from reactive psychoses and schizophreniform psychoses that have a comparatively better prognosis. The United States seems to fall between these two approaches. American diagnosis of schizophrenia using operationalized

TABLE 3.1
Results of Long-Term Follow-Up Studies

Name of Study	% Recovered or Improved	Average Follow-Up (Years)	Recovery/ Improvement Criteria
Burgholzli study (M. Bleuler, 1974)	53 (66 1st adm)	23	5-year end state determined through clinical interview by M. Bleuler
Iowa 500 study (Tsuang & Winokur, 1975)	46	35	Marital, residential, occupational, and symptom status rated on three-point scales and combined into a global measure

(continues)

TABLE 3.1 (Continued)
Results of Long-Term Follow-Up Studies

Name of Study	% Recovered or Improved	Average Follow-Up (Years)	Recovery/ Improvement Criteria
Bonn Hospital (Huber et al., 1975)	65	22	Symptoms and social functioning assessed by examination; social recovery was defined as full-time employment
Lausanne study (Ciompi, 1980)	49	37	M. Bleuler's 5-year end-state criteria
Chestnut Lodge (McGlashan, 1984a, 1984b)	36	15	Personal interview in which examiner rated subject on hospitalization, employment, social activity, psychopathology, and a global functioning score that combined these
Japanese study (Ogawa et al., 1987)	77	21–27	Follow-up interviews on psychopathology, social relationships, and residential status
Vermont study (Harding et al., 1987)	68	32	Interviews using structured instruments (Harding et al., 1987) for the collection of data on social functioning, hospital records, various symptom-based measures summarized with the Global Assessment Scale
Maine sample (DeSisto et al., 1995)	49	36	Criteria replicated the Vermont Study; (DeSisto et al., 1995) Global Assessment Scale provided a global measure of psychological and social status
Cologne study (Marneros et al., 1989)	58	25	Interviews using Global Assessment Scale, Disability Assessment Scale (Marneros et al., 1989), Psychological Impairment Rating Schedule, and Bonn criteria for categorization of psychopathological outcome
WHO International Study of Schizophrenia (Harrison et al., 2001)	48–53	15 and 25	Bleuler global assessment based on all information on course, symptoms, and functioning (Harrison et al., 2001)

criteria (Feighner et al., 1972), research diagnostic criteria (Spitzer, Endi-cott, & Robins, 1978), or the *DSM–III* (APA, 1980) is narrower than the Swiss and German concepts but does not place as much emphasis as Scandi-navian diagnosis does on separating out reactive and schizophreniform psy-choses. However, these differences do not invalidate the finding that outcomes for people with schizophrenia (variously defined) are much more varied and, on the whole, better than the Kraepelinian view would hold.

Criteria for Recovery

Different dimensions of outcome, such as symptom levels and psychosocial functioning, have generally been found to intercorrelate only to a modest degree (Harding et al., 1987; Strauss & Carpenter, 1972, 1974, 1977). For this reason, the choice of which dimensions are used as criteria for recovery is important. Some investigators (e.g., McGlashan, 1984a) believe that a study must use multiple dimensions to provide a comprehensive and valid picture. However, one could also argue that the presence of symptoms within an otherwise functional life should not disqualify an individual from being judged "recovered." Psychosocial functioning is arguably a more important criterion of recovery than being symptom free, and an overreli-ance on symptom-based criteria, together with the false assumption that symptoms and functioning are strongly correlated, may partially explain why the pessimistic Kraepelinian view of schizophrenia has persisted. Reli-ance on global ratings of outcome collapses these differences, making the exact nature of outcome unclear.

In many cases, people with schizophrenia have learned ways to cope with and manage symptoms when they arise. In cautioning against the crite-rion of presence versus absence of symptoms, Liberman et al. (2002) write that in many cases, "positive symptoms experienced during a given follow-up period may be brief, lasting days or weeks, and may have a minimal impact on social or occupational functioning" (p. 258). In addition, the Interna-tional Study of Schizophrenia (Harrison et al., 2001) found that 20% of par-ticipants maintained employment despite persisting symptoms or disability.

Treatment Outcome or Spontaneous Recovery?

Some researchers have raised the question of whether treatment played a necessary role in favorable outcomes or whether a naturally occurring "burnout" process accompanies schizophrenia that involves disappearance of positive symptoms as the person ages. This view is supported by the neu-robiological changes that accompany aging, including reduction in dopam-ine activity (Arranz, et al., 1996). However, several lines of evidence suggest that the burnout hypothesis cannot completely account for the improvements documented in the follow-up studies.

First, studies have found that a majority of older people with schizo-phrenia continue to have both positive and negative symptoms (Jeste, et al., 1997; Palmer, Heaton, & Jeste, 1999). In addition, the WHO International Study of Schizophrenia (Harrison et al., 2001) found that the greatest pre-dictor of a negative long-term outcome is a prolonged psychosis within the first 2 years following onset. When we combine these findings with the many studies that indicate that early, assertive intervention is very effective in achieving remission of psychotic symptoms (Gitlin, et al., 2001; Lieber-man, et al., 1993), treatment appears to play an obvious role in long-term outcome.

Furthermore, it seems that the type of treatment employed also makes a difference in outcomes. This is convincingly demonstrated in the Maine–Vermont Comparison Study (DeSisto, et al., 1995). Even though Vermont participants were very chronic patients from the "back wards" of the Vermont State Hospital, they had significantly better outcomes than the matched cohort from Maine and the highest recovery/improvement rate of all the follow-up studies we reviewed. The most likely explanation for this is the innovative rehabilitation/community integration program that was made available to the participants. In short, recovery can be facili-tated by treatment in two ways: assertive treatment early in the course of the disorder and comprehensive, well-coordinated services when the disor-der is more chronic (Liberman et al., 2002).

The Role of Medication

There is some disagreement in the literature on the role of antipsychotic medication on long-term outcome of schizophrenia. Judicious use of antip-sychotic medications definitely has an important role in treatment of acute psychotic disturbance. But do people with remitted symptoms have to stay on these medications for long periods? Manfred Bleuler (1974) wrote that, of all his patients who had long-standing remissions or a stable recovery, not a single one had been on long-standing neuroleptic medication. Rather, many were given neuroleptics only during active phases of psychosis and never for longer than a few weeks after they had recovered. In their assess-ment of the long-term follow-up literature, Harding and Zahniser (1994) found that at least 25% to 50% of participants were completely off medica-tions, experienced no further symptoms of schizophrenia, and were func-tioning well.

However, many clinicians feel that continuous maintenance medica-tion is necessary for continued remission of symptoms. Further research is required to determine if there is a period of symptom remission after which medications can be safely discontinued or if medications should be contin-ued indefinitely. Another possibility is suggested by Liberman (2002): that there may be an "exchangeable protection against relapse" (p. 339) between antipsychotic drugs and certain psychosocial treatments that may reduce the amount of medication that people with schizophrenia require.

THE IMPORTANCE OF SOCIOCULTURAL CONTEXT

A corollary of the Kraepelinian assumption that schizophrenia has a progressively deteriorating course is the assumption that schizophrenia is a universal human biological phenomenon that runs its course unaffected by aspects of the social and environmental surround. However, studies reviewed in this chapter indicate that the course of schizophrenia varies with sociocultural context and appears to be influenced by environmental factors. As Harding, Zubin, and Strauss (1987) concluded, the development of chronic illness "may be viewed as having less to do with any inherent natural outcome of the disorder and more to do with a myriad of environmental and other psychosocial factors interacting with the person and the illness" (p. 483). In this section, we discuss what some of these factors might be as we review evidence that suggests the need for a greater understanding of the sociocultural context of recovery from schizophrenia.

Sociocultural/Regional Differences

Beginning in the late 1960s, the WHO has conducted important cross-cultural research on schizophrenia. The first of these studies, the International Pilot Study of Schizophrenia (IPSS; WHO, 1973, 1979), examined 1,202 cases of schizophrenia at sites in nine countries. This study resulted in a surprising and controversial finding: The course and outcome of schizophrenia was better for people in the developing societies (Columbia, India, and Nigeria) than it was for people in developed societies in North America and Europe (represented in this study by Washington, London, Moscow, Prague, and Aarhus, Denmark). Overall, 52% of those in the developing countries were rated in the "best" category of outcome (defined as initial episode only, followed by full or partial remission) compared with 39% in the developed countries (Sartorius, et al., 1996). This finding was also reported in a 5-year follow-up study (Leff, Sartorius, Jablensky, Korten, et al., 1992). In this study, 73% of those in the developing countries were in the best outcome category compared with 52% in the developed countries (Sartorius, et al., 1996).

Many clinical researchers found it hard to believe that the modern health care systems of rich, industrialized societies did worse than those of the poorer, less developed countries. As with the long-term studies within Europe and North America, methodological critiques focused on the comparability of samples selected at the different sites and the adequacy of diagnostic criteria. To address these and other critiques, the WHO undertook a second study called the Determinants of Outcome of Severe Mental Disorder (DOSMD; Jablensky, et al., 1992) that used more rigorous criteria and treated incidence cohorts, defined as "cases in the early stages of the illness, evaluated as closely as possible to the point of their first contact with any service or helping agency" (p. 6). This study examined more than 1,300 cases in 10 countries and, like the IPSS, found that the highest rates of recovery occurred in the developing countries. DOSMD findings at 2-year follow-up indicated that 56% of those in the developing countries were in the best outcome category compared to 39% in the developed countries (Sartorius, et al., 1996). The finding of better outcomes in the developing countries remained whether illness onset was acute or gradual.

This study also found differences between societies in which subtypes of schizophrenia predominated. Paranoid schizophrenia (marked by delusions of persecution, grandiosity, and jealousy) was the most commonly diagnosed subtype in the study overall. However, in developing countries, the acute subtype was found twice as often (40% of all cases) as the paranoid subtype. In addition, catatonic schizophrenia (marked by motoric abnormalities such as immobility or posturing) and hebephrenic schizophrenia (marked by disorganized speech and behavior) were found much more frequently in the developing countries than in the developed countries. The investigators identified culture as an important determinant of outcome, though the precise mechanism of influence was not understood.

These findings by the WHO have been critiqued on the basis of differences in follow-up, arbitrary grouping of centers into developed and developing, diagnostic ambiguities (e.g., narrow vs. broad definition of schizophrenia), selective outcome measures, gender-related factors, and age. Recent reanalysis of the data by Hopper and Wanderling (2000) convincingly demonstrates that none of these potential areas of bias is sufficient to explain away the findings of differential course and outcome. The finding of better outcomes in developing countries is surprisingly robust.

Even in the Western studies, sociocultural environment seems to matter. Researchers have commented on the possible role of the Swiss social system or the rural environment of Vermont in the high recovery rates found in these contexts. What explains these differences? What aspects of modern industrialized Western societies may exacerbate the course of schizophrenia, blocking recovery? The remainder of this section looks at several possibilities.

Family Environment and Expressed Emotion

Researchers have suggested that variation in family systems may account for many of the differences in outcomes across cultures for people with schizophrenia. In the West, the nuclearization of the family with its associated neolocal residence pattern (pressure for children to move away and live independently) and abrogation of obligations toward family members seems crucial. This pattern, which involves the breakup of the extended family characteristic of more traditional cultures, may leave relatives with mental illness without support and socially isolated (Lin & Kleinman, 1988). Another aspect of family systems that has been found to influence the course of schizophrenia is *expressed emotion* (EE). EE is a measure of family environment that is sensitive to critical comments, hostility, and emotional overinvolvement of family members. Research suggests that people with schizophrenia who return to households with high EE are more likely to relapse than people who return to households with low EE (Bebbington & Kuipers, 1994; Brown, Birley, & Wing, 1972; Leff & Vaughn, 1985). Cross-cultural studies have found EE to be higher in Euro-American families than in Indian, British, and Mexican families (Jenkins & Karno, 1992).

Many studies of expressed emotion focus on negative family functioning that predicts relapse. Another way to understand expressed emotion is to focus on supportive aspects of family functioning that can prevent relapse (Lopez, Nelson, Snyder, & Mintz, 1999). Lopez and colleagues found that a lack of family warmth predicted relapse for Mexican Americans, whereas criticism predicted relapse for Anglo Americans. Warmth was unrelated to relapse in the Anglo American sample. However operationalized, EE has been found to vary across countries and cultures and it constitutes one possible explanation for the low relapse rate found in the developing world as compared to more industrialized societies (Jenkins & Karno, 1992; Kuipers & Bebbington, 1988).

Social Role Expectations

Another obvious difference between the developed and the developing world is the complexity and pace of modern industrialized society. One reason why criticism and other aspects of expressed emotion may be more salient for Western societies is the pressure involved in simply meeting the basic expectations of life in one of these competitive societies. For example, Jablensky and Sartorius (1988) suggest that industrialized societies impose on their members "complex and potentially conflicting cognitive tasks." Consider the increasingly complex expectations involved in modern living: operating a large motor vehicle on a busy highway, mastering the use of a computer, interacting with a diverse array of cultural groups, excelling in higher education, fitting into the expectations of the workplace, and so on. Combined with the fast pace of many industrialized societies, these complex demands may result in people who experience episodes of severe mental illness coming to perceive themselves as increasingly "off time" in comparison to role expectations for people of their age (Cohler & Ferrono, 1987). In a less culturally and technologically complex society (one that is based on agricultural work, for example), life may be much more flexible and forgiving, with less opportunity to fall behind expectations (Cooper & Sartorius, 1977). In contrast to the intimidating prospect of entering a competitive and impersonal job market accompanied by a history of psychiatric treatment, jobs in traditional village or tribal settings are more often assigned than won in competition and one's coworkers are likely to be one's relatives and friends (Lin & Kleinman, 1988).

Stigma and Discrimination

The failure of some people with schizophrenia to meet criteria for recovery is likely a result not only of the illness itself, but also the stigma associated with the illness, which results in discrimination against people with schizophrenia (Corrigan & Calabrese, in press; Corrigan & Penn, 1997). The societal stigma is also likely to exacerbate critical comments and expressed emotion in family relationships and social interactions generally. North American studies find that people are less likely to hire a person who is labeled mentally ill (Bordieri & Drehmer, 1986; Farina & Felner, 1973; Link, 1987) or to lease the person an apartment (Page, 1977, 1983, 1995). One study found that 75% of family members of a child with mental illness believed that stigmatizing attitudes decreased their child's self-esteem, ability to make friends, and ability to gain employment (Wahl & Harman, 1989). These studies illustrate some of the ways in which stigma and discrimination can limit a person's options and increase social isolation.

Research also suggests that stigmas about mental illness are widely held in the general population (Link, 1987; Phelan, Link, Stueve, & Pescosolido, 1999; Roman & Floyd, 1981) and even among mental health professionals (Heresco-Levy et al., 1999; Keane, 1990; Lyons & Ziviani, 1995; Mirabi, Weinman, Magnetti, & Keppler, 1985). Two independent factor analyses of survey results of more than 2,000 American and British citizens (Brockington, Hall, Levings, & Murphy, 1993; Taylor & Dear, 1980) yielded three stigma factors: (a) fear of people with mental illness because they are dangerous and a desire to exclude them from one's community, (b) authoritarian emphasis on controlling people who are viewed as irresponsible, and (c) benevolent desire to care for people who are seen as childlike. The social impact of these stigmatizing attitudes has been documented.

More research needs to be done to increase our understanding of cross-cultural differences in mental illness stigma and the role of these differences in recovery from schizophrenia. Several ethnographers have argued that mental illness stigma is much less prominent in traditional, nonindustrialized societies. Waxler (1977, 1979) reported that, in Sri Lanka, schizophrenia is viewed and reacted to like any other acute illness. However, the reality is probably a much more complex one than can be captured in a simple dichotomy such as "developed versus developing" or "Western versus non-Western." China, for example, is a non-Western society with a relatively high level of mental illness stigma (Lin & Kleinman, 1988). These simple dichotomies should be replaced with detailed analyses and comparisons of individual cultures as cognitive and behavioral totalities.

SUMMARY

This chapter has discussed two of the most important findings in contemporary research on schizophrenia that relate to recovery. First, long-term follow-up studies of schizophrenia have revealed more varied and positive outcomes than are typically expected by clinicians. In addition, cross-cultural studies have indicated that the course and outcome of schizophrenia varies with sociocultural context and is significantly better in developing countries than in developed countries. Each of these findings suggests that recovery is a real possibility for people with a severe mental illness such as schizophrenia. Research now needs to change its course in this area. Instead of testing the hypothesis of whether people recover, research needs to continue to look at what it means to recover and what conditions foster it. We began a discussion of the latter issue in this chapter. Clear candidates for mediators and moderators of recovery include appropriate antipsychotic medication regimens and community-based services and support. An equally important goal for research is to develop our understanding of the role of sociocultural factors in recovery. Combining these various constructs in future research will help us better understand what recovery is and how is it facilitated.

REFERENCES

American Psychiatric Association. (1952). *Diagnostic and statistical manual of mental disorders* (1st ed.). Washington, DC: Author.

American Psychiatric Association. (1980). *Diagnostic and statistical manual of mental disorders* (3rd ed.). Washington, DC: Author.

American Psychiatric Association. (1994). *Diagnostic and statistical manual of mental disorders* (4th ed.). Washington, DC: Author.

Angst, J. (1998). European long–term followup studies of schizophrenia. *Schizophrenia Bulletin, 14*, 501–513.

Arranz, B., Blennow, K., Ekman, R., Eriksson, A., Mansson, J., & Marcusson, J. (1996). Brain monoaminergic and neuropeptidergic variations in human aging. *Journal of Neural Transmission, 103*, 101–115.

Bebbington, P., & Kuipers, L. (1994). The predictive utility of expressed emotion in schizophrenia: An aggregate analysis. *Psychological Medicine, 24*, 707–718.

Bleuler, E. (1911). Dementia praecox oder die gruppe der schizophrenien. In G. Aschaffenburg (Ed.), *Hanbuch der psychiatrie*. Leipzig, Germany: Deuticke.

Bleuler, M. (1968). A 23-year longitudinal study of 208 schizophrenics and impressions in regard to the nature of schizophrenia. In D. Rosenthal & S. S. Kety (Eds.), *The transmission of schizophrenia*. Oxford, England: Pergamon Press.

Bleuler, M. (1974). The long-term course of the schizophrenic psychoses. *Psychological Medicine, 4*, 244–254.

Bleuler, M. (1978). *The schizophrenic disorders: Long-term patient and family studies* (S. M. Clemens, Trans.). New Haven, CT: Yale University Press.

Bordieri, J. E., & Drehmer, D. E. (1986). Hiring decisions for disabled workers: Looking at the cause. *Journal of Applied Social Psychology, 16*, 197–208.

Brockington, I., Hall, P., Levings, J., & Murphy, C. (1993). The community's tolerance of the mentally ill. *British Journal of Psychiatry, 162*, 93–99.

Brown, G. W., Birley, J. L. T., & Wing, J. K. (1972). Influence of family life on the course of schizophrenic disorders: A replication. *British Journal of Psychiatry, 21*, 241–258.

Ciompi, L. (1980). Catamnestic long-term study on the course of life and aging in schizophrenia. *Schizophrenia Bulletin, 6*, 606–618.

Ciompi, L., & Mueller, C. (1976). *Lebensweg und alter der schizophrenen: Eine katamnestische langzeitstudie bis ins senium*. Berlin, Germany: Springer-Verlag.

Cohler, B. J., & Ferrono, C. L. (1987). Schizophrenia and the adult life-course. In N. Miller & G. Cohen (Eds.), *Schizophrenia and aging: Schizophrenia, paranoia, and schizophreniform disorders in later life* (pp. 189–199). New York: Guilford Press.

Cooper, J. E., & Sartorius, N. (1977). Cultural and temporal variation in schizophrenia: A speculation on the importance of industrialization. *British Journal of Psychiatry, 130*, 50–55.

Corrigan, P. W., & Calabrese, J. D. (in press). Strategies for diminishing the impact of self-stigma. In P. Corrigan (Ed.), *A comprehensive review of the stigma of mental illness: Implications for research and social change*. Washington, DC: American Psychological Association.

Corrigan, P. W., & Penn, D. L. (1997). Disease and discrimination: Two paradigms that describe severe mental illness. *Journal of Mental Health, 6*, 355–366.

Cromwell, R. L. (1993). Heritage of the schizophrenia concept. In R. Cromwell & C. Snyder (Eds.), *Schizophrenia: Origins, processes, treatment, and outcome* (pp. 3–13). New York: Oxford University Press.

Davidson, K., & Bagley, C. (1969). Schizophrenic-like psychoses associated with organic disorders of the C.N.S.: A review of the literature. In R. Herrington (Ed.), *Current problems in neuropsychiatry* (pp. 113–184). Ashford, Kent, United Kingdom: Headley Brothers.

DeSisto, M. J., Harding, C. M., McCormick, R. V., Ashikaga, T., & Brooks, G. W. (1995). The Maine and Vermont three-decade studies of serious mental illness. *British Journal of Psychiatry, 167*, 331–342.

Drake, C., Levine, R., & Laska, E. (2001). Identifying prognostic factors that predict recovery in the presence of loss to follow-up. In K. Hopper, G. Harrison, A. Janka, et al. (Eds.), *Prospects of recovery from schizophrenia: An international investigation*. Madison, CT: Psychosocial Press.

Farina, A., & Felner, R. D. (1973). Employment interviewer reactions to former mental patients. *Journal of Abnormal Psychology, 82,* 268–272.

Feighner, J. P., Robins, E., Guze, S. B., Woodruff, R., Winokur, G., & Munoz, R. (1972). Diagnostic criteria for use in psychiatric research. *Archives of General Psychiatry, 26,* 57–63.

Gitlin, M. J., Nuechterlein, K. H., Subotnik, K. L., Ventura, J., Mintz, J., Fogelson, D., et al. (2001). Clinical outcome following a neuroleptic discontinuation in remitted recent-onset schizophrenia patients. *American Journal of Psychiatry, 158,* 1835–1842.

Harding, C. M., Brooks, G., Ashikaga, T., Strauss, J., & Breier, A. (1987). The Vermont longitudinal study of persons with severe mental illness. *American Journal of Psychiatry, 144,* 718–735.

Harding, C. M., & Zahniser, J. H. (1994). Empirical correction of seven myths about schizophrenia with implications for treatment. *Acta Psychiatrica Scandinavica, Supplementum, 90*(Suppl. 384), 140–146.

Harding, C. M., Zubin, J., & Strauss, J. S. (1987). Chronicity in schizophrenia: Fact, partial fact, or artifact? *Hospital & Community Psychiatry, 38,* 477–486

Harding, C. M., Zubin, J., & Strauss, J. S. (1992). Chronicity in schizophrenia: Revisited. *British Journal of Psychiatry, 161*(Suppl. 18), 27–37.

Harrison, G., Hopper, K., Craig, T., Laska, E., Siegel, C., Wanderling, J., et al. (2001). Recovery from psychotic illness: A 15- and 25-year international follow-up study. *British Journal of Psychiatry, 178,* 506–517.

Heresco-Levy, U., Javitt, D. C., Ermilov, M., Mordel, C., Silipo, G., & Lichenstein, M. (1999). Efficacy of high dose glycine in the treatment of enduring negative symptoms of schizophrenia. *Archives of General Psychiatry, 56,* 29–36.

Hopper, K., Harrison, G., Janca, A., & Sartorius, N. (Eds). (in press). *Recovery from schizophrenia: An international perspective.* Madison, CT: Psychosocial Press.

Hopper, K., & Wanderling, J. (2000). Revisiting the developed versus developing country distinction in course and outcome in schizophrenia: Results from ISoS, the WHO Collaborative Followup Project. *Schizophrenia Bulletin, 26,* 835–846.

Huber, G., Gross, G., & Schuttler, R. (1975). A long-term follow-up study of schizophrenia: Psychiatric course and prognosis. *Acta Psychiatrica Scandinavica, 52,* 49–57.

Huber, G., Gross, G., Schuttler, R., & Linz, M. (1980). Longitudinal studies of schizophrenic patients. *Schizophrenia Bulletin, 6,* 592–605.

Jablensky, A., & Sartorius, N. (1988). Is schizophrenia universal? *Acta Psychiatrica Scandinavica, 78,* 65–70.

Jablensky, A., Sartorius, N., Ernberg, G., Ankar, M., Korten, A., & Cooper, J. E. (1992). Schizophrenia: Manifestations, incidence and course in different cultures. *Psychological Medicine, 20*(Suppl.), 1–97.

Jenkins, J. H., & Karno, M. (1992). The meaning of expressed emotion: Theoretical issues raised by cross-cultural research. *American Journal of Psychiatry, 149,* 9–21.

Jeste, D. V., Symonds, L. L., Harris, M. J., Paulsen, J., Palmer, B., & Heaton, R. (1997). Non-dementia non-praecox dementia praecox? Late onset schizophrenia. *American Journal of Geriatric Psychiatry, 5,* 302–317.

Keane, M. (1990). Contemporary beliefs about mental illness among medical students: Implications for education and practice. *Academic Psychiatry, 14,* 172–177.

Kraepelin, E. (1902). Dementia praecox. In E. Kraepelin (Ed.) & A. Diefendorf (Trans.), *Clinical psychiatry: A textbook for students and physicians* (pp. 152–202). New York: Macmillan.

Kuipers, L., & Bebbington, P. (1988). Expressed emotion research in schizophrenia: Theoretical and clinical implications. *Psychological Medicine, 18,* 893–909.

Leff, J., Sartorius, N., Jablensky, A., Korten, A., & Ernberg, G. (1992). The international pilot study of schizophrenia: Five-year follow-up findings. *Psychological Medicine, 22,* 131–145.

Leff, J., & Vaughn, C. (1985). *Expressed emotion in families.* New York: Guilford Press.

Liberman, R. P. (2002). Future directions for research studies and clinical work on recovery from schizophrenia: Questions with some answers. *International Review of Psychiatry, 14,* 337–342.

Liberman, R. P., Kopelowicz, A., Ventura, J., & Gutkind, D. (2002). Operational criteria and factors related to recovery from schizophrenia. *International Review of Psychiatry, 14,* 256–272.

Lieberman, J., Jody, D., Geisler, S., Alvier, A., Loebel, S., Szymanski, M., et al. (1993). Time course and biological correlates of treatment response in first-episode schizophrenia. *Archives of General Psychiatry, 50,* 369–376.

Lin, K., & Kleinman, A. (1988). Psychopathology and clinical course of schizophrenia: A cross-cultural perspective. *Schizophrenia Bulletin, 14,* 555–567.

Link, B. G. (1987). Understanding labeling effects in the area of mental disorders: An assessment of the effects of expectations of rejection. *American Sociological Review, 52,* 96–112.

Lopez, S. R., Nelson, K., Snyder, K., & Mintz, J. (1999). Attributions and affective reactions of family members and course of schizophrenia. *Journal of Abnormal Psychology, 108,* 307–14.

Lyons, M., & Ziviani, J. (1995). Stereotypes, stigma, and mental illness: Learning from fieldwork experiences. *American Journal of Occupational Therapy, 49,* 1002–1008.

Marneros, A., Deister, A., Rohde, A., Steinmeyer, E. M., & Junemann, H. (1989). Long-term outcome of schizoaffective and schizophrenic disorders, a comparative study, I: Definitions, methods, psychopathological and social outcome. *European Archives of Psychiatry and Neurological Sciences, 238,* 118–125.

McGlashan, T. H. (1984a). The Chestnut Lodge follow-up study, I. Follow-up methodology and study sample. *Archives of General Psychiatry, 41,* 573–585.

McGlashan, T. H. (1984b). The Chestnut Lodge follow-up study, II. Long-term outcomes of schizophrenia and the affective disorders. *Archives of General Psychiatry, 41,* 586–601.

Mirabi, M., Weinman, M. C., Magnetti, S. M., & Keppler, K. N. (1985). Professional attitudes toward the chronic mentally ill. *Hospital and Community Psychology, 36*, 404–405.

Ogawa, K., Miya, M., Watarai, A., Nakazawa, M., Yuasa, S., & Utena, H. (1987). A long-term follow-up study of schizophrenia in Japan with special reference to the course of social adjustment. *British Journal of Psychiatry, 151*, 758–765.

Page, S. (1977). Effects of mental illness label in attempts to obtain accommodation. *Canadian Journal of Behavioural Science, 9*, 85–90.

Page, S. (1983). Psychiatric stigma: Two studies of behavior when the chips are down. *Canadian Journal of Community Mental Health, 2*, 13–19.

Page, S. (1995). Effects of the mental illness label in 1993: Acceptance and rejection in the community. *Journal of Health and Social Policy, 7*, 61–68.

Palmer, B. W., Heaton, S. C., & Jeste, D. V. (1999). Older patients with schizophrenia: Challenges in the coming decades. *Psychiatric Services, 50*, 1178–1183.

Phelan, J. C., Link, B. G., Stueve, A., & Pescosolido, B. (1999). *Public conceptions of mental illness in 1950 and 1996: Has sophistication increased? Has stigma declined?* New York: Columbia School of Public Health.

Roman, P. M., & Floyd, H. H. (1981). Social acceptance of psychiatric illness and psychiatric treatment. *Social Psychiatry, 16*, 21–29.

Sartorius, N., Gulbinat, W., Harrison, G., Laska, E., & Siegel, C. (1996). Long-term follow-up of schizophrenia in 16 countries: A description of the international study of schizophrenia conducted by the World Health Organization. *Social Psychiatry & Psychiatric Epidemiology, 31*, 249–258.

Spitzer, R. L., Endicott, J., & Robins, E. (1978). Research diagnostic criteria: Rationale and reliability. *Archives of General Psychiatry, 35*, 773–782.

Steinmeyer, E. M., Marneros, A., Deister, A., Rohde, A., & Junemann, H. (1989). Long-term outcome of schizoaffective and schizophrenic disorders, a comparative study, II: Causal-analytical investigations. *European Archives of Psychiatry and Neurological Sciences, 238*, 126–134.

Strauss, J. S., & Carpenter, W. T. (1972). The prediction of outcome in schizophrenia: I. Characteristics of outcome. *Archives of General Psychiatry, 27*, 739–746.

Strauss, J. S., & Carpenter, W. T. (1974). The prediction of outcome in schizophrenia: II. Relationships between predictor and outcome variables: A report from the WHO International Pilot Study of Schizophrenia. *Archives of General Psychiatry, 31*, 37–42.

Strauss, J. S., & Carpenter, W. T. (1977). Prediction of outcome in schizophrenia: III. Five year outcome and its predictors. *Archives of General Psychiatry, 34*, 159–163.

Taylor, S. M., & Dear, M. J. (1980). Scaling community attitudes toward the mentally ill. *Schizophrenia Bulletin, 7*, 225–240.

Tsuang, M. T., & Winokur, G. (1975). The Iowa 500: Field work in a 35-year follow-up of depression, mania, and schizophrenia. *Canadian Psychiatric Association Journal, 20*, 359–365.

Wahl, O. F., & Harman, C. R. (1989). Family views of stigma. *Schizophrenia Bulletin, 15,* 131–139.

Waxler, N. E. (1977). Is mental illness cured in traditional societies?: A theoretical analysis. *Culture, Medicine and Psychiatry, 1,* 233–253.

Waxler, N. E. (1979). Is outcome for schizophrenia better in nonindustrial societies?: The case of Sri Lanka. *Journal of Nervous and Mental Disease, 167,* 144–158.

World Health Organization. (1973). *The international pilot study of schizophrenia.* Geneva, Switzerland: Author.

World Health Organization. (1979). *Schizophrenia: An international follow-up study.* New York: Wiley.

4

SOCIOLOGICAL MODELS
OF RECOVERY

FRED E. MARKOWITZ

The sociology of mental illness has focused primarily on explaining the occurrence of psychiatric disorder. Although contemporary sociological thinking acknowledges the role of genetic and biochemical factors in predisposing people to mental illness, at the macro level, it places special emphasis on how larger scale political and economic conditions lead to variation in rates of mental disorder. At the individual level, sociologists emphasize how positions within the social structure (age, race, gender, and social class) shape exposure to stress, resulting in variations in symptoms of mental disorder. With limited exceptions, however, sociologists have not examined how people recover from mental illness. In this chapter, I first review the concept of recovery. I then provide an overview of sociological theories of mental illness that explain the onset of mental illness. Finally, I explore how these theories can be integrated into a sociological model of processes involved in recovery from mental illness.

THE RECOVERY CONCEPT

The concept of recovery is imported from the research literature in which the focus is directly on the services, treatment, and experiences of people with severe mental illness. For such people, controlling symptoms, regaining a positive sense of self, managing stigma and discrimination, and trying to lead a productive and satisfying life are increasingly referred to as *recovery*. Recovery is not considered an end point at which symptoms have ceased and a sense of self and quality of life are restored to some optimal level, but rather as an ongoing process where these elements *covary* over time (Anthony, 1991, 1993; Weingarten, 1994). Although recovery is complex and multidimensional, most personal accounts and attempts by researchers to explain the process point to certain core elements, involving *symptoms* of the illness, dimensions of *self-concept* (e.g., esteem, efficacy, identity), and aspects of *social and economic well-being* (e.g., relationships, employment, housing) (Anthony, 1991, 1993; Arns & Linney, 1993; Beels, 1981; Brier & Strauss, 1984; Coursey, Farrell, & Zahniser, 1991; Davidson & Strauss, 1995; Leete, 1989; Nelson, Wiltshire, Hall, Peirson, & Walsh-Bowers, 1995; Segal & VanderVoort, 1993; Uttaro & Mechanic, 1994; Weingarten, 1994). This approach to recovery is consistent with most sociological research that conceptualizes and measures mental health and illness along a continuum, rather than as discrete diagnostic outcomes (Mirowsky & Ross, 1989, 2002).

Sociologists have contributed numerous studies using the general population and clinical samples that examine relationships among many of the variables considered central to the recovery process. These studies include the relationship between social ties and symptoms (Carlton-Ford, Paikoff, Oakley, & Brooks-Gunn, 1996; Johnson, 1991; Matt & Dean, 1993; Rosenfield & Wenzel, 1997; Turner, 1981), the relationship between self-esteem and symptoms (Owens, 1994; Rosenberg, Schooler, & Schoenbach, 1989), the effects of mental health services on life satisfaction (Rosenfield, 1992, 1997), and the effects of stigma on symptoms, self-concept, and life satisfaction (Link, 1987; Link, Cullen, Frank, & Wozniak, 1987; Link, Mirotznik, & Cullen, 1991; Markowitz, 1998; Rosenfield, 1997). However, many of the studies examine these relationships in isolation from each other and often do not consider the bidirectionality of processes involved, focusing more on the causes of illness, while ignoring the consequences of illness. Below, I review some of the major sociological approaches to mental illness that form the basis of an integrated model of recovery.

SOCIAL CAUSATION AND SELECTION

Within sociology, social structural factors are central in explaining health and illness, with socioeconomic status (SES) paramount. The role of structural factors in the contemporary sociological study of mental illness is rooted in Durkheim's (1897/1951) foundational research on suicide, a presumably highly individualistic act currently understood as resulting, in large part, from depression. Durkheim showed how suicide rates throughout the mid- to late

1800s in various European countries and provinces varied by religious affiliation, marital status, and whether or not people had children. He found that suicide rates were higher for Protestants (compared to Catholics and Jews), unmarried people, and those without children. Durkheim explained these patterns according to the degree to which people are socially integrated, or bonded together and regulated by shared norms—with those less attached to social groups at greater risk of suicide. He also found that suicide rates increased during times of economic expansion and contraction. Changes in political and economic conditions create stress and a weakening of shared values and norms of behavior, leaving people in a state of normative ambiguity (anomie) that leads to an increased likelihood of depression and suicide.

As sociology took hold in the United States, classic socioecological research examined variation in rates of psychiatric hospital admissions across Chicago neighborhoods (Faris & Dunham, 1939). This research showed that rates of hospitalization for schizophrenia were higher among residents of socially disorganized neighborhoods—poorer, inner city areas with greater degrees of population turnover and higher percentages of foreign-born residents—where social ties are weak. Individual-level research on SES and mental disorder followed, including Hollingshead and Redlich's (1958) New Haven study, Srole et al.'s (1962) Midtown Manhattan study, and Brenner's (1973) study, in each case showing an inverse relationship between psychiatric illness and social class. The most recent, large-scale studies of the prevalence of mental illness (National Comorbidity Survey, Epidemiologic Catchment Area Program) are consistent with early research and show an inverse relationship between SES, as measured by education and income, and symptoms of mental disorder (Kessler et al., 1994; Robins & Reiger, 1991).

Recent research using multilevel modeling has revived interest in the role that neighborhood context plays in mental disorder. Studies using general population samples have shown that, independent of various individual characteristics, the economic status of people's neighborhoods significantly influences their level of psychological symptoms (Ross & Mirowsky, 2001; Ross, Reynolds, & Geis, 2000). Those living in economically disadvantaged or disorganized neighborhoods are more likely to report experiencing symptoms of anxiety and depression. The crime and disorder (e.g., trash, litter, graffiti, and dilapidated housing) in such neighborhoods invoke fear and create social isolation that increases the risk of mental illness. Also, studies have shown that when psychiatric patients are discharged into more "disorganized" neighborhoods, they are at an increased likelihood of violent behavior and criminal victimization (Silver, 2000).

One interpretation of the inverse association between SES and mental illness is that mental illness is a response to economic strain and lack of social attachment (Dohrenwend et al., 1992; Fox, 1990; Kessler & Cleary, 1980; Ortega & Corzine, 1990; Wheaton, 1978). This is referred to as the *social causation* perspective. More broadly speaking, social conditions—factors that involve a person's access to resources—are considered to be "fundamental causes" of mental illness (Link & Phelan, 1995). Resources include money, knowledge, power, prestige, social networks, and social support. In addition to SES, other social structural positions, such as age, race, gender, and marital status, influence people's levels of resources, affecting their risk for developing symptoms of mental disorder.

An alternative to the social causation approach is that, as a result of mental illness, people are selected into certain social positions. That is, symptoms of mental illness affect levels of education, employment status, income, the types of neighborhoods people can live in, and likelihood of forming supportive relationships and becoming married. Thus, people may drift into disadvantaged positions. Most of the research that attempts to test causation-selection processes focuses on SES. Various research strategies have been employed, including naturalistic experiments and longitudinal studies. In general, these studies find that, while both social causation and selection processes are operating, social causation may be more important in the onset of depression and anxiety, whereas selection may be more important for psychotic disorders (Dohrenwend et al., 1992; Fox, 1990; Wheaton, 1978).

STRESS-PROCESS MODEL

The stress process model is the contemporary theoretical framework that elaborates the link between social structural factors and the onset of mental illness (Pearlin, Menaghan, Lieberman, & Mullan, 1981; Turner, 1981). This approach holds that social structural positions influence the distribution of stress, in terms of the chronic strains (e.g., poverty, conflicted marriages/relationships, job overload), negative life events (e.g., deaths, divorce, unemployment, criminal victimization), and daily hassles (e.g., traffic jams, troublesome neighbors) that create disruption and threaten psychological functioning. For example, many people with low education and low occupational prestige not only experience financial stress, but are forced to live in less desirable, more disordered neighborhoods. Higher levels of depression among women are often attributed to the stresses created by the conflicting demands of paid employment and household/child care responsibilities (the double-shift). Age also acts as a prominent factor shaping life stress, with research showing a U-shaped relationship between age and depression (Mirowsky & Ross, 1989). People in their late teens and early adult years (the peak time of onset for many mental disorders) face pressures in completing their education and starting careers and families. In the middle years, stress decreases as people generally advance in their careers, income increases, and children become more self-sufficient. In old age, stress and social isolation increase as people face the loss of self-defining work roles through retirement, declines in income and physical health, and the death of spouses and others who provide social support.

The effect of stress on symptoms is, however, only moderate in size. That is, stress does not always translate into psychological problems. A central component of the stress-process model is therefore the conditional (or interaction) effect of coping resources. The impact of stress on symptoms depends on the level of people's coping resources. Key coping resources include social support, self-efficacy (i.e., sense of control), and styles of coping (e.g., emotional vs. problem solving). The effect of stress on symptoms is reduced for people with networks of family and friends who provide both emotional and instrumental types of support. Moreover, those with high self-efficacy and more rational problem-solving skills feel that they are not simply at the mercy of the stressful forces that act on them, but that, when faced with difficult circumstances, they can exert control over their consequences.

STIGMA AND RECOVERY

Stigma and discrimination are also part of a sociological approach to recovery from mental illness. The stigma that results from application of the label of "mentally ill" adversely impacts self-concept and leads to discrimination in access to the kinds of resources that influence the course of recovery, including social support, employment, income, and housing. The recent, modified version of labeling theory helps explain how stigma affects the course of illness (Link, Cullen, Struening, Shrout, & Dohrenwend, 1989; Link et al., 1987). According to the theory, generally held stereotypical attitudes about the people who are mentally ill (e.g., as incompetent and dangerous) become *personally relevant* to an individual when diagnosed (labeled) with a mental illness. Because of these attitudes, people treated for and labeled as having a mental illness expect to be devalued and discriminated against. These beliefs act as *self-fulfilling prophecies*. To avoid rejection, people who are labeled engage in various coping strategies, such as secrecy, disclosure, or social withdrawal, which may enhance the effects of expected stigma by constricting social networks and lead to unemployment and lowered income. Moreover, those labeled as having a mental illness are predicted to experience lowered self-esteem and feelings of demoralization. Drawing on the stress-process model and research, the theory further predicts that a low sense of self combined with reduced social and material resources increases stress, placing people at greater risk for continued symptoms (Pearlin et al., 1981; Turner 1981). Thus, labeling and stigmatization *indirectly* lead to sustained illness by affecting the self-concept and social outcomes (Figure 4.1). Research is generally supportive of the modified labeling theory (see Markowitz, 2003, for a review).

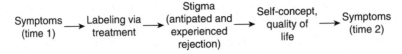

Figure 4.1. Stigma processes in the context of recovery.

TOWARD AN INTEGRATED SOCIOLOGICAL
MODEL OF RECOVERY

In Figure 4.2, I present a preliminary version of an integrated sociological model of recovery that brings together many of the theoretically specified relationships reviewed earlier. The model begins with an understanding that social demographic factors (age, race, gender, marital status, SES, and neighborhood context) serve as fundamental social positions that influence the trajectories of mental illness by shaping exposure to stressful circumstances. Stress, in turn, serves as a precipitating factor in the onset of psychiatric symptoms.

Long-term studies find that, over time, symptoms of mental illness tend to subside (Harding et al., 1987). Unfortunately, the adverse consequences of the illness are often deeply embedded in people's lives, as indicated by their lower levels of interpersonal and economic well-being. Those experiencing mental disorders are, for example, more likely to experience social isolation, be unemployed, have less income, and live in less desirable housing conditions than others (Link, 1982; Link & Cullen, 1990; Rosenfield, 1992).

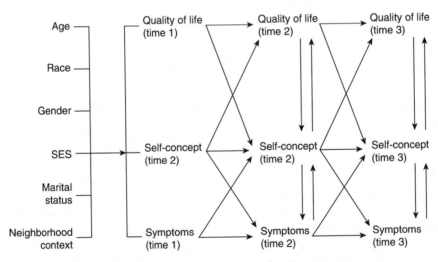

Figure 4.2. Recovery processes model integrating sociological factors.
SES = socioeconomic status.

It is, therefore, not surprising that several studies show that the most important concerns for consumers of mental health services include making and keeping friends and jobs, combating loneliness, and finding places to live (Coursey et al., 1991; Segal & VanderVoort, 1993; Uttaro & Mechanic, 1994). Consequently, much recent research on people with mental illnesses has focused on factors related to subjective interpersonal and economic quality of life, or life satisfaction (Anthony, 1991, 1993; Arns & Linney, 1993; Greenley, Greenberg, & Brown, 1997; Lehmann, 1988; Markowitz, 1998; Nelson et al., 1995; Rosenfield, 1992, 1997).

Much of the sociology of mental illness has focused on social factors related to the symptoms of illness or distress, although less attention has been given to the effects of symptoms on social well-being. Psychiatric symptoms are likely to be some of the most important factors related to life satisfaction. The effect of symptoms on life satisfaction is consistent with the social selection perspective discussed earlier. This perspective suggests that deficits in social well-being result primarily from the severity of illness. For example, the symptoms of mental illness can make social interaction more difficult, resulting in social withdrawal and rejection, and can lead to fewer and more strained social relationships (Karp, 1996; Weissman & Paykel, 1974). Also, people experiencing mental disorders may be less able to perform work roles adequately, resulting in unemployment, insufficient resources, and poor housing conditions (Huffine & Clausen, 1979). Therefore, one prediction that can be derived from this perspective is that an increase in symptoms results in decreases in interpersonal and economic well-being.

On the other hand, social causation and stress perspectives suggest that people's economic and interpersonal well-being affects the severity of their illness. For example, unemployment and the attendant lack of resources and low-quality housing combined with reduced social ties may increase stress, placing people at greater risk for increased symptoms (Pearlin et al., 1981; Perucci & Targ, 1982; Thoits, 1995; Turner, 1981). Conversely, as interpersonal and economic circumstances improve, and as support is gained, stress may be lowered, resulting in improved psychiatric condition. Therefore, it can be predicted that, to the extent that economic and interpersonal situations are favorable, symptoms will decrease. Moreover, the social stress–social support perspective also predicts that part of this relationship may operate through the self-concept.

Although they did not focus specifically on those diagnosed as having a mental illness, several longitudinal studies using general population samples indicate that processes predicted by selection, causation, and stress-process perspectives operate concurrently. For example, studies that focus on the relationship between depressive symptoms and various aspects of social relationships (e.g., social ties, social support, or perceived quality of family relationships) generally find negative reciprocal relationships between the two (Carlton-Ford et al., 1996; Johnson, 1991; Matt & Dean, 1993; Turner, 1981).

Concern with the evaluative dimension of self-concept (self-esteem and self-efficacy) has become prominent in the clinical and sociological literature on mental illness (Brown, Bifulco, & Andrews, 1990; Davidson & Strauss, 1992; Markowitz, 1998; Rosenfield, 1992, 1997; Rosenberg et al., 1989; Seilheimer & Doyal, 1996; Townsend & Rakfeldt, 1985). In one study that asked consumers of mental health services with what areas they most wanted help, 65% of the respondents indicated self-oriented concerns, such as "gaining self-confidence" (Coursey et al., 1991). Consistent with this observation, several studies have shown an inverse relationship between self-evaluation and psychiatric symptoms (Brown et al., 1990; Davidson & Strauss, 1992; Rosenberg et al., 1989). This relationship can be interpreted in various ways. For example, people higher in self-efficacy may take a more active role in their care and feel more optimistic about their prognosis (Gecas, 1989). Favorable self-evaluation may also lead to increased life satisfaction by facilitating the establishment of social relationships, employment, and housing (Bandura, 1977; Gecas, 1989; Miller & Dawson, 1965; Nelson et al., 1995; Rosenfield, 1992, 1997; Rosenfield & Wenzel, 1997; Seilheimer & Doyal, 1996). Taken together, the preceding reasoning and research underlie several predictions: As self-esteem and efficacy increase, interpersonal and economic well-being increases, and as self-esteem and efficacy increase, symptoms decrease.

The relationships just discussed have been examined primarily with recursive models, under the assumption that self-concept affects symptoms and life satisfaction. However, a reverse causal ordering is possible: Self-concept may also be affected by symptoms and life satisfaction. According to the "consistency principle" in self-esteem theory, exhibiting signs of a mental disorder may be interpreted as personal failure or inadequacy, leading people to adjust their view of self accordingly (Rosenberg et al., 1989). Some support for a self-symptom feedback loop is found in longitudinal studies of adolescents; these studies generally report significant negative reciprocal relationships between self-esteem and depressive symptoms (Owens, 1994; Rosenberg et al., 1989). Also, self-perception theory predicts that life satisfaction will affect self-evaluation. People are likely to infer their abilities and self-worth from their circumstances (Bem, 1972). For example, people who enjoy satisfying family and work lives and have more comfortable levels of income may think more highly of themselves (Gecas & Seff, 1990; Shamir, 1986). Work and family life, in particular, provide a sense of purpose and attachment. One recent study provides some support for the reciprocal effects between life satisfaction and self-concept among people with mental illnesses (Markowitz, 1998). Following from the preceding theory and research, two additional relationships are predicted: As symptoms increase, self-esteem and efficacy decrease, and as life satisfaction increases, self-esteem and efficacy increase. Moreover, consistent with the stress-process approach (Mirowsky & Ross, 1989; Pearlin et al., 1981), self-esteem and efficacy may mediate the relationship between interpersonal and economic well-being and symptoms.

One limited test of a sociological recovery model has been conducted using longitudinal (two-wave) questionnaire data from 610 people in self-help groups and outpatient treatment (Markowitz, 2001). In that study, a series of models of the relationships between key elements identified as part of the recovery process (symptoms, self-concept, and life satisfaction) were estimated. Consistent with the stress-process and social causation perspectives, the findings indicated that, as life satisfaction increases, symptoms decrease, suggesting that improvements in social relationships and economic circumstances may help improve mental condition. However, in line with a social selection perspective, the findings also showed that the reverse relationship is operating—that severity of symptoms has an adverse impact on subjective interpersonal and economic well-being. This is consistent with an understanding of the debilitating nature of mental disorder and highlights the difficulties that people with mental illnesses face. The severity of their illness may result in less adequate employment, lowered income, poorer housing conditions, and diminished social interaction and relationships. Nevertheless, improvement in these outcomes apparently helps reduce the severity of illness. These findings point to the need for sociologists to consider not only the social causes of mental disorder, but the social consequences as well, focusing on how symptoms of mental illness affect social relationships, living situations, and employment, which in turn affect the course of illness.

The findings of that study also help confirm that self-concept, as both social product and social force, is an important part of the recovery process. Consistent with self-esteem theory, Markowitz (2001) found that self-esteem has a positive effect on life satisfaction and a negative effect on symptoms. To the extent people think highly of themselves and believe that they can affect what happens to them, people may be more motivated to engage in behaviors that help improve their interpersonal, economic, and psychological well-being. Also, in line with the consistency principle of self-esteem theory, increases in symptoms have a negative effect on esteem. Self-esteem is also affected by life satisfaction, as self-perception and attribution theories predict. People look at how they think they are doing and infer self-worth accordingly. Those with friends and family to turn to, decent jobs and places to live, and sufficient funds to survive on are likely to infer a greater sense of self-worth and efficacy than those without. In addition, the results of the Markowitz (2001) study suggested that the effect of life satisfaction on symptoms operates through its effect on self-concept.

In terms of treatment interventions, sociological studies of recovery underscore the importance of continuing to develop and support *recovery-oriented* treatment systems and services for people with mental illnesses (Anthony, 1991, 1993; Blue Ribbon Commission on Mental Health Care, 1997; Campbell, 1998; U.S. Department of Health and Human Services, 1999). While not downplaying the role of effective medication, for example, such systems entail a multifaceted approach that goes beyond "medical-oriented" concern with symptom management to take into account the utility of devoting resources to social and vocational skills training to facilitate involvement in meaningful social activity (Rosenfield, 1992). Programs that are effective in developing social and vocational skills may contribute to an escalating feedback loop whereby increases in social well-being result in increased self-esteem and efficacy, which in turn decreases the symptoms of illness, leading to further increases in social well-being. These sorts of considerations become especially critical in the current era of managed care, where there may be pressure to limit nonclinical services. Moreover, allowing people with mental illnesses to receive income from paid employment in addition to income from disability programs may not only further reduce the stress associated with financial disadvantage, but may also lead to an increased sense of esteem and efficacy.

IMPLICATIONS FOR FUTURE RESEARCH

Several possibilities for sociological investigation into the process of recovery from mental illness are left open. For example, what are the mechanisms by which self-evaluation and symptoms affect each other? To what extent do symptoms affect the likelihood that people will be stigmatized and discriminated against, resulting in a diminished sense of self (Link et al., 1987, 1991)? The mechanisms through which symptoms and quality of life are related also warrant further examination. For example, to what extent does symptomatic behavior lead to rejection on the part of family and friends, and to what extent does it lead to an individual's withdrawal from social interaction? Future studies that incorporate specific measures of rejection and social withdrawal would be useful in clarifying these processes. How do styles of coping (e.g., emotion vs. problem solving) interact with how these key elements of recovery affect each other? Also, how is sense of self in terms of *identity* (e.g., "sick" vs. "well," "not normal" vs. "normal") related to symptoms and social outcomes?

Methodologically, an ideal investigation would extend recent research on the process of recovery by using data from a multiwave panel study of people with major mental illnesses. Much of the recovery-related research has been based on cross-sectional data, limiting the ability of researchers to establish causal relationships, model reciprocal effects, and determine how long it takes for symptoms to impact interpersonal and economic well-being. Although some limited research using longitudinal (mostly two-wave) data has been conducted, such research has been unable to estimate both simultaneous and cross-lagged (over time) reciprocal effects. A multiwave design would allow for the estimation of such effects and for experimentation with various causal lag specifications in recovery process models (Finkel, 1995; see Figure 4.2). Measures should include not only key demographic variables, but stressful-events indices, symptom scales, and self-concept measures including perceptions of functioning and identity provided by both respondents and significant others, such as family and friends (Matsueda, 1992). Moreover, outcomes would include a variety of objective and subjective measures of interpersonal and economic well-being (e.g., income, perceived support, life satisfaction).

In summary, *recovery* has gained prominence as an orienting concept around which the course of mental illness is understood. In this chapter, I have attempted to theoretically organize causal relationships among some of the key elements identified as part of the recovery process and suggest some directions for future research. A sociological approach to recovery begins with an assertion that social circumstances and positions are fundamental causes of stress and symptoms of mental illness, while at the same time recognizing that symptoms of illness have consequences for people's self-concepts and social well-being, which in turn, affect the course of illness.

REFERENCES

Anthony, W. A. (1991). Recovery from mental illness: The new vision of services researchers. *Innovations in Research, 1*, 13–14.

Anthony, W. A. (1993). Recovery from mental illness: The guiding vision of the mental health service system in the 1990s. *Psychosocial Rehabilitation Journal, 16*, 11–23.

Arns, P., & Linney, J. A. (1993). Work, self, and life satisfaction for people with severe and persistent mental disorders. *Psychosocial Rehabilitation Journal, 17*, 63–79.

Bandura, A. (1977). Self-efficacy: Toward a unifying theory of behavioral change. *Psychological Review, 84*, 191–215.

Beels, C. C. (1981). Social support and schizophrenia. *Schizophrenia Bulletin, 7*, 58–72.

Bem, D. (1972). Self-perception theory. In L. Berkowitz (Ed.), *Advances in experimental psychology* (Vol. 6, pp. 1–62). New York: Academic Press.

Blue Ribbon Commission on Mental Health Care. (1997). *Blue ribbon commission on mental health: Final report.* Madison: Department of Health and Family Services, State of Wisconsin.

Brenner, M. H. (1973). *Mental illness and the economy.* Cambridge, MA: Harvard University Press.

Brier, A., & Straus, J. S. (1984). The role of social relationships in the recovery from psychotic disorders. *American Journal of Psychiatry, 141*, 949–955.

Brown, G. W., Bifulco, A., & Andrews, B. (1990). Self-esteem and depression. *Social Psychiatry and Psychiatric Epidemiology, 25*, 244–249.

Campbell, J. (1998). Consumerism, outcomes, and satisfaction: A review of the literature. In R. Manderscheid & M. J. Henderson (Eds.), *Mental health, United*

States, 1998 (pp. 11–28). Rockville, MD: U.S. Department of Health and Human Services, Public Health Service, Substance Abuse and Mental Health Administration, Center for Mental Health Services.

Carlton-Ford, S., Paikoff, R. L., Oakley, J., & Brooks-Gunn, J. (1996). A longitudinal analysis of depressed mood, self-esteem and family processes during adolescence. *Sociological Focus, 29,* 135–154.

Coursey, R. D., Farrell, E. W., & Zahniser, J. H. (1991). Consumers' attitudes toward psychotherapy, hospitalization, and aftercare. *Health and Social Work, 16,* 155–161.

Davidson, L., & Strauss, J. S. (1992). Sense of self in recovery from severe mental illness. *British Journal of Medical Psychology, 65,* 131–145.

Davidson, L., & Strauss, J. S. (1995). Beyond the biopsychosocial model: Integrating disorder, health, and recovery. *Psychiatry, 58,* 44–55.

Dohrenwend, B. P., Levav, I., Shrout, P., Schwartz, S., Naveh, G., Link, B., et al. (1992). Socioeconomic status and psychiatric disorders: The causation selection issue. *Science, 255,* 946–951.

Durkheim, E. (1951). *Suicide: A study in sociology.* New York: Free Press. (Original work published 1897)

Faris, R. E. L., & Dunham, H. W. (1939). *Mental disorders in urban areas: An ecological study schizophrenia and other psychoses.* Chicago: University of Chicago Press.

Finkel, S. (1995). *Causal analysis with panel data.* Thousand Oaks, CA: Sage.

Fox, J. (1990). Social class, mental illness, and social mobility: The social selection-drift hypothesis for serious mental illness. *Journal of Health and Social Behavior, 31,* 344–353.

Gecas, V. (1989). The social psychology of self-efficacy. *Annual Review of Sociology, 15,* 291–316.

Gecas, V., & Seff, M. A. (1990). Social class and self-esteem: Psychological centrality, compensation, and the relative effects of work and home. *Social Psychology Quarterly, 53,* 165–173.

Greenley, J. S., Greenberg, J. S., & Brown, R. (1997). Measuring quality of life: a new and practical survey instrument. *Social Work, 42,* 244–254.

Harding, C., Brooks, G., Ashikaga, T., Strauss, J., & Brier, A. (1987). The Vermont longitudinal study of people with severe mental illnesses. *American Journal of Psychiatry, 144,* 718–735.

Hollingshead, A. B., & Redlich, F. C. (1958). *Social class and mental illness.* New York: Wiley.

Huffine, C. L., & Clausen, J. A. (1979). Madness and work: Short and long-term effects of mental illness on occupational careers. *Social Forces, 57,* 1049–1062.

Johnson, T. P. (1991). Mental health, social relations, and social selection: A longitudinal analysis. *Journal of Health and Social Behavior, 32,* 408–423.

Karp, D. (1996). *Speaking of sadness.* New York: Oxford.

Kessler, R. C., & Cleary, P. D. (1980). Social class and psychological distress. *American Sociological Review, 45*, 463–478.

Kessler, R. C., McGonagle, K. A., Zhao, S., Nelson, C. B., Hughes, M., Eshleman, S., et al. (1994). Lifetime and 12-month prevalence of *DSM–III–R* psychiatric disorders in the United States: Results from the National Comorbidity Survey. *Archives of General Psychiatry, 51*, 8–19.

Leete, E. (1989). How I perceive and manage my illness. *Schizophrenia Bulletin, 15*, 197–200.

Lehmann, A. F. (1988). A quality of life interview for the chronically mentally ill. *Evaluation and Program Planning, 11*, 51–62.

Link, B. G. (1982). Mental patient status, work, and income: An examination of the effects of a psychiatric label. *American Sociological Review, 47*, 202–215.

Link, B. G. (1987). Understanding labeling effects in the area of mental disorders: An empirical assessment of the effects of expectations of rejection. *American Sociological Review, 52*, 96–112.

Link, B., & Cullen, F. T. (1990). The labeling theory of mental disorder: A review of the evidence. *Research in Community and Mental Health, 6*, 75–105.

Link, B. G., Cullen, F. T., Frank, J., & Wozniak, J. F. (1987). The social rejection of former mental patients: Understanding why labels matter. *American Journal of Sociology, 92*, 1461–1500.

Link, B. G., Cullen, F. T., Struening, E., Shrout, P. E., & Dohrenwend, B. P. (1989). A modified labeling theory approach to mental disorders: An empirical assessment. *American Sociological Review, 54*, 400–423.

Link, B. G., Mirotznik, J., & Cullen, F. T. (1991). The effectiveness of stigma coping orientations: Can negative consequences of mental illness labeling be avoided? *Journal of Health and Social Behavior, 32*, 302–320.

Link, B. G., & Phelan, J. C. (1995). Social conditions as fundamental causes of disease. *Journal of Health and Social Behavior, special issue*, 80–94.

Markowitz, F. E. (1998). The effects of stigma on the psychological well-being and life satisfaction of people with mental illness. *Journal of Health and Social Behavior, 39*, 335–348.

Markowitz, F. E. (2001). Modeling processes in recovery from mental illness: Relationships between symptoms, life satisfaction, and self-concept. *Journal of Health and Social Behavior, 42*, 64–79.

Markowitz, F. E. (2003). Sociological approaches to stigma. In P. W. Corrigan (Ed.), *A comprehensive review of the stigma of mental illness: Implications for research and social change*. Washington, DC: American Psychological Association.

Matsueda, R. L. (1992). Reflected appraisals, parental labeling, and delinquency: Specifying a symbolic interactionist theory. *American Journal of Sociology, 97*, 1577–1611.

Matt, A., & Dean, G. (1993). Social support from friends and psychological distress among elderly persons: moderator effects of age. *Journal of Health and Social Behavior, 34,* 187–200.

Miller, D. H., & Dawson, W. H. (1965). Effects of stigma on re-employment of ex-mental patients. *Mental Hygiene, 49,* 281–287.

Mirowsky, J., & Ross, C. E. (1989). Psychiatric diagnosis as reified measurement. *Journal of Health and Social Behavior, 30,* 11–25.

Mirowsky, J., & Ross, C. E. (2002). Measurement for a human science. *Journal of Health and Social Behavior, 43,* 152–170.

Nelson, G., Wiltshire, C., Hall, G. B., Peirson, L., & Walsh-Bowers, R. (1995). Psychiatric consumer/survivors' quality of life: Quantitative and qualitative perspectives. *Journal of Community Psychology, 23,* 216–233.

Ortega, S. T., & Corzine, J. (1990). Socioeconomic status and mental disorders. In J. R. Greenley (Ed.), *Research in community and mental health* (Vol. 6, pp. 149–182). Greenwich, CT: JAI Press.

Owens, T. J. (1994). Two dimensions of self-esteem: Reciprocal effects of positive self-worth and self-deprecation on adolescent problems. *American Sociological Review, 59,* 391–407.

Pearlin, L., Menaghan, E. G., Lieberman, M. A., & Mullan, J. T. (1981). The stress process. *Journal of Health and Social Behavior, 22,* 337–356.

Perucci, R., & Targ, D. (1982). Network structure and reactions to primary deviance of mental patients. *Journal of Health and Social Behavior, 23,* 3–17.

Robins, L. N., & Reiger, D. A. (1991). *Psychiatric disorders in America: The epidemiologic catchment area study.* New York: Free Press.

Rosenberg, M., Schooler, C., & Schoenbach, C. (1989). Self-esteem and adolescent problems: Modeling reciprocal effects. *American Sociological Review, 54,* 1004–1018.

Rosenfield, S. (1992). Factors contributing to the subjective quality of life of the chronically mentally ill. *Journal of Health and Social Behavior, 33,* 299–315.

Rosenfield, S. (1997). Labeling mental illness: The effects of services and perceived stigma on life satisfaction. *American Sociological Review, 62,* 660–672.

Rosenfield, S., & Wenzel, S. (1997). Social networks and chronic mental illness: A test of four perspectives. *Social Problems, 44,* 200–216.

Ross, C. E., & Mirowsky, J. (2001). Neighborhood disadvantage, disorder, and health. *Journal of Health and Social Behavior, 42,* 258–276.

Ross, C. E., Reynolds, J. R., & Geis, K. J. (2000). The contingent meaning of neighborhood stability for residents' psychological well-being. *American Sociological Review, 65,* 581–597.

Segal, S. P., & VanderVoort, D. J. (1993). Daily hassles of people with severe mental illness. *Hospital and Community Psychiatry, 44,* 276–278.

Seilheimer, T. A., & Doyal, G. T. (1996). Self-efficacy and consumer satisfaction with housing. *Community Mental Health Journal, 32,* 549–559.

Shamir, B. (1986). Self-esteem and the psychological impact of unemployment. *Social Psychology Quarterly, 49*, 61–72.

Srole L., Langner, T. S., Michael, S. T., Opler, M. K., & Rennie, T. A. C. (1962). *Mental health in the metropolis: The midtown Manhattan study.* New York: McGraw-Hill.

Thoits, P. A. (1995). Stress, coping, and social support processes: Where are we? What next? *Journal of Health and Social Behavior* [Special Issue], 53–79.

Townsend, J., & Rakfeldt, J. (1985). Hospitalization and first-contact mental patients: Stigma and changes in self-concept. *Research in Community and Mental Health 5*, 269–301.

Turner, R. J. (1981). Social support as a contingency in psychological well-being. *Journal of Health and Social Behavior, 22*, 357–367.

U.S. Department of Health and Human Services, Substance Abuse and Mental Health Administration, Center for Mental Health Services, National Institutes of Health, National Institute of Mental Health. (1999). *Mental health: A report of the surgeon general*, Washington, DC: U.S. Government Printing Office.

Uttaro, T., & Mechanic, D. (1994). The NAMI consumer survey analysis of unmet needs. *Hospital and Community Psychiatry, 45*, 372–374.

Weingarten, R. (1994). The ongoing process of recovery. *Psychiatry, 57*, 369–375.

Weissman, M. M., & Paykel, E. S. (1974). *The depressed woman: A study of social relationships.* Chicago: University of Chicago Press.

Wheaton, B. (1978). The sociogenesis of psychological disorder: Reexamining the causal issues with longitudinal data. *American Sociological Review, 43*, 383–403.

5

RECOVERY FROM SCHIZOPHRENIA: A CRITERION-BASED DEFINITION

ROBERT P. LIBERMAN AND ALEX KOPELOWICZ

The Decade of the Brain of the 1990s, promoted by agencies of the federal government and consumer advocacy organizations such as the National Alliance for the Mentally Ill, fulfilled much of its promise by stimulating a vast increase in neuroscience research that casts much needed light on the structure and function of the brain as these relate to serious mental disorders. With less prominence, but of more direct, immediate, and practical relevance to the treatment of people with schizophrenia and other disabling mental disorders has been the considerable progress in developing evidence-based practices leading to optimal outcomes for these disorders. Now available to practitioners and consumers alike, the advent of vastly improved services has generated expectations for substantial progress in quality of life and psychosocial functioning for people with schizophrenia than was heretofore thought possible.

To what extent do these advances in treatment and rehabilitation presage recovery from schizophrenia as a realistic goal? In this chapter we summarize the feasibility of recovery as a therapeutic goal, provide an operational definition of recovery to facilitate research on this topic, assemble recent findings that put an operational definition in clinical perspective, identify factors that may impede or promote recovery, and conclude with a case example that highlights the recovery process and outcome.

THE TIMELINESS OF A FOCUS ON RECOVERY

A growing body of empirically based, clinical research shows that recovery from schizophrenia can be multiplied manyfold over traditional estimates if four conditions are met:

1. The disorder is treated early in its course with assertive outreach and optimal services.
2. Flexible levels of consumer-oriented case management are used.
3. Families and other natural supporters and caregivers are involved as partners in the treatment process.
4. Later stages of more chronic, relapsing, or refractory forms of the illness are treated for lengthy periods with comprehensive, well-coordinated, and continuous biobehavioral treatments that are keyed to the phase of illness (Barrowclough & Tarrier, 1998; DeSisto, Harding, McCormick, Ashikaga, & Brooks, 1995; Glynn et al., 2002; Harding, Brooks, Ashikaga, Strauss, & Breier, 1987; Lieberman et al., 1993).

Some of the evidence-based reasons for considering recovery from schizophrenia a worthwhile and cost-effective goal of research and clinical work are as follows:

- Antipsychotic drug treatment, case management, and supportive therapies have brought about almost complete remissions of positive and negative symptoms in 80% or more of persons with their first or second episodes of schizophrenia (Lieberman et al., 1993).
- Long-term, catamnestic follow-up studies of persons with severe forms of schizophrenia earlier in their lives have shown that approximately 60% of them have recovered and are living full and satisfying lives (Harding et al., 1987).
- Adding family intervention to antipsychotic drug therapy can reduce relapse rates in schizophrenia by half or more (Barrowclough & Tarrier, 1998).
- Adding structured methods of building skills, through training of social competence, has been shown to improve social functioning and autonomy of the patient (Glynn et al., 2002).
- The advent of clozapine and the newer atypical antipsychotics means that, cumulatively, more individuals with schizophrenia are now able to respond therapeutically to treatment (Davis, Chen, & Glick, 2003).

Reports have emanated from several clinical research centers demonstrating a high rate of symptomatic remission in recent onset cases, when treatment is provided in an assertive and targeted manner. For example, researchers at Hillside Hospital-Long Island Jewish Medical Center enrolled people experiencing their first schizophrenic episode into an open, standardized treatment algorithm that involved titration of neuroleptic medication to optimal doses and changing medications, if necessary, to achieve symptom control. Using a stringent definition of remission (i.e., ratings of 3 or less on the Schedule for Affective Disorders and Schizophrenia and Psychosis and Disorganization Scale psychosis items, a Clinical Global Impression severity item rating of "mild" or less, and a rating of at least "much improved" on the Clinical Global Impression improvement item), 74% of research participants were considered to be fully remitted within 1 year (Loebel et al., 1992). In a subsequent paper from the same research group (Lieberman et al., 1993), the authors concluded, "most patients recover from their first episode of schizophrenia and achieve full symptom remission" (p. 375).

At the Early Psychosis Prevention and Intervention Center in Melbourne, Australia, 91% of young people with the recent onset of psychosis were in relatively complete remission of their positive and negative symptoms (i.e., Positive and Negative Syndrome Scale scores of 3 or less) after 1 year of assertive case management, antipsychotic drugs, and cognitive–behavioral therapy (McGorry, Edwards, Mihalopoulos, & Harrigan, 1996; Edwards, Maude, McGorry, Harrigan, & Cocks, 1998). Similarly, in Nova Scotia, 89% of individuals experiencing their first episode of schizophrenia survived the first year without rehospitalization and, of these, more than half were involved in full- or part-time work or education (Whitehorn, Lazier, & Kopala, 1998). Most important, subsequent rediagnosis of the individuals from these studies revealed that more than 95% continued to meet lifetime DSM–IV (American Psychiatric Association, 1994) criteria for schizophrenia or schizoaffective disorder, thus contradicting the view that remitted individuals had been misdiagnosed originally (Hegarty, Baldessarini, Tohen, Waternaux, & Oepen, 1994).

At the other end of the acute-chronic spectrum of schizophrenia, investigators from Europe, the United States, and Asia have reported long-term follow-up studies that have documented the malleability of chronic schizophrenia to comprehensive and well-orchestrated intervention and rehabilitation programs (Bleuler, 1968; Ciompi, 1980; Harding et al., 1987; Huber, Gross, & Schuttler, 1975; Ogawa, et al., 1987). Each of these international studies followed cohorts of people with schizophrenia for at least 20 years and found rates of social restoration (i.e., Global Assessment of Functioning scores of 60 or more) of at least 50% (Harding, Zubin, & Strauss, 1992). In the most rigorous of these studies, the Vermont Longitudinal Research Project (Harding et al., 1987), the highest (68%) social recovery rate was found in a sample that contained the greatest proportion of chronic, "back ward" patients among the long-term studies. Two thirds of this sample had no psychotic symptoms when carefully interviewed 20 to 30 years after their periods of prolonged hospitalization.

We should point out that a key element in these favorable long-term outcomes was access to continuous and reasonably comprehensive mental health services including family intervention and social skills training as illustrated by a long-term follow-up study comparing a sample of well-diagnosed people with schizophrenia from Vermont to a similar cohort in Maine. The state of Vermont established a well-crafted system of accessible treatment that was flexibly linked to the needs of its chronic patients early in the 1960s, but Maine did not. After carefully matching cohorts from these two states for age, education, sociodemographic factors, and duration and severity of illness during their early periods of treatment in the Vermont and Maine state hospitals, researchers found that the rate of recovery, as defined by remission of psychotic symptoms and a score of 70 or above on the Global Assessment Scale, occurred twice as frequently in Vermont as in Maine (DeSisto et al., 1995).

DEFINING RECOVERY

We have reviewed these studies not to examine their varying definitions of recovery but to illustrate that people with schizophrenia do experience recovery regardless of how it is defined. Without reliable measurements, however, there can be no scientific advances. This applies to the construct of recovery as well as to any other aspect of psychiatry or medicine. Just as advances in etiology and treatment followed the operational definition of diagnostic categories with *DSM–III*, we can expect progress in understanding the factors that impede or promote recovery when this construct is defined in measurable terms. What, then, are the appropriate dimensions that should be used in a definition of recovery? Symptom remission alone is inadequate as seen in efforts to define recovery from depression (Frank et al., 1991). Even when symptoms are in complete remission in mood or anxiety disorders, psychosocial functioning may continue to be impaired (Mintz, Mintz, Arruda, & Hwang, 1992; Bystritsky, Liberman, Hwang, & Wallace, 2001). For example, in one recent study of 219 people with psychotic affective disorders, 98% achieved symptomatic recovery by 2 years, but only 38% achieved functional recovery by 2 years (Tohen et al., 2000). Therefore, a normative and operational definition of recovery from schizophrenia should include participation in work or school, social, family, and recreational activities and achieving symptom remission.

Because schizophrenia is so often associated with dependence on professionals, families, and other caregivers, any definition of recovery should include a dimension related to independent functioning. Whether or not the individual is living apart from the family—which could be influenced by cultural and financial factors—independent functioning could be defined as managing one's own medication, health, and money without regular supervision from others. Thus, people who have a representative payee or whose medications are administered to them would not meet this criterion for recovery. Similarly, dependence on professional networks or mental health services for social and recreational activities—for instance, long-term participation in psychosocial clubhouses or day treatment programs—would be inconsistent with a fully normative definition of recovery.

Recovery from schizophrenia is not the same as a cure. Individuals can recover and live reasonably normal and full lives while continuing to experience the vulnerability to relapse and the protective effects of indefinite treatment. Parallels are obvious for recovery from myocardial infarctions, strokes, diabetes, and rheumatoid arthritis. The participation of the individual with schizophrenia in comprehensive, coordinated, competent, and consumer-oriented services will facilitate the control of symptoms and the salutary engagement in psychosocial pursuits.

In the quest for increasing the proportion of people with schizophrenia who can attain recovery, researchers and practitioners must give up what has become a double standard in treatment; that is, pharmacological treatments are considered efficacious despite the fact that they only work while clients take them, yet psychosocial treatments are considered less than effective if they do not achieve and sustain long-term improvements in functioning when used in a time-limited manner. Expanding the proportion of people with schizophrenia who can recover will require psychosocial treatments to be accessible on a continuing basis, albeit flexibly linked in type and intensity to the phase of the person's disorder and the person's individualized goals (Kopelowicz & Liberman, 1995).

DISTINGUISHING PROCESS OF RECOVERING FROM RECOVERY AS AN OUTCOME

Just as there are clear differences between people recovering from alcoholism or drug addiction and those who have made sustained recoveries with long-term abstinence and normal psychosocial functioning, the same holds for recovery from schizophrenia. Many consumers and professionals have confounded *recovering* with *recovery* by failing to grasp the distinction between *processes and stages of preparation for recovery* from a reliable, normative, *outcome definition of recovery*. Individuals can take any of numerous pathways en route to recovery that involve many attributes at the level of personal qualities, social supports, therapies, and subjective experience.

Examples of attributes and experiences that may be associated with individuals who are progressing toward, but have not yet achieved, recovery include hope, self-responsibility, destigmatization, empowerment, self-acceptance, insight and awareness, collaboration with professionals, sense of autonomy and self-control, and participation in self-help and consumer-run programs. Subjective experiences and attributes can be viewed as mediating the process leading to recovery, but also remaining present after recovery has been achieved. For example, a treatment or self-help program may engender a feeling of empowerment in an individual that can be instrumental in motivating that person to sustain treatment and rehabilitation until criteria used to define recovery have been achieved. Once recovery has been achieved, empowerment may be even more firmly subjectively experienced, because more objective indicators of independence, employment, and freedom from psychosis would validate it.

Having hope for future improvements in quality of life may be reinforced by the enthusiasm and collaborative alliance embedded in a therapeutic relationship. Many consumers who have written first-person accounts of their recovery have pointed to the importance of a long-term relationship with a practitioner who refused to despair and reflected a beacon of hope for ultimate improvement and recovery (Spaniol & Koehler, 1994). Hope, in turn, can serve to fuel motivation for change and active participation in clinical services or self-help actions that are stepping stones toward recovery (Deegan, 1996). Once achieved, recovery can continue to reinforce a person's hope for an improved quality of life, thus facilitating self-responsibility and an attitude of "getting on with life" (Noordsy et al., 2002).

The process of recovery from severe mental illness has also been the object of qualitative research. For example, reporting on the results of a 5-year, longitudinal analysis of interviews with 12 individuals with schizophrenia, researchers at the Boston University Center for Psychiatric Rehabilitation have described four stages of recovery: overwhelmed by the disability, struggling with the disability, coping and living with the disability, and establishing a lifestyle beyond the disability (Spaniol, Wewiorski, Gagne, & Anthony, 2002). These authors identified a number of factors that appear to be associated with progression through these phases such as a supportive social network, effective treatment with antipsychotic medication, and religious faith. They also noted a number of factors that may impede progress through the stages of recovery including substance abuse, poverty and disadvantage, and early age of illness onset. Although the stages and factors described by these researchers may be viewed more as charting the phases of an overlapping, continuous, and effortful process toward symptomatic and functional recovery, the subjective variables represented by hope, empowerment, self-responsibility, and religious faith are also important accompaniments to the more objectively measured outcome variables discussed in the next section of this chapter.

It is not easy to separate *process* from *outcome* in delineating recovery from schizophrenia. Nor is it easy or useful to make fine distinctions between the objective and subjective factors in recovery since these are always in dynamic interaction with one another. Most, if not all, of the subjective attributes are influenced by the progress being made by individuals as they approximate the objective criteria being proposed for defining recovery as an outcome. Thus, the greater the person's symptomatic and functional improvement, the more one would expect subjectively experienced qualities such as hope, empowerment, self-responsibility, and autonomy to be in evidence. Furthermore, because recovery is not static or necessarily permanent, even when it meets a particular set of criteria, the processes mediating improvement may have to be remobilized to facilitate a return to the criteria used to define recovery.

OPERATIONAL DEFINITION OF RECOVERY

Although at present there are no consensually validated criteria for defining recovery from schizophrenia, we propose a multiplex criterion set of four dimensions to encourage others to propose alternative criteria. The criteria in our definition, all of which are reliably measurable, include both symptomatic and functional variables. Each variable could be set at a threshold level, with four variables at their threshold levels required to meet the critical definition for recovery. Alternatively, each criterion measure could be allowed to vary at or above a critical threshold, resulting in a quantifiable score for recovery. Two consecutive years of maintenance at or above the threshold levels are suggested as the duration required for determining recovery because few randomized controlled trials of treatment extend beyond 2 years and because 2 years represent a long enough time for clinical improvements to be translated into significant changes in subjective quality of life. For purposes of simplicity, the following criteria with their operationalized thresholds are presented as a definition of recovery from schizophrenia:

- *Psychotic symptoms:* Using the UCLA version of the Brief Psychiatric Rating Scale (BPRS; Ventura, Green, Shaner, & Liberman, 1993) with its structured interview to elicit symptoms and operationalized scale levels, recovery would require ratings of 4 (moderate severity) or below on the six scales reflecting positive and negative symptoms. A 3 is considered mild in severity, 2 very mild, and 1 nil.
- *Independence:* Whether living alone or with others, recovery represents the capacity for reliable adherence to and self-management of medications; budgeting of one's funds for supporting housing and food; meeting scheduled appointments with mental health, general health, and social agencies and personnel; and care of personal possessions and room without supervision by others.
- *Work or school:* At least half-time employment or education in normative, not sheltered or transitional, settings.
- *Social and recreational activities:* Participation at least once per week in some leisure time activity, broadly defined but in a normative

setting; conversations lasting a cumulative duration of 1 hour per week with at least one other person who is not connected or known to the recovered individual through a treatment agency.

Exhibit 5.1 lists the 10 domains from which our operational definition has been selected. Criteria for determining recovery could conceivably be drawn from any number of domains and could be either categorical or dimensional in nature. Our particular definition of recovery should be viewed as a preliminary, if arbitrary, set of criteria that could be improved on by others. In addition, one might consider a definition of recovery—especially if constructed in a dimensional fashion—as tantamount to the construct of "substantial clinical improvement."

We are not enamored of any one set of criteria for defining recovery, because our wish is to stimulate a research agenda that will rely on social and scientific validation of extant and newly emerging definitions. Future work will determine which of the domains listed in Exhibit 5.1 and which operational definitions of those domains are most closely associated with a consensual validation of recovery.

DEVELOPMENT OF DEFINITION OF RECOVERY

The four dimensions in the definition of recovery proposed earlier were selected for several reasons. First, the diagnosis of schizophrenia relies on the

EXHIBIT 5. 1
Proposed Criteria or Dimensions
Used to Operationalize Recovery From Schizophrenia

1. Remission of both positive and negative psychotic symptoms and signs

2. Working or studying in normative employment or educational settings

3. Independent living without supervision of money, self-care skills, and medication

4. Social activities with peers

5. Cordial family relations and contacts

6. Recreational activity in normative settings (i.e., not in psychosocial clubhouses or day treatment programs)

7. Resilience and capacity for problem solving when faced with stressors or challenges in everyday life

8. Subjective satisfaction with life

9. Self-esteem and stable self-identity

10. Participation as a citizen in voting, self-advocacy, neighborliness, and other civic arenas

Note. Each dimension should have a duration criterion associated with it; thus the multiplex criteria of recovery will have dual operationalization: qualitative or quantitative and temporal.

meeting of symptom criteria of clinical significance. The operational definitions of subthreshold severity on the BPRS are below what would be considered commensurate with criteria for the diagnosis of schizophrenia; for example, a 4 (moderate) on the symptom "unusual thought content" includes strange ideas that are either not strongly held or that do not disrupt psychosocial functioning; a 3 (mild) or 2 (very mild) rating on this symptom is at the level of ideas of reference or persecution and considered not delusional. For the negative symptom "emotional withdrawal" a 4, 3, or 2 rating is operationalized as "shows some affect appropriate to the topic of conversation" or "tends not to show spontaneous emotional involvement with interviewer but responds when approached and engaged in conversation."

The diagnosis of schizophrenia also requires markedly impaired functioning in work, school, interpersonal relations, or self-care—dimensions consonant with the areas of functional criteria in our proposed definition of recovery. Another source for the selection of our criteria for recovery came from a survey of individuals with well-diagnosed chronic schizophrenia at the UCLA Neuropsychiatric Hospital, a public mental health center in Los Angeles, and a community clinic in Bern, Switzerland, some of whom met all four of the recovery criteria delineated earlier (Hoffmann & Kupper, 2002). An additional rationale for our definition derived from two studies carried out in Norway during the past 15 years that were based on standardized interviews with people with schizophrenia (Torgalsboen & Rund, 2002). The interviews elicited the stability of symptom improvement and psychosocial adjustment. Twenty-seven individuals met strict criteria for full recovery from schizophrenia, including involvement in social activities, having close friends and at least one hobby, working either full or part time, and living independently or with a spouse or partner.

Finally, we conducted a survey of 55 consumers, family members, and mental health professionals and paraprofessionals all of whom were involved in schizophrenia treatment. A structured interview queried the respondents on each of the dimensions of the operational definition for recovery from schizophrenia. Three fourths of the respondents endorsed the criterion related to living independently; more than two thirds endorsed the criterion related to recreational, social, school, or work activities; and half endorsed the symptom criterion (Liberman, Kopelowicz, Ventura, & Gutkind, 2002).

DISCRIMINANT VALIDITY OF OPERATIONAL DEFINITION OF RECOVERY FROM SCHIZOPHRENIA

What evidence is available to validate the operational criteria for defining recovery from schizophrenia that are proposed in this chapter? Can the evidence be used to generate hypotheses for testing positive and negative factors that might emerge as salient for recovery? Some initial support for the utility of our definition of recovery comes from studies that have used the set of criteria for determining recovery in various samples.

One study that used our definition of recovery to discriminate people who met the criteria from those who did not matched two sets of individuals with schizophrenia according to age, sex, ethnicity, duration of illness, and parental level of education and then compared the groups on a battery of neurocognitive measures. Although the groups differed on a number of variables, the greatest differences between recovered participants and nonrecovered participants were seen on tests of executive functioning, verbal fluency, and verbal working memory. In those domains, each associated with frontal lobe functioning, recovered participants performed significantly better than nonrecovered participants and were comparable to normal control participants. The authors concluded that frontal lobe functioning appears to be the neurocognitive domain most associated with recovery from schizophrenia (Kopelowicz, Ventura, Liberman, Zarate, & Mintz, 2004).

The Hillside-Long Island Jewish Hospital schizophrenia research group applied our operational definition to their sample of 118 young adults treated and evaluated for 5 years after their first episode of schizophrenia or schizoaffective disorder. They found that 17% of their sample met all of our criteria, including the 2 years of stable remission and normal psychosocial functioning (Robinson, Woerner, Alvir, Kane, & Lieberman, 2004). Moreover, better cognitive functioning predicted full recovery.

Among 103 individuals treated in the Nova Scotia Early Psychosis Program, 67% met symptomatic criteria for remission of all psychotic symptoms after 12 months of participation in the program; 42% met criteria after 12 months for remission in the additional symptoms of anxiety, depression, and excitement. At 12 months, 50% of research participants met criteria for symptom remission and functional recovery (Whitehorn, Brown, Richard, Rui, & Kopala, 2002). Similarly, at the UCLA Aftercare Clinic, 85% of individuals with recent-onset schizophrenia achieved a return to either work or school on at least a half-time basis within 9 months of outpatient stabilization (Nuechterlein et al., 1999).

FACTORS THAT MAY IMPEDE OR PROMOTE RECOVERY FROM SCHIZOPHRENIA

A number of factors are involved in either impeding or promoting recovery. This reflects the many factors involved in the operational definition of recovery.

Family Factors

Although no studies have been conducted that directly test the hypothesis that having a supportive family is important for attaining a successful long-term outcome, two lines of research indirectly support this presumption. First, many international studies have replicated the findings that family stress—as reflected in high expressed emotional attitudes of criticism and emotional overinvolvement toward the relative with mental illness—is a powerful predictor of relapse in schizophrenia and mood disorders (Bebbington & Kuipers, 1994; Butzlaff & Hooley, 1998). Because frequency of relapse is a well-documented poor prognostic indicator, it would be predicted that individuals with schizophrenia who had supportive families that expressed acceptance, warmth, understanding, and encouragement would be more likely to recover.

Second, the relationship between family stress and relapse has led to the development of several modes of family intervention that have been designed and empirically validated for their ability to equip relatives with communication, problem-solving, and other coping skills; improve the emotional climate of the family; and reduce the incidence of relapses and rehospitalizations. More than two dozen well-controlled studies in the past decade from several countries have demonstrated that family psychoeducation and training in coping and problem-solving skills decreased the rate of relapse and subsequent hospitalization for people who participated in that type of treatment (Barrowclough & Tarrier, 1998). Moreover, individuals who participated in these types of family interventions also gained significantly more in social adjustment while requiring less overall antipsychotic medication. Together, these findings suggest that having a supportive family with realistic expectations for improvement and abundant reinforcement for incremental progress may be a critical factor in the long-term outcome of people with schizophrenia (Falloon, Held, Cloverdale, Roncone, & Laidlaw, 1999).

Substance Abuse

A National Institute of Mental Health epidemiological study estimated the prevalence of lifetime drug abuse among people with schizophrenia at 47%, well above the rate for the general population (Regier et al., 1990). The serious, clinical consequences that people with schizophrenia who use drugs face warrant special attention. People who use drugs or alcohol have been found to be more symptomatic while hospitalized, relapse more frequently, have poorer psychosocial functioning, and have poorer prognoses for recovery (Bowers, Mazure, Nelson, & Jatlow, 1990; Cleghorn et al., 1991; Swofford, Kasckow, Scheller-Gilkey, & Inderbitzin, 1996; Tsuang, Simpson, & Kronfol, 1982). They have higher rates of violence and suicide, are less likely to have their basic needs of housing and nutrition met, and are less likely to comply with treatment (Cuffel, 1994; Lyons & McGovern, 1989; Swanson, Holzer, Ganju, & Jono, 1990). These findings should be qualified by occasional reports in the research literature that limited amounts of alcohol and marijuana, when used in controlled and social contexts, may be relatively innocuous for people with schizophrenia (Warner et al., 1994).

A number of factors may contribute to the deleterious interaction of most illicit drug use and schizophrenia psychopathology. Individuals may stop taking their medication for fear of negative interactions between street drugs and neuroleptics, or because alcohol and drugs of abuse interfere with memory. Some may fail to appear for scheduled appointments in their treatment programs if they are "high," particularly if active drug use or abuse jeopardizes the benefits they obtain from treatment. People with schizophrenia who abuse drugs may have fewer resources than non-drug-abusing individuals (e.g., a home, a car) and may therefore have more difficulty adhering to their treatment program even if they are motivated to participate in services. Using cocaine may be particularly damaging to people with schizophrenia because of the severe financial and social consequences as well as the fact that cocaine, like other stimulants, operates on the dopaminergic system, which has been linked to the pathophysiology of schizophrenia psychosis and relapses (Shaner et al., 1998).

Duration of Untreated Psychosis

Longer duration of untreated psychosis (DUP), usually defined as the number of weeks from the onset of psychotic symptoms until first hospitalization or initial neuroleptic treatment, has been shown to be a predictor of poorer outcomes (Crow, MacMillan, Johnson, & Johnstone, 1986; Fenton & McGlashan, 1987; Helgason, 1990; Loebel et al., 1992; Lo & Lo, 1977). For example, a longer duration of psychotic symptoms before treatment was significantly associated with greater time to remission as well as a lesser degree of remission (Loebel et al., 1992). Longer duration of illness that included prodromal symptoms (i.e., nonspecific symptoms or behavioral changes such as difficulty sleeping, social withdrawal, and perceptual disturbances that occur before the advent of frank psychotic symptoms) was also associated with longer time to remission. A review of the literature concluded that among a list of pretreatment history variables, duration of untreated psychosis was found to be the best predictor of symptomatic and functional recovery in the studies of recent-onset schizophrenia (Wyatt, 1991).

However, it may be difficult to prove a causal relationship between longer DUP and poorer outcome or, conversely, shorter DUP and better outcome (Lieberman & Fenton, 2000). The methodological obstacles that are present when making inferences from DUP and how it may relate to recovery come from the many other factors that may be confounding this relationship. For example, those who seek treatment soon after the onset of psychosis might have more firmly established social support networks that encourage early treatment (McGlashan, 1996). Similarly, shorter DUP might be related to higher levels of premorbid functioning, higher socioeconomic status, higher intelligence, better neurocognitive functioning, or greater access to health service resources. Nevertheless, because psychosis may be associated with deleterious changes in the brain (Lieberman et al., 1993; Wyatt, 1991), early intervention in treating psychosis may be especially important for a favorable prognosis.

Evidence from prospective studies of young adults treated for their first episode of psychosis, some of whom had been followed closely during prior periods of prodromal symptoms, substantiates the value of rapid intervention in reducing the duration of untreated psychosis and aborting psychotic symptoms in achieving recovery (McGorry et al., 2002). Several investigators from these studies have reported that both positive and negative psychotic symptoms quickly clear within 6 months of initiating antipsychotic drug treatment and adjunctive psychosocial services (Gitlin et al., 2001; Lieberman et al., 1993, 2003). Moreover, the psychosocial functioning of these young adults actually shows improvement subsequent to treatment to levels higher than that exhibited prior to the psychotic episode (McGlashan, 1996). The neurocognitive functioning of these individuals also improves, often reaching the normal range. These findings suggest that rapid involvement in evidence-based treatment may actually contain the seeds of protection against the neurodevelopmental aberrations often found in people with schizophrenia.

Good Initial Response to Neuroleptics

A number of studies have found that improvement of symptoms or lack of a dysphoric effect within several days after receiving neuroleptics significantly predicts outcome after several weeks or months (Awad & Hogan, 1985; May, Van Putten, & Yale, 1980). It has been suggested that the short-term (i.e., 1-month) gains seen in people who responded positively to haloperidol within 3 days were not the result of any specific drug effects, but rather may represent a premorbid prognostic indicator related to the neurodevelopmental severity of the disorder (Klimke, Klieser, Lehmann, & Miele, 1993). More rapid clinical response to antipsychotic drugs may be mediated by lack of side effects and thus more reliable adherence to longer term medication regimens (Ayers, Liberman, & Wallace, 1984). The advent of the novel, atypical antipsychotic medications, which have fewer subjectively aversive side effects, may promote more reliable maintenance use of medication and higher rates of recovery.

Adherence to Treatment

The evidence for the efficacy of antipsychotic medication in the treatment of schizophrenia has been recognized for many years (Davis, 1975), yet failure to comply with medication regimens remains a significant problem for many individuals with the disorder (Hoge et al., 1990). Clearly, failure to take antipsychotic medication as prescribed hampers both short-term and long-term stabilization in areas such as psychopathology, rehospitalization, interpersonal relationships, illicit drug and alcohol use, frequency of violent and otherwise criminal activities, and overall quality of life (Weiden, Olfson, & Essock, 1997). Conversely, the consistent administration of antipsychotic medications—titrated judiciously to doses designed to maximize efficacy while minimizing side effects—is a necessary prerequisite to achieving optimal social and community functioning (Loebel et al., 1992).

A variety of obstacles to regular use of medication must be overcome if the benefits of treatment are to emerge. These obstacles can be found in the person, the treatment, the therapeutic relationship, and the mental health service delivery system (Corrigan, Liberman, & Engel, 1990). Although the data regarding the efficacy of psychosocial interventions are not as robust as the psychopharmacology literature, the evidence in favor of treatments such as family psychoeducation, social skills training, and vocational rehabilitation suggests that greater utilization of these modalities by practitioners and their clientele would have similar salutary effects on the long-term outcome of individuals with schizophrenia (Lehman, Steinwachs, & PORT Co-investigators, 1998; Mueser & Bond, 2000; Scott & Dixon, 1995).

Supportive Therapy With a Collaborative Therapeutic Alliance

Studies that have examined the role of psychotherapy in the lives of people with schizophrenia have found the relationship with their psychiatrists, therapists, and treatment teams to be essential to improvement (Dingman & McGlashan, 1989; Gunderson, 1978; Lamb, 1988). Supportive therapy is considered a necessary foundation for delivering all types of treatments and for therapeutic changes (Frank & Gunderson, 1990; Kopelowicz, Corrigan, Wallace, & Liberman, 1996). Supportive therapy is not, however, "nonspecific" or based solely on office-based discussions. Instead, its efficacy appears to be mediated by a spectrum of effortful and personal involvement by the psychiatrist or therapist who is capable of developing a positive, therapeutic alliance and relationship with client and family members, often in the face of considerable passivity, lack of insight, and noncooperation.

Effective psychosocial therapies in schizophrenia require competencies by the psychiatrist or therapist in active outreach to the client and family; solving problems in everyday life including *in vivo*, assertive treatments; a directive yet empathic and compassionate approach by the therapist who, when appropriate, uses his or her own life experiences and self-disclosure as a role model for the consumer; and encouragement and education of the consumer and family for proper use of antipsychotic medication and psychosocial treatment (Liberman, Hilty, Drake, & Tsang, 2001). The importance of supportive therapy to the recovery process has been corroborated by a few randomized, long-term, well-controlled studies that have demonstrated lower relapse rates and improved social functioning (Gunderson et al., 1984; Hogarty, Goldberg, & Schooler, 1974). Additional evidence comes from several first-person accounts by individuals who have recovered from schizophrenia, attributing part of their success to their relationships with their therapists (Spaniol & Koehler, 1994).

Neurocognitive Factors in the Prediction of Recovery

Neurocognitive functioning has been found to be a correlate and predictor of social learning and instrumental role outcome in schizophrenia. For example, measures of working memory (i.e., the ability to hold information "on-line" for a brief period of time), vigilance (i.e., the ability to sustain attention), and early perceptual processing (i.e., the detection and discrimination of a sensory event within 200 milliseconds of stimulus onset) were among the best predictors of work functioning after 1 year of outpatient treatment for young, recent-onset people with schizophrenia (Nuechterlein et al., 1999). Reviews of the literature have found that specific neurocognitive factors were associated with functional outcome in three areas: community outcome, social problem solving, and acquisition of social skills (Green, 1996). Secondary verbal memory, which is used to learn new information, and executive functions, such as concept formation and cognitive flexibility, emerged as the specific neurocognitive predictors of community functioning. Secondary verbal memory and vigilance were found to predict social problem solving. Immediate and secondary verbal memory and vigilance were consistently associated with acquiring social skills. Similarly, people with schizophrenia with good vocational performance did better than those with poor vocational performance on the Wisconsin Card Sorting Task, a test of executive functioning, and several measures of secondary verbal memory, but not on a variety of other neurocognitive measures (Gold, Bryant, Vladar, & Buchanan, 1997). As research accumulates in this area, it is expected that more specific linkages will emerge between selected neurocognitive factors and focal areas of psychosocial functioning.

One of the promising avenues for increasing prospects for recovery from schizophrenia comes from atypical antipsychotic medications that, because of their beneficial effects on neurocognition and their reduced neurotoxicity, enable individuals with schizophrenia to adhere better to their medication regimens and participate more actively in psychiatric rehabilitation (Kopelowicz & Liberman, 1999). Another new direction of research in this area is cognitive remediation, from which numerous studies have documented the malleability of cognitive impairments in schizophrenia to training (Liberman, 2002). An alternative strategy has been to compensate for cognitive impairments through highly structured and systematic social skills training, supported employment, and social learning programs, which appear to be able to surmount the obstacles posed by neurocognitive deficits in determining treatment outcome (Bond et al., 2001; Liberman et al., in press).

As a first pass at identifying neurocognitive correlates of recovery from schizophrenia, we administered a battery of neurocognitive tests to 28 participants (mean age: 38.2 years; 75% men; 61% European American, 25% Hispanic, 14% African American) with *DSM–IV* schizophrenia who met our operational definition of recovery from schizophrenia (Kopelowicz, Ventura, Liberman, Zrate, & Mintz, 2004). These participants were matched for age, sex, ethnicity, and parental level of education with patients with schizophrenia who did not meet recovery criteria (referred to as *nonrecovered* participants) and with normal control participants. Our recovered participants demonstrated normal or near normal functioning on tests of executive functioning (Wisconsin Card Sort Test), verbal working memory (Auditory Consonant Trigrams), and visuoperceptual skills (Rey-Osterreith Complex Figure Test). Conversely, our recovered participants performed as much as one standard deviation below normative levels on verbal learning (California Verbal Learning Test) and verbal fluency (Controlled Oral Word Fluency) and nearly two standard deviations below normative levels (similar to the scores of nonrecovered participants with schizophrenia) on early visual processing (Span of Apprehension).

These findings suggest that our recovered participants may have acquired the knowledge and skills required for successful community adjustment by pacing their learning in school and job situations, thereby compensating for their slower than normal verbal learning and fluency and visual processing. One participant who was functioning well as an elementary school teacher, for example, told of how he took copious notes and even made audiotapes of lectures in college, which he later reviewed and studied repeatedly to master the material. Another individual described his job doing computer entry in a finance company as relying on procedural learning and memory—repetitive tasks that can be done without a burden on volitional, verbal learning and attentional capacities.

Thus, despite the limitations of our methodology, our findings were consistent with previous research demonstrating a link between verbal memory and executive functioning on the one hand and community functioning on the other in individuals with schizophrenia. Although our small sample precluded statistically partialing out the relationships between specific neurocognitive functions and specific instrumental skills, anecdotally several of our participants who were using high levels of social skills in their work and friendship circles did score well on tests of vigilance as well as immediate and secondary verbal memory.

Presence of Negative Symptoms

A consistent conclusion of review articles has been that negative symptoms, such as restricted affect, diminished emotional range, poverty of speech, curbing of interests, diminished sense of purpose, and diminished social drive or the presence of the deficit syndrome (i.e., primary and enduring negative symptoms), were associated with poor outcome, cognitive impairments, and functional incapacity in social and work domains (Buchanan & Gold, 1996; Davidson & McGlashan, 1997; Glynn, 1998; Pogue-Geile & Harrow, 1987). For example, long-term outcomes in the domains of hospitalization, employment, social functioning, and global outcome were significantly poorer among people with the deficit syndrome than among individuals with nondeficit schizophrenia in the Chestnut Lodge Follow-Up Study (Fenton & McGlashan, 1994). Several cross-sectional studies have found an association between negative symptoms and pronounced frontal lobe dysfunctions (Hammer, Katsanis, & Iacono, 1995; Liddle & Morris, 1991; Strauss, 1993). Moreover, a 5-year longitudinal study in individuals with recent-onset schizophrenia found that improvements in negative symptoms correlated with improvements in cognitive test performance (Gold et al., 1997) suggesting that these domains overlap as predictors of recovery.

Social and vocational adjustment may be especially susceptible to the influence of negative symptoms, in part because negative symptoms are defined as deficits in interpersonal behavior relative to social expectations. Empirically, levels of negative symptoms have been correlated with the degree of disability in social and vocational role functioning in recent-onset schizophrenia (Johnstone, MacMillan, Frith, Benn, & Crow, 1990; Van der Does, Dingemans, Linszen, Nugter, & Scholte, 1993) and chronic schizophrenia (Lysaker & Bell, 1995; Morrison, Bellack, Wixted, & Mueser, 1990). Although intensive social skills training can have durable and substantial effects on secondary negative symptoms (Kopelowicz, Liberman, Mintz, & Zarate, 1997), no medication or psychosocial treatments have yet been documented as effective in overcoming the deficit syndrome.

Premorbid History

Extensive evidence from long-term follow-up research supports the notion that deterioration in schizophrenia occurs within the first few months and years of onset, followed by a plateau in functioning that may or may not be followed by gradual improvement later in the course of the disorder (Davidson & McGlashan, 1997; McGlashan, 1988; Robinson et al., 1999). It is difficult to say what proportion of clients will recover because it appears that wide heterogeneity of outcome predominates and because good outcome, defined as mild impairment to recovery, can range from 21% to 68% (Davidson & McGlashan, 1997). The consensus from a number of reviews of long-term follow-up studies of schizophrenia has implicated specific premorbid variables as predictors of outcome (Davidson & McGlashan, 1997; McGlashan, 1988). Premorbid factors that are predictors of poor outcome include male gender (vs. female), early age of onset, insidious onset, poor prior work history, low level of prior social adjustment, and long length of prodrome. It is not known how much treatment and rehabilitation, provided continuously and comprehensively as well as keyed to the phase of each person's disorder, can compensate for these premorbid characteristics of the person. However, social skills training provided twice a week for a minimum of 6 months has been shown to significantly improve social competence as measured in simulated situations and social adjustment in the community (Heinssen, Liberman, & Kopelowicz, 2000).

One of the important vulnerability factors most likely linked to the biologically based, genetic and neurodevelopmental abnormalities that are present in people with schizophrenia is premorbid social functioning. The prognosis for recovery among people who later develop schizophrenia is much brighter when their premorbid adjustment has been higher in school, work, and peer relationships. This source of vulnerability or resilience (Wolkow & Ferguson, 2001) can be influenced by systematic training of individuals in social and independent living skills; such training has been shown to raise the level of social competence and coping ability in individuals with schizophrenia *after* the onset of their illness (Glynn et al., 2002; Liberman et al., 1993; Marder, Wirshing, Mintz, & McKenzie, 1996; Wallace & Liberman, 1985). Buttressing clients' social competence through structured, prescriptive training programs leads to greater protection against the disability and maladjustment that otherwise would diminish social activity and quality of life.

Access to Comprehensive, Coordinated, and Continuous Treatment

The contribution of continuous, comprehensive, consumer-oriented, and coordinated treatment to good outcome in chronic schizophrenia was shown in the long-term follow-up study from Vermont and Maine described earlier (DeSisto et al., 1995). Complementing the findings from that study, reviews of psychosocial treatments in combination with antipsychotic drugs for schizophrenia have identified other studies with zero relapses and better rates of social functioning when comprehensive, continuous, and well-coordinated services were accessible and used by individuals with schizophrenia who had been diagnosed by raters trained in the use of the Structured Clinical Interview for *DSM* (Goldstein, 1999; Liberman, Vaccaro, & Corrigan, 1995; Penn & Mueser, 1996). One such study, conducted by Hogarty and colleagues (1986, 1991), randomly assigned individuals with schizophrenia to one of four groups: (a) adequate antipsychotic medication, (b) medication plus social skills training, (c) medication and family psychoeducation, or (d) medication, skills training, and family psychoeducation. Relapse rates in the first year for the first three groups were 40%, 21%, and 19%, respectively. Interestingly, not one participant in the group that received all three treatments experienced a relapse during the first year of treatment (Hogarty et al., 1986). Not surprisingly, as the psychosocial treatments were faded and then discontinued during the second year, relapse rates began to approximate the rates achieved by participants who received only medications (Hogarty et al., 1991).

Some publicly funded, mental health agencies have shifted to a capitation approach to psychiatric treatment and rehabilitation for people with schizophrenia. *Capitation* refers to a reimbursement system in which the agency receives a fixed sum per client-year rather than ongoing compensation on a fee-for-service basis. In addition to crisis intervention, supportive community-based services, medication, and other psychiatric treatments, some of these capitated programs now use transitional and supported employment, supported housing, social skills training, family education, and a major emphasis on self-help and consumer-run social and work activities. These new developments—including Assertive Community Treatment (Stein & Santos, 1998), use of evidence-based services by teams with requisite professional competencies (Liberman et al., 2001), the application of total quality improvement principles at Colorado Health Networks (Forquer & Knight, 2001), and the "wraparound services" approach practiced at the Integrated Service Agencies sponsored by the Los Angeles County Department of Mental Health (Chandler, Meiser, Hu, McGowen, & Madison, 1997)—augur well for an increased rate of recovery for participants with schizophrenia. We now take a look at a case example of recovery from schizophrenia.

CASE EXAMPLE OF RECOVERY

NOTE: Interspersed in this vignette describing Fred's recovery from schizophrenia are italicized notations of factors that predict and foster recovery, as well as the criteria that demarcate our operational definition of recovery.

After graduating from a state university with a degree in engineering, Fred accepted a commission in the U.S. Navy and served three years in the Mediterranean where he lived off-base and became fluent in Spanish. After honorable discharge and because he wanted to continue his international traveling, he joined the Peace Corps. He was stationed in Yemen for two years, assisting with construction of water, sewer, and road infrastruture (*good premorbid adjustment*). When he was 29 years old and working as a structural engineer in the aerospace industry, he suddenly and without any warning began hearing voices telling him that he was worthless and would be responsible for the world coming to an end. He also heard the voices talk amongst themselves, indicating that a plot was taking place within the Central Intelligence Agency (CIA) to blow up a major American city. He became agitated and, having full conviction in the reality of the threats the voices were making, began to search every vehicle in the city for bombs or incendiary devices. The police apprehended him while breaking into a car that he thought was rigged with explosives.

When examined by a psychiatrist in the jail (*early diagnosis and intervention*), Fred also acknowledged fears that others could tell what he was thinking, that the CIA was violating his privacy, that foreign agents were inserting alien thoughts into his mind to force him to engage in spying, and that his thoughts and actions were being controlled by laser beams directed at him by the CIA and other foreign powers. He was unable to return to work and terminated all social contacts except with his parents. During the next three years, Fred was hospitalized 18 times for acting out on his persecutory hallucinations and delusions. At no time in his life had Fred even experimented with drugs of abuse—not even cigarettes (*absence of substance abuse*). Despite repeated efforts to stabilize his illness with various types and doses of antipsychotic medication, Fred was unable to shake his psychotic symptoms and became more and more depressed. Feeling trapped and out of control of his mind, he made several suicide attempts, each of which resulted in short-term hospitalizations.

After his medical insurance ran out, Fred entered the Veterans Administration (VA) Medical Center in his city for treatment on a voluntary basis. He developed a good working relationship with a psychiatrist who was able to provide continuity of care and supportive therapy, in addition to pharmacotherapy and case management (*social skills, supportive therapy, continuous and comprehensive treatment*). His psychiatrist provided psychoeducation, utilizing the University of California at Los Angeles (UCLA) Social and Independent Living Skills modules for Symptom Management and Medication Management. In the context of their mutually respectful and trusting relationship, Fred reliably attended all of his treatment sessions, gained knowledge and skill in reliable use of his medication, negotiated with his psychiatrist on benefits and side effects of his medication, and learned ways to cope with his persistent psychotic symptoms (*adherence to treatment*). In collaboration with his psychiatrist, the two of them decided that a trial of clozapine would be desirable. Within a few months, Fred's hallucinations and delusions began to lift, ultimately going into a sustained and complete remission (*excellent response to medication*). At the same time, he attended a psychiatric rehabilitation program at the VA Medical Center that featured the Social and Independent Living Skills modules developed by Robert Liberman, MD and his colleagues at UCLA. Fred was an apt student in these "classes," rapidly acquiring knowledge and ability to self-manage his medication reliably and in partnership with his doctor and to develop a relapse prevention plan based on his understanding of warning signs of exacerbation of psychosis and basic conversation and problem-solving skills. He resumed living independently in an apartment and was able to budget his Social Security pension (*independent living criterion for recovery*).

At one point, as his depression resolved, he felt so good that he decided he had the ability to return to computer programming. In the outpatient social skills training group, Fred was willing to consider alternatives for determining his readiness for this demanding and stressful form of work. He decided that he could best judge his ability and vocational capacity by scheduling an appointment with one of his professors at the state university from which he had graduated eight years earlier. A daylong visit with this professor convinced Fred that he was not ready for such work and would be better off entering a less cognitively demanding field. His parents were extremely supportive of Fred's goals and let him know that they had no expectations that he return to a high-powered but stressful occupation. He would visit his parents on weekends for pleasant meals and an exchange of family news (*stable and supportive family*).

Because of his increasing interest in his own medication treatment, he opted to register in a 2-year training program leading to a certification as a pharmacy technician. Fred successfully completed this two-year program and obtained employment as a pharmacy technician (*normal employment criterion of recover*). He also undertook volunteer and paid opportunities to serve as a mental health advocate, traveling to Washington, DC every year to lobby for improved funds for psychiatric research. He was a most important advocate with members of Congress and their staffs because of his credibility as a person who had benefited from the nation's investment in research. He also dramatically confronted members of Congress and their staffs with their stigmas toward persons with mental illness based on stereotypes of the various disabilities, inarticulate speech patterns, and bizarre appearance (*active role as citizen and community support person—criterion of recovery*).

Several years later, Fred has maintained his independence, living alone in an apartment and fully and responsibly managing both his money and treatment with clozapine. He remains free of psychotic symptoms (*remission of psychosis criterion of recovery*) and every week attends church services and actively socializes with other members of the congregation, none of whom know that he has schizophrenia (*peer relations criterion of recovery*). However, he is a fearless advocate for reducing stigma of mental illness—participating in videos, appearing before National Alliance for the Mentally Ill groups at the local and state levels, and speaking to audiences of mental health professionals about his treatment experiences that led to recovery (*regular social activities in the community*).

Twelve years after the onset of his illness and nine years after meeting criteria for recovery, Fred continues his mainstream lifestyle. He has successfully coped with his father's death and his mother's cancer, providing considerable emotional support to his family (*cordial and mutual family relations criterion of recovery*). Preservation of selected neurocognitive functions in terms of memory, verbal learning, planning, initiative, insight, and judgment—discovered many years after his remission—helped to understand the personal attributes that promoted Fred's recovery (*intact neurocognition*). His recovery also was undoubtedly facilitated by his continuous and comprehensive treatment, which included psychosocial skills training, supportive therapy, coordinated case management, and consistent adherence to medication. His psychiatrist coordinated Fred's medication treatment with his clinicians who offered psychosocial services—giving and receiving information that permitted active and early intervention for prodromal signs of relapse and control of side effects that were interfering with his learning capacity (*comprehensive, continuous, coordinated, consistent, consumer-oriented therapy*). Family cohesion, lack of substance abuse, and good premorbid adjustment also contributed to his sustained recovery, as well as having been influences that heralded his recovery. Although remission of psychosis, employment, independent living, peer relations, cordiality with his family and integration into community life were important to Fred and an inspiration to his mental health providers, cumulatively, they exemplified a high subjective quality of life.

SUMMARY

It is hoped that by promulgating operationalized criteria and definitions of recovery one can promote research that will foster our understanding of the nature of recovery as well as the process by which recovery from schizophrenia occurs. Ultimately, what we learn from individuals who have recovered from schizophrenia should help us to develop interventions designed to enhance the likelihood of recovery, or even greater improvement, short of recovery, for those individuals who are still experiencing the ravages of this disorder. Increasing the rate of recovery from schizophrenia will also go far to destigmatize this disease, reduce the emotional burden on families, and lighten the financial weight of schizophrenia on communities, states, and the nation.

REFERENCES

American Psychiatric Association. (1994). *Diagnostic and statistical manual of mental disorders* (4th ed.). Washington, DC: Author.

Awad, A. G., & Hogan, T. P. (1985). Early treatment events and prediction of response to neuroleptics in schizophrenia. *Progress in Neuropsychopharmacology and Biological Psychiatry, 9*, 585–588.

Ayers, T., Liberman, R. P., & Wallace, C. J. (1984). Subjective response to antipsychotic drugs: Failure to replicate predictions of outcome. *Journal of Clinical Psychopharmacology, 4*, 89–93.

Barrowclough, C., & Tarrier, N. (1998). Social functioning and family interventions. In K. T. Mueser & N. Tarrier (Eds.), *Handbook of social functioning in schizophrenia* (pp. 327–341). Boston: Allyn & Bacon.

Bebbington, P., & Kuipers, L. (1994). The predictive utility of expressed emotion in schizophrenia: An aggregate analysis. *Psychological Medicine, 24,* 707–718.

Bleuler, M. (1968). A 23-year longitudinal study of 208 schizophrenics and impressions in regard to the nature of schizophrenia. In D. Rosenthal & S. S. Kety (Eds.), *The transmission of schizophrenia.* Oxford, England: Pergamon.

Bond, G. R., Becker, D. R., Drake, R. E., Rapp, C. A., Meisler, N., Lehman, A. F., et al. (2001). Implementing supported employment as an evidence-based practice. *Psychiatric Services, 52,* 313–322.

Bowers, M. B., Mazure, C. M., Nelson, J. C., & Jatlow, P. I. (1990). Psychotogenic drug use and neuroleptic response. *Schizophrenia Bulletin, 16,* 81–85.

Buchanan, R. W., & Gold, J. M. (1996). Negative symptoms: Diagnosis, treatment and prognosis. *International Clinical Psychopharmacology,* (Suppl. 2), 3–11.

Butzlaff, R. L., & Hooley, J. M. (1998). Expressed emotion and psychiatric relapse. *Archives of General Psychiatry, 55,* 547–552.

Bystritsky, A., Liberman, R. P., Hwang, S. S., & Wallace, C. J. (2001). Social and independent living and quality of life in obsessive-compulsive disorder and schizophrenia. *Anxiety & Depression, 14,* 214–218.

Chandler, D., Meiser, J., Hu, T., McGowen, M., & Madison, K. (1997). A capitated model for a cross-section of severely mentally ill clients: Employment outcomes. *Community Mental Health Journal, 33,* 501–516.

Ciompi, L. (1980). Catamnestic long-term study on the course of life and aging of schizophrenics. *Schizophrenia Bulletin, 6,* 606–618.

Cleghorn, J. M., Kaplan, R. D., Szechtman, B., Szechtman, H., Brown, G. M., & Franco, S. (1991). Substance abuse and schizophrenia: Effect on symptoms but not on neurocognitive function. *Journal of Clinical Psychiatry, 52,* 26–30.

Corrigan, P. W., Liberman, R. P., & Engel, J. (1990). From compliance to adherence in psychiatric treatment: Strategies that facilitate collaboration between practitioners and patient. *Hospital and Community Psychiatry, 41,* 1203–1211.

Crow, T. J., MacMillan, J. F., Johnson, A. L., & Johnstone, E. (1986). The Northwick Park study of first episodes of schizophrenia: II. A randomised controlled trial of prophylactic neuroleptic treatment. *British Journal of Psychiatry, 148,* 120–127.

Cuffel, B. J. (1994). Violent and destructive behavior among the severely mentally ill in rural areas: Evidence from Arkansas' community mental health system. *Community Mental Health Journal, 30,* 495–504.

Davidson, L., & McGlashan, T. H. (1997). The varied outcomes of schizophrenia. *Canadian Journal of Psychiatry, 42,* 34–43.

Davis, J. M. (1975). Overview: Maintenance therapy in psychiatry: I. Schizophrenia. *American Journal of Psychiatry, 132,* 1237–1245.

Davis, J. M., Chen, N., & Glick, I. D. (2003). A meta-analysis of the efficacy of second-generation antipsychotics. *Archives of General Psychiatry, 60,* 553–364.

Deegan, P. E. (1996). Recovery as a journey of the heart. *Psychiatric Rehabilitation Journal, 19,* 91–97.

DeSisto, M. J., Harding, C. M., McCormick, R. V., Ashikaga, T., & Brooks, G. W. (1995). The Maine and Vermont three-decade studies of serious mental illness. *British Journal of Psychiatry, 167,* 331–342.

Dingman, C. W., & McGlashan, T. H. (1989). Psychotherapy. In A. S. Bellack (Ed.), *A clinical guide for the treatment of schizophrenia* (pp. 263–282). New York: Plenum Press.

Edwards, J., Maude, D., McGorry, P. D., Harrigan, S. M., & Cocks, J. T. (1998). Prolonged recovery in first-episode psychosis. *British Journal of Psychiatry, 33*(Suppl.), 107–116.

Falloon, I. R. H., Held, T., Cloverdale, J. H., Roncone, R., & Laidlaw, T. M. (1999). Family interventions for schizophrenia: A review of international studies of long-term benefits. *Psychiatric Rehabilitation Skills, 3,* 268–290.

Fenton, W. S., & McGlashan, T. H. (1987). Sustained remission in drug-free schizophrenic patients. *American Journal of Psychiatry, 144,* 1306–1309.

Fenton, W. S., & McGlashan, T. H. (1994). Antecedents, symptom progression, and long-term outcome of the deficit syndrome in schizophrenia. *American Journal of Psychiatry, 151,* 351–356.

Forquer, S., & Knight, E. (2001). Managed care: Recovery enhancer or inhibitor? *Psychiatric Services, 52,* 25–26.

Frank, A. F., & Gunderson, J. G. (1990). The role of the therapeutic alliance in the treatment of schizophrenia: Relationship to course and outcome. *Archives of General Psychiatry, 47,* 228–236.

Frank, E., Prien, R. F., Jarrett, R. B., Keller, M. B., Kupfer, D. J., Lavori, P. W., et al. (1991). Conceptualization and rationale for consensus definitions of terms in major depressive disorder: Remission, recovery, relapse, and recurrence. *Archives of General Psychiatry, 48,* 851–855.

Gitlin, M., Nuechterlein, K., Subotnik, K. L., Ventura, J., Mintz, J., Fogelson, D. L., et al. (2001). Clinical outcome following neuroleptic discontinuation in patients with remitted recent-onset schizophrenia. *American Journal of Psychiatry, 158,* 1835–1842.

Glynn, S. M. (1998). Psychopathology and social functioning in schizophrenia. In K. T. Mueser & N. Tarrier (Eds.), *Psychosocial functioning in schizophrenia* (pp. 66–78). Boston: Allyn & Bacon.

Glynn, S. M., Marder, S. R., Liberman, R. P., Blair, K., Wirshing, W. C., Wirshing, D. A., et al. (2002). Supplementing clinic-based skills training with manual-based community support sessions: Effects on social adjustment of patients with schizophrenia. *American Journal of Psychiatry, 159,* 829–837.

Gold, J. M., Bryant, N. L., Vladar, K., & Buchanan, R. W. (1997). Successful vocational functioning in schizophrenia [Abstract]. *Schizophrenia Research, 24,* 222.

Goldstein, M. J. (1999). Psychosocial treatments for individuals with schizophrenia and related disorders. In N. E. Miller & K. M. Magruder (Eds.), *Cost-effectiveness of psychotherapy: A guide for practitioners, researchers, and policymakers* (pp. 235–247). New York: Oxford University Press.

Green, M. F. (1996). What are the functional consequences of neurocognitive deficits in schizophrenia? *American Journal of Psychiatry, 153*, 321–330.

Gunderson, J. G. (1978). Patient/therapist matching: A research evaluation. *American Journal of Psychiatry, 135*, 1193–1197.

Gunderson, J. G., Frank, A. F., Katz, H. M., Vannicelli, M. L., Frosch, J. P., & Knapp, P. H. (1984). Effects of psychotherapy in schizophrenia: II. Comparative outcome of two forms of treatment. *Schizophrenia Bulletin, 10*, 564–598.

Hammer, M. A., Katsanis, J., & Iacono, W. G. (1995). The relationship between negative symptoms and neuropsychological performance. *Biological Psychiatry, 37*, 828–830.

Harding, C. M., Brooks, G., Ashikaga, T., Strauss, J., & Breier, A. (1987). The Vermont longitudinal study of persons with severe mental illness. *American Journal of Psychiatry, 144*, 718–735.

Hegarty, J. D., Baldessarini, R. J., Tohen, M., Waternaux, C., & Oepen, G. (1994). One hundred years of schizophrenia: A meta-analysis of the outcome literature. *American Journal of Psychiatry, 151*, 1409–1416.

Heinssen, R. K., Liberman, R. P., & Kopelowicz, A. (2000). Psychosocial skills training for schizophrenia: Lessons from the laboratory. *Schizophrenia Bulletin, 26*, 21–46.

Helgason, L. (1990). Twenty years' followup of first psychiatric presentation for schizophrenia: What could have been prevented? *Acta Psychiatrica Scandinavica, 81*, 231–235.

Hoffman, H., & Kupper, Z. (2002). Facilitators of psychosocial recovery from schizophrenia. *International Review of Psychiatry, 14*, 293–302.

Hogarty, G. E., Anderson, C. M., Reiss, D. J., Kornblith, S. J., Greenwald, D. P., Javna, C. D., et al. (1986). Family psychoeducation, social skills training and maintenance chemotherapy in aftercare treatment of schizophrenia. 1. One-year effects of a controlled-study on relapse and expressed emotion. *Archives of General Psychiatry, 43*, 633–642.

Hogarty, G. E., Anderson, C. M., Reiss, D. J., Kornblith, S. J., Greenwald, D. P., Ulrich, R. F., et al. (1991). Family psychoeducation, social skills training, and maintenance chemotherapy in the aftercare treatment of schizophrenia: II. Two-year effects of a controlled study on relapse and adjustment. *Archives of General Psychiatry, 48*, 340–347.

Hogarty, G. E., Goldberg, S. C., & Schooler, N. (1974). Drug and sociotherapy in the aftercare of schizophrenia patients. III. Adjustment of non-relapsed patients. *Archives of General Psychiatry, 31*, 609–618.

Hoge, S. K., Appelbaum, P. S., Lawlor, T., Beck, J. C., Litman, R., Greer, A., et al. (1990). A prospective, multicenter study of patients' refusal of antipsychotic medication. *Archives of General Psychiatry, 47*, 949–956.

Huber, G., Gross, G., & Schuttler, R. A. (1975). Long-term follow-up study of schizophrenia: Psychiatric course of illness and prognosis. *Acta Psychiatrica Scandinavica, 52*, 49–57.

Johnstone, E. C., MacMillan, J. F., Frith, C. D., Benn, D. K., & Crow, T. J. (1990). Further investigation of the predictors of outcome following first schizophrenic episodes. *British Journal of Psychiatry, 157*, 182–189.

Klimke, A., Klieser, E., Lehmann, E., & Miele, L. (1993). Initial improvement as a criterion for drug choice in acute schizophrenia. *Pharmacopsychiatry, 26*, 25–29.

Kopelowicz, A., Corrigan, P., Wallace, C., & Liberman, R. P. (1996). Biopsychosocial rehabilitation. In A. Tasman, J. Kay, & J. A. Lieberman (Eds.), *Psychiatry* (pp. 1513–1534). Philadelphia: W. B. Saunders.

Kopelowicz, A., & Liberman, R. P. (1995). Biobehavioral treatment and rehabilitation of schizophrenia. *Harvard Review of Psychiatry, 3*, 55–64.

Kopelowicz, A., & Liberman, R. P. (1999). Biobehavioral treatment and rehabilitation of persons with serious mental illness. In J. R. Scotti (Ed.), *New directions in behavioral interventions: Principles, models, and practices* (pp. 123–128). Baltimore: Brookes Publishing.

Kopelowicz, A., Liberman, R. P., Mintz, J., & Zarate, R. (1997). Efficacy of social skills training for deficit versus nondeficit negative symptoms in schizophrenia. *American Journal of Psychiatry, 154*, 424–425.

Kopelowicz, A., Ventura, J., Liberman, R. P., Zarate, R., & Mintz, J. (2004). Neurocognitive correlates of recovery from schizophrenia. Manuscript submitted for publication.

Lamb, H. R. (1988). One-to-one relationships with the long-term mentally ill: Issues in training professionals. *Community Mental Health Journal, 24*, 328–337.

Lehman, A. F., Steinwachs, D. M., & PORT Co-investigators. (1998). Translating research into practice: The schizophrenia patient outcomes research team (PORT) treatment recommendations. *Schizophrenia Bulletin, 24*, 1–10.

Liberman, R. P. (2002). Cognitive remediation in schizophrenia. In H. Kashima, I. R. H. Falloon, M. Mizuno, & M. Asai (Eds.), *Comprehensive treatment of schizophrenia* (pp. 254–278). Tokyo: Springer-Verlag.

Liberman, R. P., Gutkind, D., Mintz, J., Green, M., Marshall, B. D., Robertson, M. J., et al. (in press). Impact of risperidone vs. haloperidol on activities of daily living in treatment refractory schizophrenia. *Comprehensive Psychiatry*.

Liberman, R. P., Hilty, D. M., Drake, R. E., & Tsang, H. W. H. (2001). Requirements for multidisciplinary teamwork in psychiatric rehabilitation. *Psychiatric Services, 52*, 1331–1342.

Liberman, R. P., Kopelowicz, A., Ventura, J., & Gutkind, D. (2002). Operational criteria and factors related to recovery from schizophrenia. *International Review of Psychiatry, 14*, 256–272.

Liberman, R. P., Vaccaro, J. V., & Corrigan, P. W. (1995). Psychiatric rehabilitation. In H. I. Kaplan & B. J. Sadock (Eds.), *Comprehensive textbook of psychiatry*. Baltimore: Williams & Wilkins.

Liberman, R. P., Wallace, C. J., Blackwell, G., Eckman, T. A., Vaccaro, J. V., & Kuehnel, T. G. (1993). Innovations in skills training for the seriously mentally ill: The UCLA Social & Independent Living Skills modules. *Innovations and Research, 2*, 43–60.

Liddle, P. F., & Morris, D. L. (1991). Schizophrenic syndromes and frontal lobe performance. *British Journal of Psychiatry, 158*, 340–345.

Lieberman, J. A., & Fenton, W. S. (2000). Delayed detection of psychosis: Causes, consequences and effect on public health. *American Journal of Psychiatry, 157*, 1727–1730.

Lieberman, J., Jody, D., Geisler, S., Alvir, J., Loebel, A., Szymanski, S., et al. (1993). Time course and biological correlates of treatment response in first-episode schizophrenia. *Archives of General Psychiatry, 50*, 369–376.

Lieberman, J. A., Tollefson, G., Tohen, M., Green, A. I., Gur, R. E., Kahn, R., et al. (2003). Comparative efficacy and safety of atypical and conventional antipsychotic drugs in first-episode psychosis: A randomized, double blind trial of olanzapine versus haloperidol. *American Journal of Psychiatry, 160*, 1396–1404.

Lo, W. H., & Lo, T. (1977). A ten-year followup study of Chinese schizophrenics in Hong Kong. *British Journal of Psychiatry, 131*, 63–66.

Loebel, A. D., Lieberman, J. A., Alvir, J. M. J., Mayerhoff, D. I., Geisler, S. H., & Szymanski, S. R. (1992). Duration of psychosis and outcome in first-episode schizophrenia. *American Journal of Psychiatry, 149*, 1183–1188.

Lyons, J. S., & McGovern, M. P. (1989). Use of mental health services by dually diagnosed patients. *Hospital and Community Psychiatry, 40*, 1067–1069.

Lysaker, P., & Bell, M. (1995). Negative symptoms and vocational impairment in schizophrenia: Repeated measurements of work performance over six months. *Acta Psychiatrica Scandinavica, 91*, 205–208.

Marder, S. R., Wirshing, W. C., Mintz, J., & McKenzie, J. (1996). Two-year outcome of social skills training and group psychotherapy for outpatients with schizophrenia. *American Journal of Psychiatry, 153*, 85–1592.

May, P. R., Van Putten, T., & Yale, C. (1980). Predicting outcome of antipsychotic drug treatment from early response. *American Journal of Psychiatry, 137*, 1088–1089.

McGlashan, T. H. (1988). A selective review of recent North American long-term followup studies of schizophrenia. *Schizophrenia Bulletin, 14*, 515–542.

McGlashan, T. K. (1996). Early detection and intervention in schizophrenia: Research. *Schizophrenia Bulletin, 22*, 327–345.

McGorry, P. D., Edwards, J., Mihalopoulos, C., & Harrigan, S. M. (1996). EPPIC: An evolving system of early detection and optimal management. *Schizophrenia Bulletin, 22*, 305–326.

McGorry, P. D., Yung, A. R., Phillips, L. J., Yuen, H. P., Francey, S., Cosgrave, E. M., et al. (2002). Randomized clinical trial of interventions designed to reduce the risk of progression to first-episode psychosis in a clinical sample with sub-threshold symptoms. *Archives of General Psychiatry, 59*, 921–928.

Mintz, J., Mintz, L. I., Arruda, M. J., & Hwang, S. S. (1992). Treatments of depression and the functional capacity to work. *Archives of General Psychiatry, 49*, 761–768.

Morrison, R. L., Bellack, A. S., Wixted, J. T., & Mueser, K. T. (1990). Positive and negative symptoms in schizophrenia: A cluster-analytic approach. *Journal of Nervous and Mental Disease, 178*, 377–384.

Mueser, K. T., & Bond, G. R. (2000). Psychosocial treatment approaches for schizophrenia. *Current Opinion in Psychiatry, 13*, 27–35.

Noordsy, D., Torrey, W., Mueser, K., Mead, S., O'Keefe, C., & Fox, L. (2002). Recovery from severe mental illness: An interpersonal and functional outcome definition. *International Review of Psychiatry, 14*, 318–326.

Nuechterlein, K. H., Subotnik, K. L., Gitlin, M., Dawson, M. E., Ventura, J., Snyder, K. S., et al. (1999). Neurocognitive and environmental contributors to work recovery after initial onset of schizophrenia: Answers from path analyses. *Schizophrenia Research, 36*, 179.

Ogawa, K., Miya, M., Watarai, A., Nakazawa, M., Yuasa, S., & Utena, H. (1987). A long-term follow-up study of schizophrenia in Japan with special reference to the course of social adjustment. *British Journal of Psychiatry, 151*, 758–765.

Penn, D. L., & Mueser, K. T. (1996). Research update on the psychosocial treatment of schizophrenia. *American Journal of Psychiatry, 153*, 607–617.

Pogue-Geile, M. F., & Harrow, M. (1987). The longitudinal study of negative symptoms in schizophrenia. In R. R. Grinker & M. Harrow (Eds), *Clinical research in schizophrenia: A multidimensional approach* (pp. 189–199). Springfield, IL: Charles C. Thomas.

Regier, D. A., Farmer, M. E., Rae, D. S., Locke, B. Z., Keith, S. J., Judd, L. L., et al. (1990). Comorbidity of mental disorders with alcohol and other drug abuse: Results from the Epidemiologic Catchment Area (ECA) study. *Journal of the American Medical Association, 264*, 2511–2518.

Robinson, D. G., Woerner, M. G., Alvir, J. M., Bilder, R., Goldman, R., Geisler, S., et al. (1999). Predictors of relapse following response from a first episode of schizophrenia or schizoaffective disorder. *Archives of General Psychiatry, 56*, 241–247.

Robinson, D. G., Woerner, M. G., Alvir, J. M. J., Kane, J. M., & Lieberman, J. A. (2004). Symptomatic and functional recovery from a first episode of schizophrenia or schizoaffective disorder. *American Journal of Psychiatry, 161*, 473-479.

Scott, J. E., & Dixon, L. B. (1995). Psychological interventions for schizophrenia. *Schizophrenia Bulletin, 21*, 621–630.

Shaner, A., Roberts, L. J., Eckman, T. A., Racenstein, J. M., Tucker, D. E., Tsuang, J. W., et al. (1998). Sources of diagnostic uncertainty for chronically psychotic cocaine abusers. *Psychiatric Services, 49*, 684–690.

Spaniol, L., & Koehler, M. (1994). *The experience of recovery*. Boston: Center for Psychiatric Rehabilitation, Boston University.

Spaniol, L., Wewiorski, N. J., Gagne, C., & Anthony, W. A. (2002). The process of recovery from schizophrenia. *International Review of Psychiatry, 14*, 327–336.

Stein, L. J., & Santos, L. B. (1998). *Assertive community treatment of persons with severe mental illness*. New York: Norton.

Strauss, M. (1993). Relations of symptoms to cognitive deficits in schizophrenia. *Schizophrenia Bulletin, 19*, 215–232.

Swanson, J. W., Holzer, C. E., Ganju, V. K., & Jono, R. T. (1990). Violence and psychiatric disorder in the community: Evidence from the Epidemiologic Catchment Area surveys. *Hospital and Community Psychiatry, 41*, 761–770.

Swofford, C. D., Kasckow, J. W., Scheller-Gilkey, G., & Inderbitzin, L. B. (1996). Substance use: A powerful predictor of relapse in schizophrenia. *Schizophrenia Research, 20,* 145–151.

Tohen, M., Hennen, J., Zarate, C. M., Baldessarini, R. J., Strakowski, S., & Stoll, A. L. (2000). Two year syndromal and functional recovery in 219 cases of first episode major affective disorder with psychotic features. *American Journal of Psychiatry, 157,* 220–228.

Torgalsboen, A. K., & Rund, B. R. (2002). Lessons learned from three studies of recovery from schizophrenia. *International Review of Psychiatry, 14,* 312–317.

Tsuang, M. T., Simpson, J. C., & Kronfol, Z. (1982). Subtypes of drug abuse with psychosis: Demographic characteristics, clinical features, and family history. *Archives of General Psychiatry, 39,* 141–147.

Van der Does, A. J., Dingemans, P. M., Linszen, D. H., Nugter, M. A., & Scholte, W. F. (1993). Symptom dimensions and cognitive and social functioning in recent-onset schizophrenia. *Psychological Medicine, 23,* 745–753.

Ventura, J. V., Green, M. F., Shaner, A., & Liberman, R. P. (1993). Training and quality assurance in the use of the Brief Psychiatric Rating Scale: The "drift busters." *International Journal of Methods in Psychiatric Research, 3,* 221–244.

Wallace, C. J., & Liberman, R. P. (1985). Social skills training for patients with schizophrenia: A controlled clinical trial. *Psychiatry Research, 15,* 239–247.

Warner, R., Taylor, D., Wright, J., Sloat, A., Springett, G., Arnold, S., & Weinberg, H. (1994). Substance use among the mentally ill: Prevalence, reasons for use and effects on illness. *American Journal of Orthopsychiatry, 64,* 465–476.

Weiden, P., Olfson, M., & Essock, S. (1997). Medication noncompliance in schizophrenia: Effects on mental health service policy. In B. Blackwell (Ed.), *Treatment compliance and the therapeutic alliance* (pp. 35–60). New York: Harwood Academic.

Whitehorn, D., Brown, J., Richard, J., Rui, Q., & Kopala, L. (2002). Multiple dimensions of recovery in early psychosis. *International Review of Psychiatry, 14,* 273–283.

Whitehorn, D., Lazier, L., & Kopala, L. (1998). Psychosocial rehabilitation early after the onset of psychosis. *Psychiatric Services, 49,* 1135–1137.

Wolkow, K. E., & Ferguson, H. (2001). Community factors in the development of resiliency. *Community Mental Health Journal, 37,* 489–498.

Wyatt, R. J. (1991). Neuroleptics and the natural course of schizophrenia. *Schizophrenia Bulletin, 17,* 325–351.

6

VERBAL DEFINITIONS AND VISUAL MODELS OF RECOVERY: FOCUS ON THE RECOVERY MODEL

RUTH O. RALPH

Many definitions of recovery exist; some focus on the process and others point toward the outcomes of recovery. Process and outcome in recovery are part of the same continuum. The process of working through recovery is necessary to achieve the outcomes of a normal, healthy life. This chapter examines both the verbal definitions and visual models of recovery. Some of the most cogent definitions come from the verbal products of people who have experienced mental illness, who have lived through this experience, and who are working to overcome the difficulties that accompany it. Several of these personal accounts have been reviewed or qualitatively analyzed to determine some common themes of recovery.

Some people find that a picture or graphic helps them to better understand a concept. Visual definitions have also been developed as models of recovery. Visual models expand on the individual definitions found in personal accounts. They bring together ideas and concepts from a number of sources. These visual models provide a theoretical base for the concept of recovery. A number of these models are described in this chapter to indicate the variety of ideas presented. Finally, we look at the Recovery Advisory

Group Recovery Model in more detail: its development and the set of visual and verbal definitions prepared to portray important aspects of the recovery process and outcomes. The Recovery Advisory Group was composed of a number of consumer leaders who were invited by the U.S. Center for Mental Health Services to spend some time discussing recovery from their own perspectives and the perspectives of those with whom they worked.

Each definition of recovery enriches the concept and helps us better understand this very complex but individual experience. If recovery is to become a regular part of the fabric of mental health services, more research is required to determine how and when people recover and to develop methods to help people recover. It is important to continue the development of verbal definitions and visual models of recovery to move the vision of recovery into the mental health system so that individuals can be encouraged and assisted in their recovery experience.

VERBAL RECOVERY DEFINITIONS

Recovery in mental health is verbally defined in the writings of consumers. People who experience mental illness need to realize that to heal they must grow in their understanding of the illness and themselves, must discover ways of coping and living they may not have used before, and must make changes to incorporate their growth and discovery. Deegan (1988) elaborates on this concept with the idea that recovery is "a way of approaching the day's challenges" (p. 15). She also points out that recovery is not always straightforward, but that one must keep trying even when he or she falters. The desire to establish a sense of integrity and purpose, and to live beyond the disability is clear, as is making a contribution to the community in which one lives. "Recovery is a process, a way of life, an attitude, and a way of approaching the day's challenges. It is not a perfectly linear process. At times our course is erratic and we falter, slide back, regroup and start again. . . . The need is to meet the challenge of the disability and to re-establish a new and valued sense of integrity and purpose within and beyond the limits of the disability; the aspiration is to live, work, and love in a community in which one makes a significant contribution" (Deegan, 1988, p. 15).

People who experience mental illness often lose the belief that they are able to make their own decisions. This is the focus of Chamberlin's (1997) comment: "One of the elements that makes recovery possible is the regaining of one's belief in oneself" (p. 9). Hope is the theme of Leete's (1988) comments—hope to overcome symptoms, hope to live independently, hope to contribute to society: "Having some hope is crucial to recovery; none of us would strive if we believed it a futile effort.... I believe that if we confront our illnesses with courage and struggle with our symptoms persistently, we can overcome our handicaps to live independently, learn skills, and contribute to society, the society that has traditionally abandoned us" (p. 32). Stocks (1995) points out that recovery is not static, that it is "an ongoing process of growth, discovery, and change" (p. 89).

A number of common themes have been identified through literature review or qualitative analysis of consumer personal accounts and commentary. In a qualitative inquiry, Ridgway (2001) analyzed four early consumer recovery narratives (Deegan, 1988; Leete, 1989; Lovejoy, 1982; Unzicker, 1989) with a constant comparative method to find eight common themes. These themes are expanded on here with examples from the narratives:

- *Recovery is the reawakening of hope after despair.* A psychiatric diagnosis can lead one to despair, particularly when accompanied by common negative expectations and stereotypes of lifetime disability from an incurable illness. Hope is found in many ways: through the support and love of family, through learning about and from other recovering individuals, and by finding out that there is employment and life beyond the diagnosis.
- *Recovery is breaking through denial and achieving understanding and acceptance.* A normal reaction to a psychiatric diagnosis or recognition of psychiatric problems is denial, to avoid dealing with them. However, learning what the challenges are and how to deal with and overcome them is an important part of recovery.
- *Recovery is moving from withdrawal to engagement and active participation in life.* Isolation is one reaction to a psychiatric diagnosis and symptoms. It is also the pattern of some closed program environments. It is described as "numbness" and "a perpetual suspended animation that is better than never-ending pain" (Unzicker, 1989, p. 71). People may have to push themselves into socializing with others—and finding ways to do this—to break out of the isolation. Consumer narratives indicate more comfort with people with similar interests and experiences. They also highlight employment or educational situations where one can relate to fellow employees or students.
- *Recovery is active coping rather than passive adjustment.* It is important for the individual to take personal responsibility for his or her own well-being. To do so requires self-awareness including paying attention to sources of stress and positive reinforcement. People need to keep in touch with their own feelings and deal with difficulties as quickly as possible.
- *Recovery means no longer viewing oneself primarily as a person with a psychiatric disorder and reclaiming a positive sense of self.* Rather than being shaped by a psychiatric diagnosis, a person needs to see one's self in the larger picture, the picture that exists beyond the diagnosis. Thus, psychiatric problems are

only a part of life. Recovery makes it possible to see yourself in a positive sense, to feel important to someone or something, and to realize that you are a valuable person.

- *Recovery is a journey from alienation to a sense of meaning and purpose.* Prior to recovery, there is a great sense of being alone, being alienated from the world around you. Mental health treatments are often barren, boring, and lifeless and hence contribute to this alienation. However, consumers who wrote these narratives agreed that although they were able to find personal meaning in meeting their own personal goals, they also found deep meaning and purpose in helping others who experience psychiatric disabilities.

- *Recovery is a complex and nonlinear journey.* Recovery is accomplished in small, concrete steps, and not in one big leap. Leete (1989) felt accomplishment when she crossed things done off a list. Deegan (1988) began by "simple acts of courage" such as taking a ride in a car or talking to a friend for a few moments each day. Recovery is an evolving process and does not follow a straight course. There may be setbacks after which one must begin again on the journey.

- *Recovery is not accomplished alone; the journey involves support and partnership.* Recovery does not happen in a vacuum. Family, friends, peers, and mental health providers are all important because they "cheer" a person on their road to recovery. Sometimes this support consists simply of being there and never giving up; at other times, it is encouragement to participate in self-help or other self-stimulating activities. Providers who believe the client can improve his or her life are important components in the recovery journey. However, all of the "cheerleaders" in a person's life must strive to be just that, and not to attempt to assume control.

In a review of recovery literature prepared as background for *Mental Health: A Report of the Surgeon General* (U.S. Department of Health and Human Services, 1999), four dimensions of recovery found in personal accounts were identified (Ralph, 2000):

1. *Internal factors* are those factors which are within the consumer such as the awakening, insight, and determination it takes to recover.
2. *Self-managed care* is an extension of the internal factors in which consumers describe how they manage their own mental health and how they cope with the difficulties and barriers they face.
3. *External factors* include interconnectedness with others; the supports provided by family, friends, and professionals; and

having people who believe that they can cope with and recover from their mental illnesses.

4. *Empowerment* is a combination of internal and external factors, in which internal strength is combined with interconnectedness to provide self-help, advocacy, and caring about what happens to ourselves and to others.

VISUAL RECOVERY MODELS

A number of visual models have been developed to explain or describe recovery. These are theoretical models developed from different perspectives. In all cases, narrative explains the concepts on which the model is based. The examples described here do not include models described in other chapters in this book, nor are program models that assist people in their recovery considered here.

Several versions of a model have been published by the National Empowerment Center. It was first called the Empowerment Vision of Recovery from Mental Illness (Fisher, 1994–1995) and later the Empowerment Model of Recovery from Mental Illness (Fisher & Ahern, 1999). Severe emotional distress anchors the beginning of this model. On the one hand, sufficient social supports, resources, or coping skills lead to maintaining a social role even under emotional distress and finally to emotional healing and recovery from mental illness. On the other hand, insufficient social supports, resources, or coping skills lead to a person being diagnosed with a mental illness, loss of social role, dependency, and being treated as a nonperson.

The narrative that accompanies the diagram illustrating this model includes the following concepts:

> People are labeled with mental illness through a combination of severe emotional distress and insufficient social supports/resources/coping skills to maintain the major social role expected of them during that phase in their life. The degree of interruption in a person's social role is more important in affixing the label "mental illness" to someone than his or her diagnosis. Recovery is possible through a combination of supports needed to (re)establish a major social role and the self-management skills needed to take control of the major decisions affecting one. This combination of social supports and self-management help the person regain membership in society and regain the sense of being a whole person. (Fisher & Ahern, 1999, p. 13)

A Public Health Model for the Recovery of Adult Mental Health Consumers, developed by Dornan, Felton, and Carpinello (2000), presents hope as the central theme. This model begins with will to survive; continues through anguish, awakening, action plan, self, and shared determination; and ends with recovery. The will to survive must be present to recover from any life-changing illness, whether a physical illness or mental illness. Anguish is described as disorder, shame, isolation, imprisonment, disability, and discrimination. Awakening is a positive step in which the person awakens: to trust in at least one other person, to their own anger, to a belief in self, and to moments of clear thinking. To get back to a normal, healthy life, the individual must have a plan that outlines actions and decisions to be made. Determination to follow this plan and accomplish a more normal life is important and is easier if it can be shared and augmented by support from a loved one, a friend, or even a provider. Dornan and colleagues (2000) define recovery "as the act of gaining and taking back hope, personal identity and abilities—from loss due to disorder, injury, or submission to powerlessness. It is also a taking back of trust in one's own thoughts and choices so as to restore mental, emotional, social and biological order. It may be lifelong, intermittent or short-term" (p. 2).

In studies of how people change in terms of addiction, Prochaska, DiClemente, and Norcross (1992) indicate a four-phase process of precontemplation, contemplation, preparation, and action. Precontemplation occurs when there is no recognition of the problem or intention to change. When a person is aware that a problem exists, is thinking about doing something about it, but has not made a commitment, they have moved to the contemplation stage. Preparation includes both intention and some activity toward dealing with the problem. For example, smokers who delay their first cigarette of the day or smoke a few less are both intending to quit and beginning to take action. Action occurs when a person modifies his or her behavior or environment to overcome the problem. Prochaska et al. (1992) present these stages in a spiral model showing that people can go back to precontemplation from action and, therefore, must start the cycle over again to overcome their problems.

The Medicine Wheel is a relational or cyclical worldview that has its roots in the tribal cultures of the Native American Indian. As described by Cross, Earle, Echo-Hawk-Solie, and Manness (2000):

> It is intuitive, non-time oriented and fluid. Balance and harmony in relationships is the driving force of this thought system, along with the interplay of spiritual forces. The relational worldview sees life in terms of harmonious relationships; health or wellness is achieved by maintaining balance among the many interrelating factors in one's circle of life. Every event relates to all other events regardless of time, space or physical existence. Health exists only when all elements are in balance or harmony. (p. 8)

The Medicine Wheel's relational worldview model appears as a circle or sphere with four quadrants. These quadrants—called context, mind, body, and spirit—represent the four major forces or sets of factors that together must come into balance. *Context* includes culture, community, family, peers, work, school, and social history. *Mind* includes intellect, emotion, memory, judgment, and experience. *Body* includes all physical aspects, such as genetic inheritance, gender, and condition, as well as sleep, nutrition, and substance use. The *spirit* area includes both positive and negative learned spiritual teachings and practices, dreams, symbols, stories, negative forces, and gifts and intuition. In this model, we recognize that all life is in constant flux and change, even from morning to night. We must work to keep a constant balance and rebalance whenever necessary. Balance is harmony, and we must keep all of our relationships, behaviors, feelings, thoughts, and physical and spiritual states in balance to keep our lives healthy. When something changes this balance, we must examine each quadrant to see what is out of harmony, and work toward change and health.

THE RECOVERY ADVISORY GROUP RECOVERY MODEL

The Recovery Advisory Group included consumer leaders[1] who were invited by the Center for Mental Health Services to form a discussion group with the purpose of defining recovery and possibly identifying ways to measure it. During 12 monthly teleconferences, these consumer leaders discussed recovery from their own experiences and the experiences of those with whom they worked. The group also exchanged and reviewed a considerable amount of literature on recovery. During the course of their work, the group realized that there needed to be some visual method to portray recovery so they discussed what such a visual should look like. The consumers from Maine in the group developed initial models that the group subsequently discussed and modified to result in the current Recovery Advisory Group Recovery Model (Ralph & Recovery Advisory Group, 1999).

This Recovery Model, shown in Figure 6.1, describes and defines recovery through a number of stages: anguish, awakening, insight, action plan, determination to be well, and well-being, empowerment, and recovery. The path is not linear, and people do not move through one stage to the next, but may move back and forth among the various stages. Although the arrows in Figure 6.1 are shown between adjacent stages, consumers indicate that one may move from any stage to any other stage, both backwards and forwards, depending on where individuals are in their mental health journeys. The circles in Figure 6.1 that represent each stage are placed in such a

---

[1]The consumer leaders in the Recovery Advisory Group were Jean Campbell, PhD, Missouri; Sylvia Caras, PhD, California; Jeanne Dumont, PhD, New York; Daniel Fisher, MD, Massachusetts; J. Rock Johnson, JD, Nebraska; Carrie Kaufmann, PhD, Pennsylvania; Kathryn Kidder, MA, Maine; Ed Knight, PhD, Colorado; Ann Loder, Florida; Darby Penny, New York; Jean Risman, Maine; Ruth O. Ralph, PhD, Maine; Wilma Townsend, Ohio; and Laura Van Tosh, Maryland.

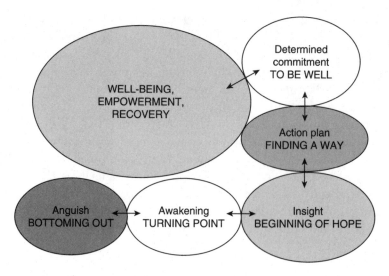

Figure 6.1. The Recovery Advisory Group Recovery Model.

way as to begin a spiral. Consumers of mental health services often speak of their lives as being in a spiral; they may slip back all the way to anguish, but during their next phase of recovery, their insight and action plan may be on a different plane than it was the first time they began this journey.

Consumers who developed this model indicate that recovery is both internal and external as reflected in the Recovery Model chart shown in Exhibit 6.1. The internal is what happens within oneself, whereas the external includes interactions with others. Internal dimensions include cognitive, emotional, spiritual, and physical. Cognitive dimensions are areas of knowing, recognition, or insight through the stages of recovery. Emotional dimensions include areas of feeling and learning to be hopeful. Spiritual dimensions give meaning to a person's life and help that person to realize he or she is not alone. Physical dimensions are those areas that affect the body, which can also affect the mind. The external dimensions consist of a person's actions and reactions to external influences, as well as interactions with people and situations as one moves across and through the stages of recovery. Dimensions used to describe the external aspect of recovery are activity, self-care, social relationships, and social supports. Activity includes listening, watching, learning, and doing things that support or increase your mental health. Self-care includes caring for oneself both physically and emotionally and may include asking for help. Social relationships are those interactions with other people, accepting and giving support, and establishing meaningful contacts with friends, family, and coworkers. Social supports include housing, income, employment, and education, including learning

EXHIBIT 6.1
Recovery Model Chart

Stages / Domains	ANGUISH	AWAKENING	INSIGHT	ACTION PLAN	DETERMINED COMMITMENT TO BECOME WELL	WELL-BEING/ EMPOWERMENT
	Experience of despair because of the "mentally ill" label	*Awareness that things can change*	*I understand that change is possible*	*I must do something to make things better*	*I will recover*	*I am empowered to help myself and others. This gives me a feeling of well-being*
Cognitive	Negative thoughts	Recognition of anguish and what causes anguish	Insight that there is something better	Searching for what will work: intellectual search and study	Recognize I am capable of making own decisions. I have self-determination, self-knowledge, and self-worth	Positive self-regard: best use of intellectual power
Emotional	Hopelessness	Realization that change can take place	Positive self-talk: "I can do it, I will try today"; beginning of hope	Learning to cope with difficult feelings	I am hopeful; the future looks promising	Acceptance of ups and downs and not being disabled by them
Spiritual	No meaning or purpose	Recognizing that the pain of staying where you are is greater than the pain of changing	Seeking help from a "higher power"; possibility of meaning	Finding spiritual satisfaction	My life has meaning and value	Compassion for self and others; acceptance of other's compassion; connectedness
Physical	Pain/ dysfunction	Realization that it will take physical and emotional effort to change	Recognition you can start with physical activity; hurting for a reason	Learning basis for physical pain	I am committed to respecting my body and taking care of it	Taking care of physical being

INTERNAL

(continues)

EXHIBIT 6.1 (Continued)
Recovery Model Chart

Stages	ANGUISH	AWAKENING	INSIGHT	ACTION PLAN	DETERMINED COMMITMENT TO BECOME WELL	WELL-BEING/ EMPOWERMENT
	Experience of despair because of the "mentally ill" label	*Awareness that things can change*	*I understand that change is possible*	*I must do something to make things better*	*I will recover*	*I am empowered to help myself and others. This gives me a feeling of well-being*
Domains						
Activity	Limited/ constrained Loss of competence Excessive/ disruptive	Listening, watching, and learning	Purposeful movement. Experimenting, taking small steps	Searching for meaningful activities, social activism, etc.	Complex activity— increasing competence, movement toward work positive behavior change	Meaningful work—paid, volunteer, hobbies
Self-care	Lack of physical, emotional, and spiritual care	Expressing the need for self-care. Asking for assistance	Starting to care for self in one or two dimensions	Learning ways to care for self better	Attending to nutrition, getting appropriate medical and mental health care	Integrated in everyday activities, ensuring physical, emotional, and spiritual aspects are given attention
Social relationships	Isolation and alienation	Accepting encouragement	Wanting social interactions	Looking for meaningful social interactions with those who understand	Establishing meaningful contacts with friends, family, and coworkers	Interaction with others by choice; advocating for important things
Social supports	Homelessness, poverty, destitution	Learning there may be a way out of poverty, homelessness, and destitution	Learning about what social supports can help me	Asking for help you want	Safe living arrangements, housing, and financial supports	Stability in housing, finances; capacity to maintain comfort

EXTERNAL

about such supports and asking for help when needed. Internal insight, "self-talk," and growth must take place, but there also needs to be interaction with the world in which one lives. Statements were developed to describe each stage of recovery in each of the dimensions listed in Exhibit 6.1.

External influences (e.g., family, friends, community, mental health system) are very important for recovery and can support or deter recovery. Negative influences lead to discrimination, prejudice, and stigma, whereas positive influences lead to collaboration, respect, and trust. These influences cover a wide range: from mental health services, through social supports and natural supports such as family and friends, to peer supports. Negative influences in mental health services include lack of choice of treatment, lack of information about treatment such as side effects, involuntary treatment, forced medication, and control and abuse by the mental health system and staff. In contrast to this, positive influences include providers who listen and collaborate in treatment, efforts to find treatment that works and is available, alternative healing methods, respect of cultural issues and beliefs, information about medication and treatment, and respect for consumer choice. In the area of social supports, negative influences include poverty, homelessness, substandard or no housing support, work limits because of benefits, and cultural and racial discrimination. Negative influences also include the lack of funding for treatment, providers who will not accept Medicaid, and inability to pay for care. On the positive side, social supports include adequate income supports, housing assistance including reuniting families, and employment and education opportunities. People supports show up negatively in lack of understanding of the illness, lack of resources and education, overprotection, self-blame, denial, and with competition among peers rather than collaboration. On the positive side, family and friends provide an open door without coercion, emotional and spiritual support, financial assistance, and housing as needed. Peer supports include collaboration, emotional and physical support, and advocacy. Figure 6.2 depicts external influences and shows both the positive and negative sides of these influences. Positive influences are shown as circles or ovals in Figure 6.2, whereas negative influences are shown as squares or oblongs.

In the big picture (Figure 6.3), the person who is recovering is shown in the center, with the stages or phases of recovery as part of the growth and process in his or her recovery journey. The person is surrounded by external influences that are both positive and negative. There must be efforts to find as many positive influences as possible to overcome the negative influences that may be present. As mentioned earlier in this chapter, people do not go through their journeys to recovery in a vacuum. They must react and interact with people and systems that can influence their lives. Thus, people moving toward recovery cannot be seen as being separate from those with whom they interact.

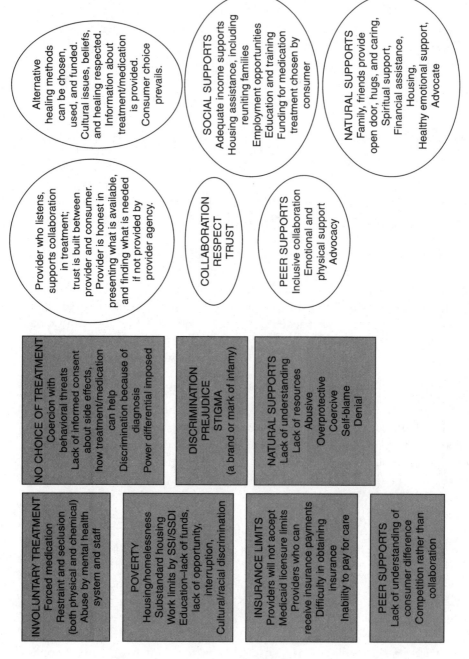

Figure 6.2. External influences that affect recovery. *SSI,* Social Security income; *SSDI,* Social Security disability income.

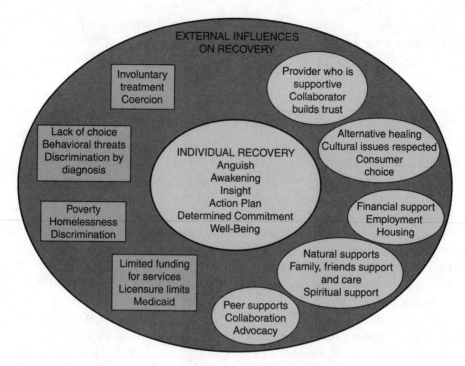

EXTERNAL INFLUENCES
ON RECOVERY

Involuntary
treatment
Coercion

Provider who is
supportive
Collaborator
builds trust

Lack of choice
Behavioral threats
Discrimination by
diagnosis

INDIVIDUAL RECOVERY
Anguish
Awakening
Insight
Action Plan
Determined Commitment
Well-Being

Alternative healing
Cultural issues respected
Consumer
choice

Poverty
Homelessness
Discrimination

Financial support
Employment
Housing

Limited funding
for services
Licensure limits
Medicaid

Natural supports
Family, friends support
and care
Spiritual support

Peer supports
Collaboration
Advocacy

Figure 6.3. The big picture—the recovering person is influenced by his or her environment.

Because of the need for research and measurement of recovery, efforts have been directed at developing a measurement tool based on this model. A group of consumers from Maine developed items for each block of the Recovery Model chart. People completing the items will indicate if the statement is very much like them, somewhat like them, or not at all like them. This has resulted in a 90-item tool that is still to be tested.

SUMMARY

Each definition, whether verbal or visual, is rich in meaning, and in these definitions we find similar and different emphases, which, when taken as a whole, help to give us a picture of recovery. As we think about defining recovery, let us think about the strengths of these definitions and models and how they can help us live our own recovery and assist others in finding balance and health in their lives. Although it is an individual experience, recovery does not happen in a vacuum. There must be some stimulus, some source of strength and encouragement for it to take place. Thus, the family members of a person with a psychiatric disorder and providers of mental health services need to embrace the concepts of recovery and provide the support and encouragement needed for a person to recover. One of the most important supports is for someone to believe in the person with a psychiatric disorder, that he or she is a person, and that she or he can recover (Fisher, 1997). The visual models described in this chapter may help family members and direct care providers to better understand recovery and to incorporate behaviors that support recovery into their belief systems and interactions with people with psychiatric disorders.

To build evidence that recovery does take place, research on recovery must be done, and instruments to measure the processes and outcomes must be developed and tested. Models described in this chapter and in other chapters in this book can be helpful in developing research paradigms to study. Measurements may also be based on these models.

How can these verbal definitions and visual models be used to further recovery of individuals? Can they be used by consumers to check where they are in their own recovery process? Can they be used by professionals to communicate with consumers in terms of how they are doing, and where they can be most helpful? Can consumers and their family members communicate more freely if they agree on what helps and what hinders their recovery? Do other models or verbal definitions exist that would be helpful to consumers, family members, providers, and researchers? How can these definitions and models be used to inform and enhance research on recovery? All of these questions are important to the growth and development of recovery both as an individual process and as an outcome. Answers may lead to changes in the way mental health providers think about and interact with people with psychiatric disorders.

REFERENCES

Chamberlin, J. (1997, Summer/Fall). Confessions of a non-compliant patient. *National Empowerment Center Newsletter*, 9–10.

Cross, T., Earle, K., Echo-Hawk-Solie, H., & Manness, K. (2000). Cultural strengths and challenges in implementing a system of care model in American Indian communities. In *Systems of care: Promising practices in children's mental health, 2000 series* (Vol. I, pp. 8–14).Washington, DC: Center for Effective Collaboration and Practice, American Institutes for Research.

Deegan, P. E. (1988). Recovery: The lived experience of rehabilitation. *Psychosocial Rehabilitation Journal*, *11*(4), 11–19.

Dornan, D. H., Felton, C. J., & Carpinello, S. E. (2000, November). *Mental health recovery from the perspectives of consumers/survivors*. Paper presented at the annual meeting of the American Public Health Association, Boston, MA.

Fisher, D. B. (1994–1995, Winter). The empowerment model of recovery: Finding our voice and having a say. *National Empowerment Center Newsletter*, 5–6.

Fisher, D. B. (1997, Summer/Fall). Someone who believed in them helped them to recover. *National Empowerment Center Newsletter*, 3–4.

Fisher, D. B., & Ahern, L. (1999, Spring). People can recover from mental illness. *National Empowerment Center Newsletter*, 13–14.

Leete, E. (1988). A consumer perspective on psychosocial treatment. *Psychosocial Rehabilitation Journal, 12*, 45–52.

Leete, E. (1989). How I perceive and manage my illness. *Schizophrenia Bulletin, 15*, 197–200.

Lovejoy, M. (1982). Expectations and the recovery process. *Schizophrenia Bulletin, 8*, 605–609.

Prochaska, J. O., DiClemente, C. C., & Norcross, J. C. (1992). In search of how people change: Applications to addictive behaviors. *American Psychologist, 47*, 1102–1113.

Ralph, R. O. (2000). Recovery. *Psychiatric Rehabilitation Skills, 4*, 480–517.

Ralph, R. O., & Recovery Advisory Group. (1999). *The Recovery Advisory Group Recovery Model*. Paper presented at the National Conference on Mental Health Statistics, Washington, DC.

Ridgway, P. A. (2001). Re-storying psychiatric disability: Learning from first person recovery narratives. *Psychiatric Rehabilitation Journal, 24*, 335–343.

Stocks, M. L. (1995). In the eye of the beholder. *Psychiatric Rehabilitation Journal, 19*(1), 89–91.

Unzicker, R. (1989). On my own: A personal journey through madness and re-emergence. *Psychological Rehabilitation Journal, 13*, 70–77.

U.S. Department of Health and Human Services, Substance Abuse and Mental Health Services Administration, Center for Mental Health Services, National Institutes of Health, & the National Institute of Mental Health. (1999). *Mental health: A report of the Surgeon General*. Rockville, MD: Author.

7

QUALITATIVE STUDIES OF RECOVERY: WHAT CAN WE LEARN FROM THE PERSON?

LARRY DAVIDSON, DAVID SELLS,
STEPHANIE SANGSTER, AND MARIA O'CONNELL

"Why don't you ever ask me what I do to help myself?"

—*Woman with schizophrenia talking with interviewer*
(Strauss, 1989, p. 182)

"Among the many goals of the ex-patient's movement . . . is to play a part in devising mental health policy, rather than to be merely the passive objects of policies designed by others. . . . Unless planning groups and councils are made up of at least one-third mental health consumers, they are failing to live up to what we consider the mandate of the [Mental Health Planning Act (Public Law 99-660) which required states to plan the implementation of community-based systems of care incorporating the input of various constituency groups]."

—*Judi Chamberlain and Joseph Rogers*
(1990, pp. 1241–1243)

The authors gratefully acknowledge the assistance of John Strauss, MD, and Richard Weingarten, RPRP, in critiquing prior drafts of this paper.

147

"Nothing about us without us!"

—*Slogan of the Disability Rights Movement*
(cited in Charlton, 1998)

The order of the preceding quotations reflects an evolution in assertion of the agency, independence, and eventual self-determination of people with psychiatric disabilities. This evolution—from the fact that people with schizophrenia can do things to help themselves, to requiring decision-making bodies to involve at least one third of the consumers, to people with disabilities taking over complete control of their own lives—speaks to an important principle underlying the recovery movement that serves as the focus of this volume. This principle asserts that people with psychiatric disabilities—just like all those who do not have psychiatric disabilities—are the experts on the topic of their own experiences, needs, and preferences, and thus are best able to identify what would be helpful—or not—in promoting their own recovery. Like the proverbial customer, they know best when it comes to their own lives, including their own efforts in struggling and coping with severe psychiatric disorders.

What this principle suggests in relation to psychological studies of recovery is that people with psychiatric disorders may have important information, if not also expertise, to contribute to the research enterprise itself. Thus far, two predominant approaches have been used regarding the inclusion of people with psychiatric disabilities in recovery research: The first and more common of these has involved eliciting the perspectives, experiences, and voices of people with psychiatric disabilities through qualitative research methods that rely on first-person accounts, open-ended narrative interviews, and ethnographic observation. The second approach involves the emerging paradigm of *participatory action research* (PAR). Regardless of whether or not the generation of scientific knowledge is itself explicitly viewed as a social or political change process (i.e., the "action" in participatory action research), PAR includes people with psychiatric disabilities as collaborators in all aspects and phases of the research enterprise.

This chapter focuses on the first of these approaches and offers an integrative summary of existing qualitative studies on processes of recovery in serious mental illness. The absence of findings from PAR in this summary does not reflect our assessment of their relative value as much as it does their relative scarcity in the field. Although committed in the conduct of our own investigations to the fundamental principle of inclusion on which PAR is based (e.g., Davidson, Stayner, Lambert, Smith, & Sledge, 1997), we recognize the newness of PAR to the fields of clinical psychology and community mental health, fields that have a history of viewing people with psychiatric disorders as objects, rather than as participants, of study. We therefore leave this topic for another occasion, and turn to see what light has been shed on processes of recovery by people living with psychiatric disabilities through the methods of qualitative inquiry.

A BRIEF OVERVIEW OF QUALITATIVE RESEARCH ON SERIOUS MENTAL ILLNESS

In contrast to PAR, qualitative inquiry focused on serious mental illness is not a new phenomenon. In fact, several of the classic and most influential texts to be produced during the era of institutional care for people with these disorders incorporated qualitative methods, at least in part, if not in their entirety. Stanton and Schwartz's (1954) seminal study of the mental hospital was based on ethnographic observation informed by psychoanalytic theory and organizational psychology, whereas Goffman's (1961, 1963) important investigations of processes of stigmatization and institutionalization, later elaborated by Wing, Monck, Brown, and Carstairs (1964), were based on ethnography and narrative informed by sociological theory. It was in Sue Estroff's (1981) groundbreaking study of community care in Madison, Wisconsin, in the 1970s (entitled *Making It Crazy: An Ethnography of Psychiatric Clients in an American Community*), based on her own observations and first-hand experiences living as a client of an assertive community treatment team for 9 months, that these methods were first transferred from the institutional to the community context. Since that time, qualitative research methods have gone through what Estroff (1995) characterized as their own process of deinstitutionalization, shifting from studies of disorder, and of individual and social psychopathology, to studies of recovery. In the following, we review what the body of qualitative research has generated since Estroff's initial work taught us about the processes involved in the phenomenon of recovery.

WHAT WE CAN LEARN FROM FIRST-PERSON ACCOUNTS OF RECOVERY

To learn how recovery has been described by people with psychiatric disabilities, we first collected and conducted a thematic analysis of first-person accounts of recovery appearing in the consumer–survivor and psychiatric rehabilitation literature. This search involved review and analysis of all first-person accounts related to recovery, improvement, and adaptation in serious mental illness identified through both MEDLINE and PsychINFO searches.

The first thing we discover when we turn to these accounts—which admittedly represent only that select sample of people who are interested in and willing to tell their stories to the public—is that *recovery involves a redefinition of one's illness as only one aspect of a multidimensional sense of self that is capable of identifying, choosing, and pursuing personally meaningful goals and aspirations even when continuing to experience the effects and side effects of mental illness.* Such a definition of recovery obviously differs from the sense of recovery used in clinical research, in which recovery involves alleviation of the symptoms that cause a person distress or ill health and a return to his or her premorbid level of functioning (Young & Ensing, 1999). Recovery, from this clinical perspective, is an absence of illness or symptoms or the removal of something that was not part of a person's life prior to the illness, such as medication (White, 2000; Whitwell, 2001). Although this model also may include more positive indicators of improvement such as employment and relationships, the focus remains nonetheless on removing obstacles to an otherwise normal or healthy state (Davidson, 2003; Davidson & Strauss, 1995; Jacobson & Curtis, 2000).

From the perspective of many consumer/survivors, however, recovery is not understood in this way as an "end product or result" (Deegan, 1988, p. 15). It is neither "synonymous with cure" nor does it involve a return to a premorbid state (Deegan, 1993; Walsh, 1996). Rather, it is a lifelong process that involves an indefinite number of incremental steps in various life domains (Frese & Davis, 1997). As a result, many people view the process of recovery as a uniquely personal process or as a way of life (Deegan, 1988, 1996) rather than as a return to health.

An additional reason that recovery is not typically viewed as a return to a previous state is that advocates often view the experiences of disability, treatment, hospitalization, stigma, and discrimination associated with their mental illness as having changed their lives irrevocably. Like trauma survivors who can never simply return to their lives prior to the traumatic event, mental illness in its more severe forms may be experienced as a life-altering condition. Walsh (1996), for example, argues that: "We can never go back to our 'premorbid' selves. The experience of disability and stigma attached to it, changes us forever" (p. 87). Some people, in addition, would not want to go back to their lives prior to their experiences of illness because that would in effect deny an important part of their existence (Corrigan & Penn, 1998) or negate gains they have made in the process of recovery (Davidson & Strauss, 1992). This last element speaks to the fact that recovery—in contrast to an absence of symptoms, relief from effects of illness, or amelioration of difficulties—often involves growth and an expansion of capacities.

Because this sense of recovery may be different for different people, it is difficult to come up with one set of essential ingredients that will be true for all. Our review of these personal accounts reveals several common aspects of the journey of recovery, however. In addition to redefining self, these include being supported by others, renewing a sense of hope and commitment, accepting illness, being involved in meaningful activities and expanded social roles, managing symptoms, resuming control over and responsibility for one's life, overcoming stigma, and exercising one's citizenship. We review each briefly in the following subsections.

Being Supported by Others

Despite appearances, at times, recovery is not a solitary, but an inevitably social, process. Beyond the value of medications, people most often describe the importance of having someone believe in them when they could not believe in themselves or of having someone else stand by them even when they felt they had had been subsumed by their illness (Davidson, 2003). Having supportive others, whether they are family members or friends, professionals, community members, or peers, to provide encouragement through the difficult times, to help celebrate the good, and to keep the person feeling like a worthwhile human being despite the ravages of the illness has been reported to be critical to recovery (Smith, 2000).

People in recovery also speak of the importance of having another person in recovery as a mentor as they go through their own journey. Such role models can give people a sense of what recovery may entail and require of them, and also may give them ideas about what to hope and strive for (Baxter & Diehl, 1998; Fisher, 1994; Mead & Copeland, 2000; Young & Ensing, 1999). Finally, these supportive others do not necessarily have to be flesh-and-blood people; they can also be beloved pets or God. Many people in recovery, in fact, emphasize the importance of their having faith in God when everything else was at its bleakest. This faith offers them a sense of being loved and supported and a sense of belonging, even when they feel abandoned by others (Davidson, 2003; Sullivan, 1994).

Renewing Hope and Commitment

On the basis of the foundation provided by supportive others, the importance of having hope and believing in the possibility of a renewed sense of self and purpose emerges as the next essential component of recovery (Deegan, 1996; Fisher, 1994; Mead & Copeland, 2000; Smith, 2000). Without hope, people remain demoralized, despairing, and lost to the illness, whereas hope without renewed commitment produces passivity and impotence. For hope to be channeled into effective efforts toward improvement of one's condition and situation, it must be translated into a desire and commitment to recover (Smith, 2000; Young & Ensing, 1999).

Accepting Illness and Redefining Self

As noted earlier in our initial definition, the redefinition of one's self as a person of whom mental illness is simply one part is probably the most over-arching aspect of recovery. Given its tendency to subsume the entirety of the person experiencing it, psychiatric disorder has been described as a disease of the self (Estroff, 1989). Not only does a person experience psychiatric symptoms and resulting impairments, social consequences, and stigma, but he or she may be socialized into assuming the role and identity of a "mental patient." This role is reinforced by a system that has historically valued and rewarded compliance and passivity over signs of autonomy and independence. Although acceptance of illness is described in this way as essential to recovery (Munetz & Frese, 2001; Smith, 2000; Sullivan, 1994; Young & Ensing, 1999), this should not be taken to mean that one must accept a particular framework or conceptual model of illness (e.g., a narrow biomedical view) to recover. It also and emphatically does not mean accepting the identity of a "mentally ill person." To the contrary, accepting one's illness instead involves redefining how a person understands this particular one of life's challenges within the context of a broader and more multifaceted life and sense of self.

Being Involved in Meaningful Activities and Expanded Social Roles

Once the person feels supported, hopeful, and committed to and capable of recovery, he or she has to have something to do. An additional and important aspect of recovery is thus involvement in meaningful activities and the development or expansion of valued social roles (Young & Ensing, 1999). Here again it is not so important what activities or roles people choose to become involved in or to pursue as much as it is important for them to participate in personally meaningful and gratifying activities that also afford them a sense of making worthwhile contributions to their community. This kind of participation also affords the person a sense of purpose and direction in his or her life. In addition to a person's own particular interests, education, employment, and spirituality are some of the primary, socially sanctioned ways in which people can acquire more meaning and purpose in their lives (Rogers, 1995; Sullivan, 1994).

Managing Symptoms

Although complete remission of symptoms is not necessary for recovery to occur, people often do report that being able to manage symptoms in some way is essential for them to be able to take an active role in their own recovery (Fisher, 1994). The methods by which people manage symptoms differ substantially from one person to the next—whether it be through medication, therapy, or their own coping strategies—and the methods themselves are not as important as the freedom and latitude the person regains by bringing the symptoms under some degree of control. Recovery in this sense is about people *using* treatment, services, medication, or coping skills in an active way as a major force in their own recovery rather than as a recipient of services and a beneficiary of the efforts of others (Deegan, 1996).

Resuming Control and Responsibility

Just as recovery is about what a person *does* and not something that can be done *to* a person by others, people must assume responsibility for their transformation from a patient with a mental illness or a disability to a person in recovery (Baxter & Diehl, 1998; Frese, Stanley, Kress, & Vogel-Scibilia, 2001; Leete, 1994; Lovejoy, 1982; Mead & Copeland, 2000; Smith, 2000). Taking back control of one's life helps reduce the feelings of helplessness and perceptions of victimization while increasing the person's sense of efficacy in his or her life (Fisher, 1994; Lovejoy, 1982; Young & Ensing, 1999; Walsh, 1996). For the person to take control of, and responsibility for, his or her life and regain a sense of agency and efficacy, however, she or he must be afforded opportunities and must have meaningful options from which to choose (Walsh, 1996; Young & Ensing, 1999).

Overcoming Stigma

Recovery involves more than overcoming the devastation of one's mental illness. For many people, it also involves recovering from the social consequences and devastation of the stigma of mental illness as well. Societal stigma has been identified as one of the major barriers to recovery both by the surgeon general and by people in recovery themselves (U.S. Department of Health and Human Services, 1999). A person's immediate social context exerts tremendous influence on that person's developing sense of self and identity. One especially problematic result of the impact of stigma is the process of internalization some people go through in accepting their community's notions of serious mental illness and withdrawing into a "mental patient" role and identity. Recovery, on the other hand, requires developing resilience to stigma or actively fighting against it.

Exercising Citizenship

Recovery involves the restoration not only of the rights of community living but also of the responsibilities that go with them. Part of recovery therefore involves participating as full, contributing, and responsible members of society, whether this is through working and paying taxes or through voting, volunteerism, and participation in other civic activities. Resuming the role of citizen may require advocacy as well as activity, however, because there are numerous legislative, attitudinal, and material barriers to full participation in civic life for people with disabilities (Rowe, 1999).

WHAT WE CAN LEARN FROM NARRATIVE
INTERVIEWS AND ETHNOGRAPHY

Although providing a useful point of departure, the collection and analysis of published first-person accounts does not exhaust the potential contributions of qualitative inquiry. In fact, given the selection bias mentioned earlier and, more importantly, the fact that autobiographical narratives rely entirely on the person's conscious awareness of and reflection on his or her own experiences, first-person accounts tend to stay on the surface of the phenomena in question. We actually are consciously and reflectively aware of very little that happens in our lives, even less so of the reasons for what happens or for what we ourselves choose to do (Davidson et al., 2003; Dennett, 1991). We can expect to learn more, then, from in-depth interviews that elicit rich descriptive details from informants—details they might not have thought to provide otherwise—and from combined intensive observation and interviewing, as in ethnographic approaches. We now summarize the findings these methods have generated regarding elements of, and barriers to, recovery, beginning with the processes from which informants have had to recover.

Loss of Self

The first and most striking component of in-depth interviews conducted with people with psychiatric disabilities is the way in which they describe the impact of the illness on their lives, including the disruptions and losses associated with it. Primary among these appears to be the loss of their pre-illness sense of self. How do people lose their sense of self in the context of severe mental illness and what are the implications of this loss for recovery?

Qualitative findings suggest at least two answers to these questions. First, internal personal processes such as how people account for their psychiatric problems can affect the extent to which they come to identify themselves as "mentally ill." For example, a person who thinks of his psychiatric difficulties in terms of neurobiological problems may be more likely to identify himself as "ill" than if he conceives of his difficulties as a response to job stress. Second, interpersonal processes comprising the social milieu can significantly impact the sense of self in relation to chronic illness in general, and severe mental illness in particular (Charmaz, 1983). For example, a person with psychiatric problems who is continually treated as "sick" by those around her is more likely to identify herself as such than if she were afforded respect for her strengths and talents. Although internal and social processes of identification with mental illness are thought to be interdependent, we attempt to distinguish between them here in the interests of clarifying what qualitative investigations have revealed about each.

Internal Processes

In terms of internal processes, Estroff, Lachicotte, Illingworth, and Johnston (1991) explored mechanisms of autobiographical revision among people with severe mental illness. Specifically, investigators interviewed 90 women and 79 men receiving inpatient psychiatric care at the time of consent. Most of the 169 informants were under age 35 and carried diagnoses of schizophrenia, affective disorder, or a personality disorder. Each informant provided interviews five times over a 2-year period at 6-month intervals. All narrative data were transcribed and rated according to text analysis and inductively derived coding schemes of illness descriptions and self-labeling tendencies. These descriptions and self-labeling tendencies appeared to vary according to how informants accounted for their problems.

Informants with the highest tendency to label themselves as mentally ill included those who accounted for their problems in terms of medical or emotional-developmental processes. For example, one informant stated: "I have chronic bipolar illness" (Estroff et al., 1991, p. 348), invoking an objective clinical description of psychiatric difficulties as reflected in the possessive *have*. Another informant stated: "I found out my high blood pressure medicine had side effects that kept me depressive . . . the other part is being alcoholic" (Estroff et al., 1991, p. 348). Like the preceding statement, this informant's illness identification was offered in clinical vernacular; unlike the other informant, however, the account reflected a subjective identification with illness, suggested by the depiction of "being" alcoholic and depressive.

Informants with the lowest tendency to label themselves as mentally ill were those using social-situational, "no problem," and religious-spiritual accounts for their difficulties. Those using situational accounts appeared to see their difficulties as a function of social and environmental stresses, as opposed to internal processes. As one informant stated: "If my life situation were fine, I'd be fine" (Estroff et al., 1991, p. 350). By contrast, those who maintained that they had no problem or provided religious-spiritual accounts for their difficulties did not acknowledge the existence of psychiatric difficulties. For example, one informant who reported being possessed by a ghost asserted: "I have tried, struggled to see the possibilities of this [as] mental illness, and I just can't believe that it is" (Estroff et al., 1991, p. 351).

Given informants' self-labeling tendencies, the degree to which mental illness absorbs the self appeared to span from none, as evidenced by those who maintained that they had no problems, to subjective identification with a psychiatric designation itself, as given by those who suggested they *were* schizophrenic, alcoholic, or otherwise. Estroff and colleagues (1991) observed some fluctuation in stability of self-labeling depending on accounts informants gave for their difficulties. In many instances, however, self-labeling tendencies were observed to be relatively stable, and might be construed as reflecting varying degrees of loss of self within a mental illness designation ranging from minimal to apparent engulfment. *Engulfment* refers to the point at which people with psychiatric disorders begin to think of themselves more or less entirely in terms of mental illness categories. Here, we use the term to represent a high degree of loss of self. What, then, is the relationship between loss of self as reflected by illness identification statements and recovery?

Findings of qualitative research appear to dispute the notion of a simple linear relationship between illness identification and recovery. That is, at one extreme, subjective identification with an illness category seems most likely to impede recovery, particularly given qualitative research suggesting that an enhanced sense of self is positively associated with recovery (Davidson & Strauss, 1992). At the other extreme, denial of any relationship between self and illness is also a potential impediment to recovery, especially if it prevents the person from taking measures to address his or her difficulties. This last point was illustrated by Estroff and colleagues (1991) through a not uncommon case vignette of an informant who had continually resisted the label of mental illness despite (or perhaps because of) his confinement on a psychiatric inpatient unit. This stance, however, appeared to lead him to discount his difficulties in maladaptive ways after discharge, such as not taking prescribed medications. On meeting and speaking with this informant when he returned to inpatient care, an investigator speculated that he remained in the process of "coming to terms with himself" (Estroff et al., 1991, p. 336) particularly with regards to having a mental illness.

Given the findings of qualitative investigations such as Estroff and colleagues' (1991), the relationship between illness identification and recovery may be best described as *curvilinear*. That is, as suggested in Figure 7.1, we propose that an optimal level of illness identification with respect to recovery may be found in between the extremes of denial and engulfment of identification as mentally ill. Though this optimal middle ground should vary for each individual, it may broadly represent the capacity to recognize the presence of mental illness without becoming wholly defined by it.

Social Processes

With respect to the role of the social milieu in the loss of self, Barham and Hayward (1998) explored the effects of stigma on the social lives of people with severe mental illness living in the United Kingdom. Specifically, 20 male and 4 female informants provided individual interviews and participated in group-level discussions, both of which were recorded and later rated to assess difficulties in adaptation to social and community life. The authors found that both explicit and implicit processes of stigma can have devastating effects on a person's sense of who she or he is. For example, Ian,

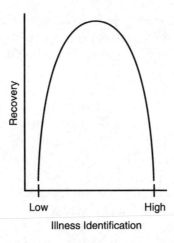

Figure 7.1. Proposal for a curvilinear relationship between illness identification and recovery.

an informant with schizophrenia, relayed a discussion with his psychiatrist in which he shared an interest in pursuing community work of some sort. His psychiatrist responded by telling him that he "must be content to be 'on the sick' and cope and manage as best he could" (Barham & Hayward, 1998, p. 165). Such discouraging messages embody what Deegan (1997) referred to as "spirit-breaking." As she described, spirit-breaking may be exercised "in any environment in which there are people who have power and people who have been stripped of their power to direct their own lives and make their own choices" (p. 353). In this instance, the psychiatrist's message of hopelessness led Ian to internalize the stigma of his mental illness.

Ian also reflected on his attempts to obtain a volunteer job in the local school system, stating: "I applied and told them I had been a student teacher and told them I had had nervous trouble and been in the hospital, and they never wrote back and never offered me a position. So that was volunteer work!" (Barham & Hayward, 1998, p. 165). In this example, Ian presented himself to a prospective employer as both a teacher and as a person who has had psychiatric difficulties. The rejection perceived in the lack of response from the employer was felt to discredit his identity as a teacher, again leaving him to question his value as anything but a psychiatric patient.

Discrediting experiences like Ian's appear most likely to be internalized into a person's sense of self at times of particular vulnerability or at moments in which a person perceives from interactions or events suggestions of an alternative, diminished self-definition (Charmaz, 1983). Perhaps nowhere is such internalization more probable than in the context of hospitalization. Lally (1989) used a qualitative approach to detail the effects of hospitalization on the self-image of people with severe mental illness, finding frequency and duration of psychiatric hospitalization to be significant determinants of adoption of a patient identity. For example, one informant in Lally's (1989) study described his reactions to being hospitalized by invoking past views of a classmate who he learned had once been hospitalized, noting: "I would always look down on him, for just being in a place like this. Then when I got here, it was like my life had ended" (p. 259). In this situation, the discrediting event was the informant's first hospitalization, in which his sense of vulnerability was high and he identified with a person he had once disparaged for being in a similar situation. Correspondingly, the informant's statements suggest a profound revision of his sense of self.

In this way, the cumulative effects of social stigma and internalization can be felt to dismantle a person's sense of self and, thereby, compromise possibilities for recovery. Charmaz (1983) suggested that this process implicates an eventual restriction of activity and social isolation. That is, a person who has experienced painful and repeated insults over the course of social interactions is likely to restrict her or his activities to those that are less likely to involve contact with others. This restriction can range from going only to public places in which social contact is minimal to becoming entirely homebound. Particularly in the latter case, social isolation is likely to impede recovery, ultimately contributing to a vicious cycle of loss, social restriction, and exacerbation of difficulties.

Supportive Others

In our own previous work (e.g., Davidson, et al., 2001), we systematically investigated the specific mechanisms by which social support contributes to recovery through qualitative research based on studies of *supported socialization*. Supported socialization parallels other recent advances in community-based care such as supported housing and employment, which are known to foster community adaptation of people with severe mental illness. One study included conditions in which individuals who were experiencing mental illness and living in the community in relative social isolation were paired with volunteer partners. Over a 9-month period, these pairs spent a few hours each week engaging in social and recreational activities such as going out together to dinner, movies, or for coffee. Both informants and volunteers were provided a stipend of $28 a month to offset the costs of recreational activities. Qualitative interviews were conducted with 14 individuals who received partners. The interviews were later rated by investigators for thematic prominence.

In these interviews, salient themes with respect to processes of recovery included partner acceptance, refuge from mental illness, mutuality, and an emergent sense of belonging. In terms of acceptance, many informants suggested that what they perceived as openness to their life circumstances and indeed, who they were, on the part of their partners greatly facilitated forging a relationship with them. Of course, some of this openness may be conceived as a programmatic contract for participation in this study; that is, partners volunteered specifically to befriend participants and informants were aware of this, making it easier to connect initially than it might have been under other circumstances. Acceptance was further manifest in the consistency with which informants met with their partners (i.e., weekly) throughout the 9-month intervention and emerged almost as a precondition to the development of other positive aspects of the relationship.

Informants noted that time spent with their partners often provided a refuge from viewing themselves as mentally ill. Often, refuge was found simply through "getting out" into the community with their partners and experiencing a sense of enjoyment and comfort, regardless of the nature of the activity. As one informant asserted: "The more you get out, the better you feel" (Davidson et al., 2001, p. 284). In the context of other informants' statements, this remark also implied distraction from the social isolation and stigma often punctuating informants' daily lives. Moreover, getting out appeared to facilitate a discovery of alternative things to focus on and do besides having a psychiatric disorder, as reflected in one informant's comment that "It just opened my eyes that there are other things to think about besides mental illness . . . [that] I could go places and have fun" (Davidson et al., p. 284).

In addition to a sense of getting out, refuge from mental illness was also reflected in informants' feelings of having positive things to look forward to. In this latter sense, the type of community activities emerged as an important factor. As one informant described: "We did a lot of hiking in parks and stuff . . . I love nature, I love the outdoors . . ." (Davidson et al., 2001, p. 284). The implications of this informant's comment stretch beyond the benefits of "getting out" and extend to a sense of moving toward particular interests and activities. Over time, the engagement of such interests and activities may foster an exploration of identities that are more salutary than that of mental patient.

Informants frequently alluded to a sense of having things to offer in their relationships with partners, inspiring feelings of mutuality not often experienced in other relationships in their lives, such as those with family and mental health providers. Although most informants valued the opportunity to be in reciprocal relationships, they noted that doing so entailed work, which was observed to range from compromises in deciding where to go out together to taking care of the other person. For example, one informant who had been paired with a consumer partner discovered both challenges and rewards in listening to his partner's descriptions of difficulties with continuing psychotic symptoms. He remarked that, on the one hand, the stress of doing so tended to exacerbate his own symptoms, whereas on the other he became a "more receptive and caring" person because of it. Prior to this relationship, he said, "There was nothing there. I just didn't feel for the [other] person" (Davidson, Haglund, et al., 2001, p. 285). In this example, the informant's efforts to care for another unearthed a previously lost or forgotten sense of emotional connection to other people, the rediscovery of which was felt to be worth the temporary disturbance it caused in his life. This informant's experience seems consistent with Deegan's (1993) conceptualization of relapse in recovery as a "breaking through" as opposed to "breaking down" (p. 10). That is, without knowledge of this informant's life, we might make a critical error in understanding his exacerbation of symptoms as a mechanism of failure rather than as reflective of his success in recovering a sense of social connection.

Phrases such as *getting out* into the community, *moving toward* new interests, and *breaking through* invoke an overarching theme of favorable reengagement as reflected in informants' reports; that is, the cultivation of a sense of belonging in the world that many informants had not known for a long time, often since first becoming ill. Moreover, within this new space of belonging, informants experienced an enhanced sense of competency, as was evident in one informant's comment that after the program he felt "like a more presentable person who can do things in the world" (Davidson et al., 2001, p. 287). Such experiences, in turn, were noted by informants to enhance their sense of self-esteem, as another pointed out: "The project has just sort of opened up some doors for me in terms of dealing with people . . . [now] I feel like I have something to offer . . ." (Davidson et al., p. 288). Ultimately, such feelings appeared to provide a needed foundation for further efforts at recovery.

Reconstruction of Self

The majority of additional efforts that informants made in their own recovery can be captured broadly under this rubric of reconstructing an effective sense of self as a social agent. An earlier qualitative study that we conducted expressly provides a framework for understanding these various efforts toward reconstruction of self and their role in fostering recovery, describing processes of self-reconstruction among a sample of 32 women and 34 men, aged 20 to 55 (M = 29) who were experiencing severe mental illness (Davidson & Strauss, 1992). For this study, we collected data from each of these 66 informants using intensive semistructured follow-along interviews conducted over a 2- to 3-year period focusing on work, social life, living situations, psychiatric difficulties, and coping. Interviews were transcribed and later analyzed and coded qualitatively for common themes.

Review of interview data suggested that reconstruction of the self fosters recovery through processes of (a) discovery of potentials of the self, (b) examination of strengths and weaknesses in the self, (c) putting aspects of the self into action while integrating the results as indicative of actual capabilities, and (d) using a developed sense of self as refuge from mental illness and a toxic social milieu. These processes are neither necessarily sequential nor mutually exclusive, but rather overlapping and likely interactive.

Discovery of potentials of the self refers to the perception, however tentative, of who one may be apart from mental illness. Such a perception can be afforded by rediscovery of aspects of self that have remained unaffected by mental illness or by discovery of new qualities brought to bear in challenges presented by mental illness. In either case, the perception refers to aspects of the self that are neither yoked with mental illness nor currently in active use. For one informant, the perception of her own potential was prompted by a nurse who was particularly supportive of her while she was in seclusion during an episode of inpatient care. This informant remarked that the nurse "knew I had potential and talent and all this and that I could get better" (Davidson & Strauss, 1992, p. 135).

Examination of a person's own strengths and weaknesses represents a goal-oriented inventory of qualities and potentials in the self prior to taking more concrete action. This process is akin to Strauss and colleagues' (1985) notion of *moratorium*, wherein significant subjective changes take place in a person during periods of self-reflection. On the other hand, the process of taking inventory can also take place within social contexts in which a person's assessment of his or her own potentials is considered concurrently with significant others' assessments of those same potentials. People engaging in this facet of the process may encounter significant tension when their assessment of their own potential conflicts with the assessments of others. In one such situation, a study informant recounted his readiness to take a job as a dishwasher at a diner at a time when his clinicians and family felt that he was not prepared to do so. The informant's own assessment ultimately led him to take the job against the advice of others, a decision he later credited as a positive turning point in his recovery.

Putting the self into action refers to concrete behavior stemming from a prior period of self-assessment. The results of this behavior may foster either further action or reassessment, or some combination of the two, depending on how the outcomes are understood. In any case, the results may serve as evidence of the person's actual capacities (or lack thereof) with respect to particular behaviors and goals. To continue with the example introduced earlier, the informant who took the job at the diner found that working a regular schedule and handling the pressures of coworkers and a boss did in fact reflect his actual capacities at that time. Moreover, this informant discovered that not only could he handle the basic demands of his job, but he could also cultivate friendships with coworkers and expand his social life beyond prior expectations.

Using a developed sense of self as a tool with which to manage mental illness and a toxic social milieu entails active coping stemming from a relatively clear subjective understanding of who one is apart from mental illness. In this process, psychiatric symptoms do not jeopardize one's identity so much as warn the person of threats in the immediate environment. The way in which the person decides to deal with such threats may be determined in part on the basis of the outcomes of previous efforts made in similar situations in the past. Over time, a widening of one's repertoire of successful responses to situational stresses may enhance perceived self-efficacy. An enhanced sense of efficacy, in turn, may lead to broader considerations of one's potentials, current strengths and weaknesses, actions, and so forth. What appears to emerge from this set of processes is a solid foundation on which to seek refuge not only from the illness itself, but also from the detrimental aspects of the social milieu, and from which to launch continuing efforts at recovery.

Coping and Adaptation

Finally, coping and adaptation refer to the remaining things that people can do in terms of daily activities to foster recovery from mental illness. Such efforts are typically directed toward the illness itself rather than the person. Corin's (1990, 1998) and Corin and Lauzon's (1992, 1994) qualitative research represents one of the richest examinations of this topic. Briefly, Corin interviewed 45 male informants (ages 25 to 50) diagnosed with schizophrenia between 5 and 15 years prior to the study. Corin assumed that community tenure reflected adaptation to community life and hence grouped informants' narratives according to high, medium, and low rates of rehospitalization during the prior 4 years, using structural and discourse analyses across narratives. Given our interest in coping and adaptation, we focus here on findings obtained for those in Corin's investigation with low rates of rehospitalization.

Corin (1990, 1998) found similarities in activities across people with high community tenure. These activities included spiritual pursuits, frequenting public places, and linguistic tactics. With respect to spiritual pursuits, activities ranged from one informant's occasional participation in a meditation group to another's founding and leading a congregation following the tenets of a religion he created. Across narratives, spiritual activities appeared to foster friendships in the community and shift informants' attention from external to internal personal values.

In their qualitative investigations, Barham and Hayward (1998) found that spirituality was most beneficial to coping when distinguished from mental illness. The authors noted that this task hinges on a person's understanding of her or his illness in either principally existential (I am) or materialistic (I have) terms. Barham and Hayward (1998) pointed out that while adopting an existential framework may lead one to conceive an illness such as schizophrenia as an extension of one's spirituality, a materialistic framework is more likely to separate the illness from other aspects of personhood, including spirituality. As such, understanding mental illness as something one *has* as opposed to something one *is* may best promote spirituality as a mechanism of coping and adaptation.

Corin (1990) observed that informants with higher community tenure tended to visit particular types of public places regularly. These places tended to be impersonal settings such as malls and fast-food restaurants, where people quickly stop and go and where social interactions are generally brief if not superficial. Nonetheless, Corin observed that frequenting such places held meaning for informants in adapting to community life. Lovell (1997) elaborated on this idea in her research detailing how homeless people with schizophrenia expanded the notion of "home" beyond shelters and soup kitchens to include entire cities. Such an expansion, argued Lovell, can inspire a sense of movement and development through space and over time. It is possible that informants in Corin's investigation experienced similar feelings of development at a social level if one views public places as avenues for being with others in safe and rewarding ways.

Several of the informants in Corin's investigation with high community tenure used language in particular ways that appeared to foster coping. For example, one informant described himself as "withdrawn," noting that "I would rather stay home . . . one has to find satisfaction in oneself . . . before, I was always after people to get something" (Corin & Lauzon, 1994, p. 27). According to the authors, a quality of this statement associated with informants with high community tenure is introducing a new meaning to a signifier; in this case, "withdrawn" took on the novel dimension of self-satisfaction. A second quality has to do with introducing a historical perspective to the present context. That is, the informant was once "always after people," but has now developed autonomy. At a broader level, the statement reflects an intentional and positive distance from the social world, one that for this informant made it possible for him to lead a rewarding life in the community.

Two related mechanisms through which coping and adaptation strategies appear to foster recovery from mental illness are the negotiation of contact with the social world and the reconstruction of personal experience. Negotiation of contact with the social world has been termed by Corin and Lauzon (1992) as *positive withdrawal*, which they describe as representing a stance of simultaneous involvement in, and distance from, the social milieu. In each of the activities reviewed earlier, the notion of positive withdrawal punctuates informants' behavior, whether it is negotiating spatial contact within the community, cultivating a shared spiritual transcendence, or using common language in uncommon ways.

The overarching mechanism in strategies of positive withdrawal appears to be a reconstruction of experience; that is, casting one's existence into a larger frame of reference than that of "mental patient." As reviewed earlier, the existing social milieu tends to curtail space for recovery in its objectification and discrediting of people with mental illness. The work of recovery, therefore, must take place within more expansive intersubjective spheres, in which the present can be understood in relation to a personal past, and in which one can establish a sturdy sense of place and belonging in the world.

In Figure 7.2, we attempt to summarize the qualitative findings of our review by delineating the various aspects of recovery from mental illness described by participants in these interviews. The figure is not meant to be exhaustive, but is offered as one possible means of organizing the complex set of situations and experiences elucidated in the qualitative studies reviewed here. Beginning at the middle far left of Figure 7.2, we make reference to the person's life prior to the onset of illness. Using this as a point of departure, the person begins to experience symptoms reflecting distress, impairment, or some combination of the two. These experiences contribute to a decline in functioning in one or more aspects of the person's life (e.g., interpersonal, professional). As this happens, the person begins to struggle with the question of how to account for her or his difficulties. As pointed out by Estroff et al. (1991), ways of accounting for illness appear to have an impact on its course; so we consider this a critical juncture in the recovery process. We note both Estroff's (1989) description of schizophrenia as an "I am" illness, as well as Barham and Hayward's (1998) distinction between materialist and existentialist views of illness in this model by differentiating a position of "I have" versus a position of "I am" as one key to the recovery process.

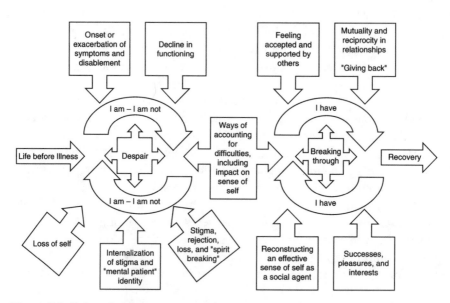

Figure 7.2. Roles of various aspects of the recovery process.

Adopting an "I am" stance is likely to lead one to internalize stigma, resulting in a loss of self as illustrated by Lally's (1989) work. At the other extreme, maintaining that "I am not" mentally ill may lead one to discount her or his difficulties in ways that might prevent her or him from taking steps to address them. Within our model, we propose that the extant tension between stances of "I am" and "I am not" can contribute to a vicious cycle of exacerbation of difficulties, decline in functioning, loss, internalization of social stigma, and loss of self. We propose the hub of this cycle be represented by despair, both in becoming numbed down by the onslaught of distress and impairment, and at another level, in attempting to reconcile one's identity to newly felt limitations.

Adopting an "I have" position with respect to mental illness, however, appears to serve as a bridge toward recovery. Such a position is both facilitated by and facilitative of the presence of supportive others, which, under favorable circumstances, leads to experiences of mutuality and the recognition of having positive things to offer others as revealed in the work of Davidson et al. (2001). The recognition of one's own positive qualities is likely to lead to pleasure and the cultivation or recultivation of interests, ultimately fostering a reconstruction of self as outlined by Davidson and Strauss (1992). We borrow from Deegan (1993) to describe the hub of this cycle as an experience of breaking through, where even an exacerbation of difficulties related to mental illness can be considered integral to the recovery process. We suggest that this cycle ultimately facilitates the process of recovery, in terms of a redefinition of illness as only one aspect of a person's overall and evolving sense of self. With this result we come full circle to the perspective on recovery expressed through the consumer and first-person accounts we reviewed in the first part of this chapter, in which we defined recovery as involving a redefinition of one's illness as only one aspect of a multidimensional sense of self. What our qualitative review has now added to this definition are insights into some of the processes and pathways by which this may be accomplished.

SUMMARY

Having now reviewed the key elements of first-person accounts and our integrative summary of findings of qualitative studies on recovery, the reflective reader might well be harboring the reasonable question of how all, if any, of this information is specific to people with serious mental illness. In shifting from investigations of the illness per se to studies of the role of the person emerging, as it were, from behind the illness, have we lost sight of the illness altogether? It would appear, in fact, that the processes we describe as involved in the recovery of people with serious mental illness are processes that may be equally relevant to all of us, whether or not we experience a serious mental illness. For example, when we propose that redefining the self may play a critical role in recovery, we must also recognize that all of us are in the process of constantly redefining ourselves with each new activity and experience. Similarly, like people in recovery, we all tend to embrace hope in striving for challenging goals. Additionally, we are all essentially social and find experiences such as acceptance, mutuality, and a sense of belonging beneficial to our sense of self-esteem and self-worth. In summary, to borrow from Harry Stack Sullivan's (1954) bold pronouncement from a half century ago, when we study the person with the illness we find that we are all much more simply human than otherwise. Rediscovering this fact might lead us to question what then we truly have learned about mental illness as a result of these investigations. Here too, the answer is complicated, and here too, we are not the first to make this sobering observation.

After years of directing several different Italian community mental health systems, Franco Basaglia, the noted mental health reformer, asserted that we cannot really know yet what mental illness *is* because most of the difficulties we see in people who have been diagnosed with it are the effects of institutionalization and the social stigma that is its legacy (rather, that is, than effects of the illness per se) (Scheper-Hughes & Lovell, 1986). To make things even more complicated, once people shed the negative effects of institutional life, they tend, most simply, to resemble people. Therefore, we should not be surprised that most of the activities and experiences found to foster the recoveries of people diagnosed with mental illness are much the same ones that the "rest of us" find helpful or pleasurable throughout our lives (Davidson, 2001). During the course of the last half century of deinstitutionalization and the development of community-based care, many of the lessons we have learned have proven to be more or less recapitulations of Basaglia's fundamental insight. That is, much of what we currently find to characterize the challenges people with serious mental illness encounter in their everyday lives can be attributed to the effects of stigma, poverty, alienation, chronic unemployment, political oppression and discrimination, and the demoralization and social isolation that result from their effects (Davidson et al., 1997). Given the depth of the shadow cast by these societal factors, we still cannot begin to articulate what mental illness—apart from the toxic social milieu that surrounds it—is (Davidson et al., 2001).

What implications do these ideas hold for practice and research? Given this ambiguity in defining mental illness per se, we might do well to adopt an attitude of openness to both illness and recovery on the basis of the unique experiences and capacities of individuals engaged in such processes. With respect to practice, this translates to the adoption of less illness- and deficit-based models of treatment in favor of more person-centered approaches. These approaches suggest a collaborative, rather than directive, treatment relationship, wherein the person's strengths and talents are regarded as tools for recovery. They suggest knowing the person well enough to be able to connect her or his personal history to current goals in a manner that fosters an overarching experience of life continuity and purpose. And they demand willingness on the part of clinicians to move with the person through the various stages of recovery and to consider—when fitting and in collaboration with the person—the next one or two steps along the path (Davidson et al., 2003).

Similarly, with respect to research, these findings suggest that we continue to consider the person, rather than the illness, as the subject of our scientific inquiries. This entails, as Strauss and colleagues (1985) proposed, further consideration of the person's role in her or his own recovery both within and outside of the context of formal treatment. As introduced by one of the opening quotes for this chapter, we need to ask our research participants what it is they do to foster their own recoveries. This consideration, both in topic and in method, signifies a break from traditional models of psychological research, as represented in part by an emphasis on the person's subjective experiences. As suggested earlier, it is precisely for such subject matter that qualitative research approaches may be uniquely well suited.

REFERENCES

Barham, P., & Hayward, R. (1998). In sickness and in health: Dilemmas of the person with severe mental illness. *Psychiatry, 61*, 163–170.

Baxter, E. A., & Diehl, S. (1998). Emotional stages: Consumers and family members recovering from the trauma of mental illness. *Psychiatric Rehabilitation Journal, 21*, 349–355.

Chamberlain, J., & Rogers, J. A. (1990). Planning a community-based mental health system: Perspective of service recipients. *American Psychologist, 45*, 1241–1244.

Charlton, J. (1998). *Nothing about us without us*. Berkley: University of California Press.

Charmaz, K. (1983). Loss of self: A fundamental form of suffering in the chronically ill. *Sociology of Health and Illness, 5*, 168–195.

Corin, E. (1990). Facts and meanings in psychiatry. An anthropological approach to the lifeworld of schizophrenics. *Culture, Medicine, and Psychiatry, 14*, 153–188.

Corin, E. (1998). The thickness of being: Intentional worlds, strategies of identity, and experience among schizophrenics. *Psychiatry, 61*, 133–146.

Corin, E., & Lauzon, G. (1992). Positive withdrawal and the quest for meaning: The reconstruction of experience among schizophrenics. *Psychiatry, 55*, 266–278.

Corin, E., & Lauzon, G. (1994). From symptoms to phenomena: The articulation of experience in schizophrenia. *Journal of Phenomenological Psychology, 25*, 3–50.

Corrigan, P., & Penn, D. (1998). Disease and discrimination: Two paradigms that describe severe mental illness. *Journal of Mental Health, 6*, 355–366.

Davidson, L. (2001). Us and them. *Psychiatric Services, 52,* 1579–1580.

Davidson, L. (2003). *Living outside mental illness: Qualitative studies of recovery in schizophrenia.* New York: New York University Press.

Davidson, L., Haglund, K. E., Stayner, D. A., Rakfeldt, J., Chinman, M. L., & Tebes, J. K. (2001). "It was just realizing that life isn't one big horror": A qualitative study of supported socialization. *Psychiatric Rehabilitation Journal, 24,* 275–292.

Davidson, L., Stayner, D., Lambert, M. T., Smith, B., & Sledge, W. H. (1997). Phenomenological and participatory research on schizophrenia: Recovering the person in theory and practice. *Journal of Social Issues, 53,* 767–784.

Davidson, L., Stayner, D. A., Nickou, C., Styron, T. H., Rowe, M., & Chinman, M. L. (2001). "Simply to be let in": Inclusion as a basis for recovery. *Psychiatric Rehabilitation Journal, 24,* 375–388.

Davidson, L., & Strauss, J. S. (1992). Sense of self in recovery from severe mental illness. *British Journal of Medical Psychology, 65,* 131–145.

Davidson, L., & Strauss, J. S. (1995). Beyond the biopsychosocial model: Integrating disorder, health, and recovery. *Psychiatry, 58,* 44–55.

Davidson, L., Tondora, J., Staeheli, M., O'Connell, M., Frey, J., & Chinman, M. (2003). Recovery guides: An emerging model of community-based care for adults with psychiatric disabilities. In A. Lightburn & P. Sessions (Eds.), *Community-based clinical practice.* London: Oxford University Press.

Deegan, P. E. (1988). The lived experience of rehabilitation. *Psychosocial Rehabilitation Journal, 11,* 11–19.

Deegan, P. E. (1993). Recovering our sense of value after being labeled. *Journal of Psychosocial Nursing, 31,* 7–11.

Deegan, P. E. (1996). Recovery as a journey of the heart. *Psychiatric Rehabilitation Journal, 19,* 91–97.

Deegan, P. E. (1997). The helping culture. In L. Spaniol, C. Gagne, & M. Keohler (Eds.), *Psychological and social aspects of psychiatric disability* (pp. 348–357). Boston: Center for Psychiatric Rehabilitation.

Dennett, D. C. (1991). *Consciousness explained.* Boston: Little, Brown.

Dixon, L. (2000). Reflections on recovery. *Community Mental Health Journal, 26,* 443–447.

Estroff, S. E. (1981). *Making it crazy: An ethnography of psychiatric clients in an American community.* Berkley: University of California Press.

Estroff, S. E. (1989). Self, identity, and subjective experiences of schizophrenia: In search of the subject. *Schizophrenia Bulletin, 15,* 189–196.

Estroff, S. E., Lachicotte, W. S., Illingworth, L. C., & Johnston, A. (1991). Everybody's got a little mental illness: Accounts of illness and self among people with severe, persistent mental illnesses. *Medical Anthropology Quarterly, 5,* 331–369.

Fisher, D. V. (1994). Health care reform based on an empowerment model of recovery by people with psychiatric disabilities. *Hospital & Community Psychiatry, 45,* 913–915.

Frese, F. J., III, & Davis, W. W. (1997). The consumer-survivor movement, recovery, and consumer professionals. *Professional Psychology Research & Practice, 28,* 243–245.

Frese, F. J., III, Stanley, J., Kress, K., & Vogel-Scibilia, S. (2001). Integrating evidence-based practices and the recovery model. *Psychiatric Services, 52,* 1462–1468.

Goffman, E. (1961). *Asylums: Essays on the social situation of mental patients and other inmates.* Garden City, NY: Doubleday.

Goffman, E. (1963). *Stigma: Notes on the management of spoiled identity.* Englewood Cliffs, NJ: Prentice Hall.

Harding, C. M., Zubin, J., & Strauss, J. S. (1987). Chronicity in schizophrenia: Fact, partial fact, or artifact? *Hospital & Community Psychiatry, 38,* 477–486.

Lally, S. J. (1989). "Does being in here mean there is something wrong with me?" *Schizophrenia Bulletin, 15,* 254–265.

Leete, E. (1994). Stressor, symptom, or sequelae? Remission, recovery, or cure? *The Journal of the California Alliance for the Mentally Ill, 5,* 16–17.

Lovejoy, M. (1982). Expectations and the recovery process. *Schizophrenia Bulletin, 8,* 605–609.

Lovell, A. (1997). "The city is my mother": Narratives of schizophrenia and homelessness. *American Anthropologist, 99,* 355–368.

Mead, S., & Copeland, M. (2000). What recovery means to us: Consumers' perspectives. *Community Mental Health Journal, 36,* 315–328.

Munetz, M., & Frese, F. J., III. (2001). Getting ready for recovery: Reconciling mandatory treatment with the recovery vision. *Psychiatric Rehabilitation Journal, 25,* 35–42.

National Alliance for the Mentally Ill. (n.d.). *Omnibus Mental Illness Recovery Act.*

Rogers, J. (1995). Work is a key to recovery. *Psychosocial Rehabilitation Journal, 18,* 5–10.

Rowe, M. (1999). *Crossing the border: Encounters between homeless people and outreach workers.* Berkeley: University of California Press.

Scheper-Hughes, N., & Lovell, A. M. (1986). Breaking the circuit of social control: Lessons in public psychiatry from Italy and Franco Basaglia. *Social Science Medicine, 23,* 159–178.

Smith, M. (2000). Recovery from a severe psychiatric disability: Findings of a qualitative study. *Psychiatric Rehabilitation Journal, 24,* 149–159.

Stanton, A., & Schwartz, M. (1954). *The mental hospital: A study of institutional participation in psychiatric illness and treatment.* New York: Basic Books.

Strauss, J. S. (1989). Subjective experiences of schizophrenia: Toward a new dynamic psychiatry—II. *Schizophrenia Bulletin, 15,* 179–187.

Strauss, J. S., Hafez, H., Lieberman, P., & Harding, C. M. (1985). The course of psychiatric disorder, III: Longitudinal principles. *American Journal of Psychiatry, 142,* 289–296.

Sullivan, H. S. (1954). *The psychiatric interview*. New York: Norton.

Sullivan, W. A. (1994). A long and winding road: The process of recovery from severe mental illness. *Innovations and Research, 3*, 19–27.

U.S. Department of Health and Human Services, Substance Abuse and Mental Health Services Administration, Center for Mental Health Services, National Institutes of Health, & the National Institute of Mental Health. (1999). *Mental health: A report of the surgeon general*. Rockville, MD: Author.

Walsh, D. (1996). A journey toward recovery: From the inside out. *Psychiatric Rehabilitation Journal, 20*, 85–90.

White, W. L. (2000, April). *Toward a new recovery movement: Historical reflections on recovery, treatment, and advocacy*. Paper presented at the meeting of the Recovery Community Support Program Conference, Arlington, VA.

Whitwell, D. (2001). Recovery as a medical myth. *Psychiatric Bulletin, 25*, 75.

Wing, J. K., Monck, E., Brown, G. W., & Carstairs, G. M. (1964). Morbidity in the community of schizophrenic patients discharged from London mental hospitals in 1959. *British Journal of Psychiatry, 110*, 10–21.

III

DIVERSITY AND RECOVERY

8

MUTUAL-HELP GROUPS AND RECOVERY: THE INFLUENCE OF SETTINGS ON PARTICIPANTS' EXPERIENCE OF RECOVERY

KATIE WEAVER RANDALL AND DEBORAH A. SALEM

The purpose of this chapter is to describe how settings can influence individuals' beliefs about or models of recovery from serious mental illness. We demonstrate the power of settings on beliefs about recovery by exploring the characteristics of one type of setting, mutual-help groups, and how these

The Schizophrenics Anonymous Evaluation study referenced in this chapter was conducted by Deborah A. Salem and Thomas M. Reischl at Michigan State University, Department of Psychology, and done in collaboration with the Mental Health Association in Michigan and Schizophrenics Anonymous (SA). This research was supported by the Ethel and James Flinn Foundation, Detroit, Michigan. Portions of the information presented in the case study were presented earlier at the 1998 and 1999 SA Leaders Conference and the 1998 and 2000 Society for Community Research and Action. A manuscript presenting a more detailed cross-case analysis of SA members' stories of recovery is in preparation.

characteristics are related to members' definitions and understandings of recovery. Mutual-help groups differ from other types of consumer-run organizations, and from professionally run organizations, in that they have unique structures and processes for sharing experiential knowledge (Borkman, 1990), or knowledge based on one's experience with recovery and mental illness.

The value placed on experiential knowledge allows mutual-help groups to develop beliefs about recovery that are quite distinct from those held by people involved with professionally run settings. These beliefs are communicated to mutual-help group members through the development of community narratives (Rappaport, 1993). Community narratives articulate specific ideologies about a problem and its solution (Antze, 1976). In mutual-help groups, these narratives are reinforced by the presence of role models, the support of others, and the availability of valued organizational roles. As a result, members of mutual-help groups are likely to incorporate the community narrative into their personal understanding of recovery. Schizophrenics Anonymous (SA), a mutual-help group for people experiencing a schizophrenia-related illness, is described as a case example of this process.

BACKGROUND

The groups, organizations, and institutions with which we identify shape how we understand the world and ourselves, interpret our experiences, and help us formulate goals, plans, and dreams (Hooper, 1982; Sherif, 1962). This is no different for people who have been diagnosed with a mental illness and must figure out how to go about the process of recovery. The experience of mental illness is not something that most people have an understanding of prior to confronting it, and they have no or little frame of reference for making sense of what they are experiencing (Corin & Lauzon, 1994). Therefore, one of the difficult tasks they face is developing a framework within which to understand their experience so they can begin the process of recovery (Corin & Lauzon, 1992, 1994). As a result of stigma, discrimination, and limitations due to psychiatric disability, the number and types of settings available to assist individuals with a mental illness in developing these frameworks of recovery tend to be quite limited. This is particularly true for people diagnosed with schizophrenia, a highly stigmatized (Fraser, 1994; Wahl, 1998) and often debilitating illness.

For most individuals with a psychiatric diagnosis, the settings (i.e., programs, organizations, services, or groups) in which they receive treatment, information, and support for living with their illness have a powerful effect on their understanding of mental illness and their beliefs about recovery (Deegan, 1988, 1993; Houghton, 1982; Lovejoy, 1984; Unzicker, 1989; Weingarten, 1994). These settings help shape what they learn about mental illness, what it will mean for their lives, whether or not recovery is possible, and how to engage in the process of recovery.

Although not always explicit, these settings function based on institutional belief systems about mental illness and recovery, which influence their culture, structure, and activities (Meyer & Rowan, 1977; Scott, 1995). These ideologies and assumptions are communicated to participants through both the explicit messages that settings convey about mental illness and recovery (e.g., what it means, how and whether one can recover from it) and the implicit messages inherent in the opportunity role structure of the setting (Maton & Salem, 1995). *Opportunity role structure* refers to the opportunities that organizations provide for participation in meaningful roles and activities. These include the organization of relationships (e.g., hierarchical or egalitarian), available roles and activities (e.g., opportunities to be both the provider and recipient of help), and opportunities to be involved in organizational decision making. The roles and opportunities available to mental health consumers communicate a great deal about how individuals with a mental illness are valued and what contributions they can make to their own recovery and the recovery of others. In summary, for those diagnosed with mental illness, the beliefs about mental illness and recovery and the structures and activities available to them in treatment, rehabilitation, and support settings can have a powerful effect on individuals' personal beliefs and definitions of recovery from mental illness.

These beliefs, structures, and activities are highly influenced by the predominant ideologies within the setting's sector or organizational niche (Meyer & Rowan, 1977; Scott, 1995). To increase their legitimacy and access to resources, organizations within the same sector (e.g., mental health) come to look and behave like other organizations in that sector (DiMaggio & Powell, 1983). Because of this, the ideologies of settings and their accompanying organizational structures and practices do not tend to vary tremendously within a given service sector. Historically, traditional mental health service settings have functioned based on ideologies that emanate from the medical model (Corrigan et al., 2002; Fisher, 1994; Zinman, 1987). The medical model emphasizes expert knowledge gained through professional training and education. Davidson et al. (1999) argued that traditional mental health settings function based on the belief that mental illness can only be ameliorated by professionals and professional technologies. Adherence to this medical or clinical model leads to hierarchical settings (Arntson & Droge, 1987), which are structured to give professionals control and power both over the setting and the setting's participants (Chamberlin, 1978). There are few meaningful roles for mental health consumers in such settings and no venue for the voice of consumers to influence how mental illness is understood or how recovery is defined.

Settings that rely solely on the medical model as a way to understand mental illness tend to focus on pathology and disease (Mead, Hilton, &

Curtis, 2001) and to define recovery as a set of predetermined outcomes that emphasizes symptom elimination and a return to premorbid functioning. This model of illness and recovery can be detrimental to a person's experience of recovery, because it undermines hope (Chamberlin, 1978; Lovejoy, 1984), which has been described as one of the cornerstones of recovery (Deegan, 1988). This has been particularly true with regard to the treatment of schizophrenia, where the goal of returning to life as it was prior to the onset of the illness has resulted in great professional pessimism about the possibility of recovery (e.g., *Diagnostic and Statistical Manual of Mental Disorders*, 4th ed. [DSM–IV]; APA, 1994).

Consumers' personal narratives, which provide accounts of their experiences living with their mental illness, describe how their interactions with the mental health system can instill a sense of hopelessness and pessimism about their futures (Deegan, 1988, 1993; Houghton, 1982; Lovejoy, 1984; Unzicker, 1989; Weingarten, 1994). Spaniol and Koehler (1998), through their work with individuals with mental illness, identified specific treatment practices that traumatize individuals. These include negative professional attitudes, lack of appropriate assisting skills of professionals (e.g., undermine self-determination), devaluing and disempowering programs, and lack of enriching opportunities (e.g., valued work or social roles). Although mental health programs and treatments are designed with good intentions, the beliefs about mental illness and recovery communicated by these settings are often pessimistic and disempowering. They do not help consumers develop personal understandings of recovery that, in turn, allow them to move forward with optimism and to deal with the challenges posed by a serious mental illness.

Mutual-help organizations, in contrast, have a tradition of operating outside of the formal mental health system and without professional involvement.[1] They function according to belief systems that are based on lived experience with mental illness or experiential knowledge (Borkman, 1990). The empirical literature on experiential knowledge is extremely limited, but a few studies have documented its presence in mutual-help groups as well as its value to members (Salem, Bogat, & Reid, 1997; Salem, Reischl, Gallacher, & Randall, 2000; Schubert & Borkman, 1994). For example, in a study of a self-help group for parents of children who were both gifted or talented and also had learning disabilities, Schubert and Borkman (1994) identified eight categories of experiential knowledge that the group

---

[1]It is important to note that not all mutual-help groups operate outside of the formal mental health system and many groups that call themselves mutual- or self-help groups have varying degrees of professional involvement. An increasing professional involvement in mutual-help groups is apparent, but such interest may undermine their ability to promote experientially based definitions of recovery.

had developed. They found that the experiential knowledge was highly valued by the group and that group members reported that they would be more likely to turn to experienced parents for assistance with issues related to their children, than to professionals, family, or friends.

As a result of the value placed on experiential knowledge, mutual-help groups are structured to reflect the assumption that all participants have something of value to contribute to the setting. People diagnosed with mental illness are viewed as having valuable knowledge and skills gained from their own experiences (Borkman, 1990), which can be used in assisting others in learning to live with mental illness (Riessman, 1965). The value placed on experiential knowledge results in a more egalitarian organizational structure, which creates a variety of meaningful roles and participation opportunities (Maton & Salem, 1995). Within such settings, participants have the opportunity to reflect on and share their experiences of recovery (Rappaport, 1993). Consequently, within these settings, definitions of recovery can reflect the lived experiences of people who are recovering from a mental illness. These definitions are more likely to reflect a sense of hopefulness and possibility. They tend to focus on the process of transforming one's sense of self, changing one's beliefs and attitudes, and enhancing wellness and quality of life (Spaniol & Koehler, 1998). Next we describe some of the characteristics of mutual-help organizations that make them well suited for promoting a hopeful view of recovery.

CONSUMER-OPERATED SETTINGS AND MUTUAL-HELP GROUPS

Consumer-operated services were originally developed outside of the formal mental health system by the consumer/survivor/ex-patient movement or the mental health consumer movement (Davidson et al., 1999). However, in the past 20 years, there has been increasing support and pressure to establish and legitimize consumer-operated settings as either adjuncts or alternatives to the more traditional, professionally run services within the public mental health system. The pressure to include consumer-operated services as part of the continuum of care offered by public mental health systems has come from the consumer mental health movement and has been supported by federal agencies, such as the Substance Abuse and Mental Health Services Administration (SAMHSA), and by state mental health authorities, who provide funding earmarked to develop and implement such settings. Although consumer-operated settings vary widely in program philosophy, ideology, mission, and range of activities (Katz & Bender, 1990; Emerick, 1991), they do share some commonalities.

Solomon and Draine (2001) defined consumer-operated services as those that are planned, managed, and provided by consumers. Consumer-operated services include drop-in centers, peer-run case management services, crisis and respite services, vocational services, advocacy services, supported education, residential programs, psychoeducational programs, and mutual-help groups. These settings share an emphasis on expertise gained through experience, voluntary participation, self-determination, self-reliance, and self-empowerment (Kurtz, 1997). Involvement in consumer-operated settings can counteract the feelings of powerlessness that are often experienced in the mental health system (Chamberlin, 1990; Chamberlin & Rogers, 1990) by promoting autonomy (Chamberlin, 1978; Zinman, 1987), self-definition (Slack, 1995), and self-determination (Walker-Davis, 1995).

Because consumer-operated settings value knowledge gained through experience (Salem et al., 1997, 2000; Schubert & Borkman, 1994), people involved with consumer-operated settings may have different beliefs about mental illness and recovery than those espoused in professionally controlled settings. However, in spite of the many similarities among consumer-operated settings, important differences do exist that may influence the adoption of experiential knowledge and, as a consequence, participants' beliefs about and experiences of recovery. One of the characteristics of consumer-operated services that is particularly salient for understanding how these settings influence beliefs about recovery is their affiliation with the formal mental health sector.

Organizations are affiliated with a specific sector when they receive funding from that sector; are responsible for following rules, guidelines, certification procedures, and regulations that are mandated by that sector; or are supervised or overseen by a larger umbrella organization that is affiliated with that sector. To the extent that a setting is dependent on a particular sector for resources and legitimacy, its beliefs, structures, and practices are more likely to align with those of its institutional environment (Meyer & Rowan, 1977; Pfeffer & Salancik, 1978; Scott, 1995). Settings that are located outside of the mental health sector are less likely to be influenced by the mental health sector's institutional ideologies, including its reliance on the medical model for understanding mental illness and recovery.

One of the qualities that sets mutual-help organizations apart from many other types of consumer-operated services or settings (e.g., drop-in centers, peer-to-peer counseling) is that they tend to exist outside of the formal mental health system. They are typically grassroots organizations that do not rely on funding from the mental health system or on professional support or expertise (Kurtz, 1997). Because they are not dependent on the formal mental health system for their survival, mutual-help groups have more freedom to develop their own beliefs and understandings about mental illness and recovery and to challenge the status quo. Mutual-help groups provide a unique setting in which mental health consumers can develop personal frameworks for understanding mental illness that enable them to view recovery as an ongoing process of personal change and adaptation.

Participation in self-help or mutual-help groups has become increasingly popular in the United States as a way to address a variety of problems, including psychiatric problems and their associated traumas. It is estimated that more than 25 million Americans have participated in a self-help group at some time in their lifetime, and that groups for individuals with a mental illness or emotional problems are the second most frequented type of group, after groups for people with substance abuse problems (Kessler, Mickelson, & Zhao, 1997). Mutual-help groups can be defined as voluntary associations or organizations of people who share some status, problem, or common predicament that results in difficulties that the groups try to address (Borkman, 1990; Humphreys & Rappaport, 1994). Although they have been defined and conceptualized in many different ways, the term *mutual-help group* is used in this chapter to express the egalitarian and communal aspect of such groups (Humphreys & Rappaport, 1994) and to reflect the presence of the mutual exchange of information and support. Mutual-help groups are settings that are developed, controlled, and run by people experiencing the problem or issue.

By virtue of their independence from the formal mental health system, mutual-help settings have the freedom to develop different beliefs around mental illness and recovery. Most have well-articulated beliefs about recovery and specific mechanisms to develop, transmit, and sustain these beliefs (e.g., Emotions Anonymous, 1973; GROW, 1982; Recovery Inc., 1985; SA, 1999). Within mutual-help groups, beliefs about mental illness and recovery are communicated and learned through the creation of community narratives and the telling and retelling of personal stories (Rappaport, 1993). They are reinforced by the presence of role models, the support of others, and the availability of organizational roles that reflect the assumptions articulated in the community narrative (Maton & Salem, 1995). These mechanisms facilitate the adoption of personal stories of recovery that reflect the community narrative.

Personal Stories and Community Narratives

Steinman and Traunstein (1976) argued that one of the most fundamental aspects of mutual-help groups is that stigmatized individuals come to perceive and define their problem as less deviant and less stigmatizing than the rest of society does. Mutual-help groups facilitate this process by providing a community narrative (Cain, 1991; Humphreys, 1993; Rappaport, 1993; Rappaport & Simkins, 1991), which articulates specific ideologies about the problem and its solution (Antze, 1976). Through participation in mutual-help groups, individuals come to adopt the community narrative as their own, thus altering their personal understanding of the problem (i.e., personal narrative) and their sense of self (Rappaport, 1993).

Several studies have examined the role of community narratives in facilitating positive change in people's lives. Using a content analysis of organizational materials and 22 narratives of leaders from GROW, a mutual-help organization for people diagnosed with mental illness, Corrigan et al. (2002) demonstrated that the leaders integrated components of the community narrative into their own personal narrative. Cain (1991) showed that over time, members of Alcoholics Anonymous (AA) altered the story of their alcoholism until it more closely reflected that of AA's community narrative, which is essential for achieving success and recovery through the AA program. Rappaport and Simkins (1991) examined the role of community narratives in healing and empowering individuals within religious settings and concluded that the stories that are told within a setting are powerful mechanisms that shape self-understanding and identity. Conceptualizing mutual-help groups as normative narrative communities (Rappaport, 1993) (i.e., a setting's stories about itself) helps provide a framework for understanding how these settings can promote the process of recovery by helping people make sense of their experiences in a less stigmatizing and less deviant way than understood by formal systems of care and the general population and that includes the possibility of recovery.

One of the ways that mutual-help groups convey their community narratives about mental illness and recovery is through the telling and retelling of personal stories of mental illness and recovery. Many mutual-help groups (e.g., AA, SA) have formal mechanisms that facilitate the sharing of stories, which are often not found in other types of consumer-operated settings. Davidson et al. (1999), in their review of peer support among individuals diagnosed with mental illness, pointed to the importance of having mechanisms by which mental health consumer providers (i.e., mental health consumers hired to provide services within traditional mental health settings) can incorporate their personal experiences with mental illness and recovery into their work with clients. They raised this question: How does the experiential knowledge of consumer providers get conveyed to clients? In mutual-help groups, the telling of personal stories is an important mechanism for sharing experiential knowledge. Such sharing is encouraged by providing a jumping off spot for one's story (e.g., "I am Bob and I am an alcoholic"); group norms around listening, responding, and taking turns (e.g., no cross-talk); and written materials that recount individual's stories.

The personal stories that are told and retold in these settings serve many purposes. Sharing one's personal story can be cathartic and can help a person to reflect and make sense of the problem that brought them to the group (Arntson & Droge, 1987). In the presence of peers who are not judgmental and may have had similar experiences, it is often easier to share events or thoughts that may be considered deviant or shameful by others who have not experienced the problem (Katz, 1993). Slack (1995) argued that listening to stories of pain, suffering, courage, and recovery, and articulating and making sense of one's own story within this context of sharing, is necessary for recovery. The telling and retelling of personal stories also fulfills the reciprocal function of helping to create and change the setting or community narrative, which in turn provides a map for participants' personal narratives. The presence of role models, meaningful roles, and the support of others help to reinforce the messages communicated by these community narratives.

Role Models

Role models are individuals who we admire and seek to emulate. We look to role models for guidance as to how we should behave and how we should view the world. Mutual-help groups provide role models for their participants in two important ways. First, both group and organizational leaders are individuals who are experiencing the shared problem, but who are coping with it well enough to take on a leadership role (Kurtz, 1997; Powell, 1975). Hearing from these leaders that they "have been there" and seeing them in a position of leadership helps participants to believe that they too can take on leadership roles and help themselves and others. If a person feels he or she shares similar life experiences with the role model, the model's influence may be greater (Katz, 1993). Because of the stigma of mental illness, opportunities to have a personal relationship with someone who is coping well with a mental illness may be limited. Social comparison theory (Festinger, 1954) suggests that people seek out others who are similar to help them make sense of the world. Comparisons between themselves and others who are perceived as doing better are used to learn new skills and coping strategies and to increase a sense of hope for improvement (Bandura, 1986).

Second, knowing other members who are in recovery provides a sense of hope (Davidson et al., 1999; Spaniol & Koehler, 1998), which is paramount to the recovery process (Deegan, 1993). Listening to the stories of others who have been there can be inspiring, motivating, and instructive (Deegan, 1988, 1993; Leete, 1987). From the experiences of others, people can learn practical strategies for coping with their mental illnesses.

Opportunity Role Structures

Mutual-help groups also promote recovery through the opportunity role structures that they provide (Maton & Salem, 1995). These opportunity role structures emanate from the value placed on expertise gained through lived experience with a problem (Borkman, 1990; Kurtz, 1997). Mutual-help groups lack the hierarchy and reliance on professional expertise that characterizes professional mental health settings (Kurtz, 1997). In addition, they are based on the belief that every member of the group has something of value to offer because of their experience living with the problem. As a result, they provide people diagnosed with mental illness opportunities to engage in valued activities and social roles that may not be available in other spheres of their life (Levine, 1988; Riessmann, 1965).

Mutual-help groups operate on assumptions that all members can be both helper and helpee (Maton, 1988; Rappaport, Reischl, & Zimmerman, 1992) and both the recipient and provider of social support (Roberts et al., 1991, 1999). The benefit derived from helping others is referred to as the *helper-therapy principle* (Riessman, 1965) and is especially salient to people diagnosed with mental illness who, in most settings, are likely to be the recipients of help. Being the provider of help is a more valued role in our culture than being the recipient of help, and feeling valued and worthy are identified as being especially important in the recovery process (Deegan, 1988; Houghton, 1982; Leete, 1987; Lovejoy, 1984).

Mutual-help settings also offer participants the opportunity to engage in other roles that are not available in professionally run mental health settings (Levine, 1988; Riessman, 1965). They have the opportunity to be leaders of groups; to participate in the decision making that impacts the group, organization, or setting; and to have equal status with all other setting participants. This allows for self-definition and self-determination. It also allows people diagnosed with a mental illness to develop and maintain their own understandings of recovery.

In addition to formal roles, mutual-help groups and organizations tend to be underpopulated settings or settings in which there are more roles or tasks available than there are people to fill the roles or perform the tasks (Rappaport et al., 1992). Zimmerman et al. (1991) argued that GROW, a mutual-help organization for people diagnosed with mental illness, intentionally creates roles for newer members as a means of expanding their organization. Because these settings offer more roles than there are people to fill them, opportunities for involvement tend to be numerous and barriers to participation tend to be low.

Social Support, Sense of Belonging, and Connection

Although mutual-help groups stress that individuals must take responsibility for their own recovery, they also believe that it is not something that someone can do alone. Mutual-help groups provide social support (Humphreys, 1997; Maton, 1988; Rappaport et al., 1985; Roberts et al., 1999) and a sense of connection (Humphreys, 1997), belonging, and community that is often lacking in the lives of people diagnosed with mental illness (Slack, 1995). They provide members with the important feeling that they are not alone and that what they have experienced is not unique to them—others have experienced it too. This simple realization can help to reduce feelings of social isolation and enhance feelings of belongingness.

In addition to the sense of positive well-being that comes from being surrounded by people who understand and support you, the attitudinal, cognitive, and emotional changes that individuals must go through in the process of recovery are not easily accomplished in isolation. Recovery has been described in the consumer literature as something that you do with other people (Deegan, 1988, 1993; Fisher, 1994; Lovejoy, 1984; Unzicker, 1989). It is essential that settings provide this sense of connection to other people and support for the difficult changes people must undergo.

In summary, mutual-help groups are not subject to the same institutional ideological influences that shape settings within the mental health system. As independent settings, stemming either from the general self-help movement (Katz, 1993) or the consumer mental health movement, they function based on a belief in the value of experiential knowledge. Through the creation of community narratives and the telling of personal stories, beliefs about mental illness and recovery are shaped by and communicated to members. These beliefs are reinforced by the presence of role models, the availability of meaningful roles and responsibilities, and the presence of a supportive context in which one can make sense of their experience through their interaction with others. Taken together, these characteristics enable members to develop a framework for understanding their illness and engaging in the process of recovery.

SCHIZOPHRENICS ANONYMOUS: A CASE EXAMPLE

In this section, we will use SA, a mutual-help organization for people experiencing a schizophrenia-related illness, as an example of the ideological and organizational characteristics described in the preceding section. SA was the focus of a longitudinal evaluation, which included evaluation of both organizational-level characteristics and individual member experiences. Having access to both levels of information has allowed for an exploration of the relationship between organizational characteristics and structure and individual beliefs and experiences. SA's well-documented ideology around mental illness and recovery and its well-articulated organizational structure and meeting processes make it an excellent setting for exploring the relationship between settings and individuals' beliefs about recovery.

The evaluation used multiple methods to examine organizational-level characteristics and individual member experiences, including participant observation, archival document reviews, surveys of participants and leaders, and qualitative open-ended interviews with group members and leaders. For the purposes of this discussion, we will focus on three types of information:

1. An analysis of the organization's literature provides an understanding of the organization's community narrative, including its ideology around mental illness and recovery.
2. Organizational literature, data from participant observations of individual groups, and members' stories of their experiences in SA help us to understand the role models, opportunity role structure, and social support that facilitate and support the settings' beliefs around mental illness and recovery.
3. Cross-case and within-case content analysis of 46 qualitative, open-ended interviews with members provides examples of how participants understand mental illness and recovery and have incorporated SA's beliefs into their personal belief systems. These interviews were designed to elicit members' stories of their mental illness and their experience in SA.

In the following description, first we describe the SA organization, followed by a description of its community narrative. Next, we discuss how the structure of SA supports its members in changing the way they view their mental illness and recovery. Finally, we describe how SA members understand and experience recovery and link this back to SA's community narrative around mental illness and recovery.

Description of Schizophrenics Anonymous

SA is a mutual-help organization for people with schizophrenia and schizophrenia-related illnesses. It was founded in 1985 in the Detroit area by a woman who had been diagnosed with schizophrenia. The organization has grown substantially over the years and currently there are more than 140 groups meeting throughout 20 states, Canada, Mexico, Venezuela, and Brazil. (Visit the Schizophrenics Anonymous Web site at http://www.sanonymous.org/.) There are no dues to attend meetings and anyone who wishes to recover from schizophrenia or a schizophrenia-related illness is invited to participate.

The organization's format and ideology were modeled in part after that of AA, in that there are weekly meetings for members, steps for recovery, a program philosophy, and mutual support between meetings (John, 1997). Also, similar to AA, SA does not engage in advocacy for individuals with mental illness or allow the name of the organization to be used to endorse political causes. A difference between SA and some other 12-step programs is that religious discussions are not encouraged, except in the broad sense of spirituality. SA members are encouraged to recognize their spirituality as it pertains to finding meaning or a higher purpose in their lives, but not to promote a specific religion or religious identity. Participants in SA groups are invited to share their experiences, feelings, and hopes in a confidential and nonjudgmental environment. SA has been described as providing a home for individuals with schizophrenia and a setting in which to receive peer support and acceptance (John, 1997).

Each SA group meets at a set time and place (typically weekly) and is headed by a SA leader and in some cases also a coleader. SA leaders are, in most cases, members of SA who have schizophrenia and who take primary responsibility for leading the group. Although the SA program has a suggested format for running groups, there is flexibility in how this format is implemented. Groups vary considerably with regard to attendance, leader experience, use of the program and literature, and social context or group setting (e.g., groups meet in churches, community mental health centers, and office buildings).

Schizophrenics Anonymous's Community Narrative[2]

SA's belief system was initially based on the experience of the organization's founder, Joanne V. Joanne V. has a diagnosis of schizophrenia and after making significant progress toward her own recovery, she made it her mission to help others by providing support, fellowship, and a belief system around schizophrenia and recovery that was based on her personal experience. Since the organization's inception in 1980, others have joined the founder in creating written materials and further developing SA's community narrative. It is communicated to members through a variety of written venues. The most important of these is SA's how-to manual (SA, 1999). This small booklet, referred to in SA as the "Blue Book," contains SA's mission, guiding principles, program structure, and stories of personal recovery. Other materials include the SA brochure (highlights the key elements of the SA program), videos about SA, the *Group Leader's Circular* (monthly leadership newsletter), the *E-Letter* (a weekly informational e-mail), a Web site, newspaper and magazine articles, a collection of personal stories, and conference presentation materials. In general, the SA program, as indicated in their mission statement, promotes recovery through the use of a six-step program and a variety of guiding principles. The six steps are "(1) I surrender... I admit I need help. I can't do it alone; (2) I choose... I choose to be well. I take full responsibility for my choices and realize that the choices I make directly influence the quality of my days; (3) I believe... I now come to believe that I have great inner resources, and I will try to use these resources to help myself and others; (4) I forgive... I forgive myself for all the mistakes I have made. I also forgive and release everyone who has

---

[2]The summary of members' beliefs about recovery that is presented in this section is based on the qualitative analysis of 46 open-ended semistructured interviews with SA members.

injured or harmed me in any way; (5) I understand… I now realize that erroneous, self-defeating thinking contributes to my problems, unhappiness, failures, and fears. I am ready to have my belief system altered so my life can be transformed; (6) I decide… I make a decision to turn my life over to the care of God, as I understand Him, surrendering my will and false beliefs. I ask to be changed in depth" (SA, 1999, 7–11). SA's Blue Book provides the foundation for the organization's community narrative, which is then reinforced by these other sources.

Content analysis of the program literature reveals some specific beliefs about schizophrenia and recovery that are at the core of the community narrative of SA: (a) Schizophrenia is a lifelong, no-fault biological illness; (b) recovery is possible and all people can engage in recovery regardless of symptom severity or other circumstances; (c) recovery consists of changing one's attitudes, beliefs, and approach to life; (d) people have inner strength and resources that can be used in their recovery and the recovery of others; (e) recovery can only be achieved with the help of others; and (f) recovery is an ongoing process with ups and downs. Interestingly, SA's belief system around the origin and cause of schizophrenia is based on the medical model understanding of mental illness as a biological illness. However, SA's understanding of recovery, what it means, and how to achieve it is based on experiential knowledge. SA's dual beliefs that schizophrenia is a lifelong, no-fault biological illness and that all people have a right to recovery imply that a person can experience recovery and still be living with the symptoms of schizophrenia. The view that a problem can be enduring, but that recovery is still possible, is found in many mutual-help groups (e.g., consider AA's view that alcoholism is a lifelong illness, but that recovery is still possible). This is a very different understanding of recovery than that which is conveyed by the medical model. Examples of how each of the key aspects of the community narrative is represented in the SA literature are provided next, along with quotes from SA members that reflect their incorporation of these aspects of SA's belief system into their own understanding of mental illness and their experience of recovery.

Schizophrenia is a lifelong, no-fault biological illness. This belief is reflected in the SA community narrative primarily with regard to the "facts" that members are taught about schizophrenia. For example, the following statements appear in the Blue Book (SA, 1999) and on the SA Web site:

> Schizophrenia is a biologically based psychological and emotional disorder that impairs normal brain function. (p. 2)

> A number of theories regarding the cause are now focused on biochemical and physical abnormalities in the brain. Chemical messengers carry signals from one nerve branch to another. Researchers believe that an imbalance in these chemicals contributes to schizophrenia-related symptoms. (SA Web site)

Members' personal stories of mental illness and recovery have incorporated the idea that schizophrenia is a lifelong illness:

> Well, if they've got schizophrenia they've got to realize that it isn't going to go away. And you've gotta live with it.

and that it is a biological illness:

> But I said no, it's a chemical imbalance in the brain. . . . Somebody might say, well, it's all my mother's fault. What I would say to them is, "I thought it was, too." I blamed my mother for years. But my mother did the best she could and I realize that this is a no-fault illness. . . . A lot of them thought it was a weakness of character, like I did.

Understanding schizophrenia as a lifelong illness within the context of the medical model's understanding of recovery may lead to hopelessness. In the context of SA's belief system, however, it helps people to accept their diagnosis and to move forward in other areas of their lives, even while still experiencing symptoms.

Recovery is possible and all people can engage in recovery regardless of symptom severity or other circumstances. The SA community narrative stresses that recovery is possible for everyone. This belief is reflected in the following statements in the Blue Book (SA, 1999):

> We believe that recovery is a personal thing: each person living up to his or her potential. Anyone who has a schizophrenia-related illness is invited to . . . join our ranks on the road to recovery. (p. 2)

> [Recovery] might include living independently, forming meaningful relationships, being financially self-supporting, and not having to be rehospitalized for psychiatric reasons. . . . But can aspects of recovery exist at less high levels of functioning? Can a person be considered as "recovering" if he or she is unable to maintain employment or live independently? At SA we believe that some level of recovery is achieved if that person is functioning at that person's highest possible level. (p. 10)

> One thing that we want to express to the newcomer is a sense of HOPE. What SA members have seen over the years is that people with schizophrenia are capable of making giant strides in recovery, and are able to find a place for themselves in this world. Life is a promise, even for those who have been afflicted with our difficult illness. (p. 32)

These beliefs are also reflected in members' stories of recovery. Members describe their belief in recovery and their hopes for the future:

We don't completely recover but we do recover, we do get well. We do get better. We can be successful people in society. . . . There is hope for recovery.

I'm coming from a mental illness, going off medication, going back to work, oh yeah, I've got a lot to look forward to.

Recovery consists of changing one's attitudes, beliefs, and approach to life. This belief, stated clearly in SA's purpose—"To improve our own attitudes about our lives and our illness" (SA, 1999, p. 3)—is reflected most fundamentally in SA's Steps for Recovery (see p. 185). Each step offers a new way to think about one's life and one's illness. According to the Blue Book, the steps help members to "forgive others and ourselves, to reject our misconceptions, to acknowledge spiritual values, and to take other affirmative steps" (p. 5). With regard to changing one's attitude about schizophrenia, SA goes so far as to point out that having schizophrenia can have positive benefits, as stated in the Blue Book (SA, 1999):

In the process we grow in a way that might not have been possible if we had not been stricken with the illness. (p. 5)

While the limitations [of schizophrenia] are well known, the advantages usually go unrecognized. For example, shared concern and empathy for mentally ill persons and for all society's down-trodden members is very evident among people with schizophrenia. (p. 12)

For members, this is reflected in many ways in their stories about SA and recovery. Attitude and worldview changes include developing a greater sense of empathy and compassion,

Before when I was a kid and not having any really bad symptoms, if I saw somebody who really looked [odd], stood out, I might giggle like the rest of the kids. Now, I would have compassion for the person.

It [having schizophrenia] made me more human . . . it made me really have compassion and empathy.

accepting one's illness and choosing to be well,

Accepting the illness and know that it's not so devastating. That there's hope for recovery.

I choose to be well. Because making the choices is really up to you. And if you don't make the choices to be well and be positive, then you won't overcome anything.

rethinking one's life goals and setting new priorities,

I still had to struggle with was I ever going to get a Bachelor's degree and go on and do all that? Would I ever have kids and I've come to terms with those two things—no and no. I'm not gonna have any kids and I'm not gonna probably ever have a career that's full time. Strangely enough, it doesn't bother me. I just felt a release of negative energy when I gave up those aspirations. . . . It all depends on how bad our illness is and how realistic we are in accepting the illness.

Before I got sick, I wanted to be a chief executive officer for a company so I had high goals for myself. And SA kept reminding me that I had an illness. That maybe that dream wasn't realistic for me anymore. And maybe I had to start re-dreaming and start, start setting new goals and be more practical to what I could actually accomplish, rather than what I wanted to accomplish.

and seeing the positive benefits of having schizophrenia,

Well, it, my illness, actually got me writing poetry. For which I've been published. I got some recognition.

As a 22-year-old woman am a lot stronger than any other 22-year-old woman I have ever met.

People have inner strength and resources that can be used in their recovery and the recovery of others. This belief is most strongly expressed in Step 3 of the SA program:

I now come to believe that I have been provided with great inner resources and I will try to use these resources to help myself and others. (SA, 1999, p. 7)

In a discussion of this step, the Blue Book goes on to state:

We believe that all of us have inner strengths that are useful in overcoming difficulties. . . . By accepting Step Three we are each saying "I believe in myself—I can get better." (p. 7)

This belief is seen in the narratives of SA members:

Though I have a mental illness, I have some strengths that I didn't know I had.

And it made me realize that if you're a strong person, you can go ahead and achieve whatever you need to achieve.

Recovery can only be achieved with the help of others. This belief is fundamental to SA and most mutual-help groups. It is stated in the first step of the SA program,

I surrender . . . I admit I need help. I can't do it alone. (SA, 1999, p. 5)

and in SA's statement of purpose,

> To offer fellowship, positive support, and companionship in order to achieve good mental health. (SA, 1999, p. 3)

SA is based on the belief that people need a caring, supportive, nonjudgmental environment to face difficult issues and make difficult changes. As stated in the Blue Book (SA, 1999):

> A large segment of society views people with schizophrenia as outcasts or second-class citizens. . . . At SA we offer a place to meet and socialize where persons with schizophrenia are not judged, but are accepted for who we are. (p. 11)

They also recognize that sharing one's experiences with others who understand is a powerful tool in recovery. As stated in the Blue Book:

> Those who have schizophrenia have a whole world of experiences that others don't know about. . . . We have these things in common. In a way it's like a homecoming. You are welcome here. (p. 32)

Reflections on the importance of being able to share their experiences with those who understand and the value of the support received in SA are abundant in members' stories. Members reflect on the importance of realizing that they are not alone in their experiences and that there are people who understand and will not judge them:

> Then everybody went around and told their story and I told my story, too. And when I left, I had this great feeling of relief, you know. Everything's gonna be OK. There are more people like me. . . . I had something in common with them, that I had with nobody else in my life.

> I could understand that people were going through the same thing that I was and I didn't feel so isolated which was a big step right there . . . there was nobody sitting around the table to judge you. . . . And just that feeling of not being alone is something, because there were experiences that I was scared to talk about. You know, like I mean, you tell somebody that you're gonna sit and watch the TV and you think it's talking at you, they're gonna bust out laughing, like who's this idiot? But when you go to a group and you sit down and tell people, oh, I'm not so different after all. I think the bottom line with people is they want to feel accepted and common, you know?

Recovery is an ongoing process with ups and downs. SA's community narrative clearly communicates that recovery is a process. The six-step model is a process model of recovery. Participants work through the steps as they move toward recovery. In the Blue Book (SA, 1999), new members are invited to "join our ranks on the road to recovery" (p. 2). Notably, there is no expectation in SA that members will work the steps sequentially (Walsh, 1994). This conveys the belief that there is no right place to start recovery and that it is up to the individual to choose the step that is most relevant to his or her life. The SA narrative also conveys the belief that there is no predetermined end point or final outcome that all members are expected to reach. Each person works to reach his or her own personal potential. As stated in the Blue Book:

> SA believes that each member should work towards the goals of achieving the objective measures of recovery: work, independent living, the development of interpersonal relationships. However we also believe that no member should be arbitrarily pushed beyond his current ability to achieve these goals. Put simply, our hope is that all members will eventually enjoy the fullest life possible. (p. 10)

It is also clearly communicated that setbacks are a normal and expected part of the recovery process:

> At SA we feel that setbacks are a normal, expected part of our usually chronic illness. We view them as a temporary intensification of symptoms which will often pass. (p. 11)

When members reflect on their recovery, they talk about it as a process that involves working the steps,

> But had I never taken that first step, to admit I was schizophrenic and join the group, nothing would have developed. . . .

setting goals,

> [I've started] making goals for myself. Even though I sometimes wouldn't meet those goals, it gave me something to look forward to. And I started changing, every six months, I started changing. . . . I set some goals for this year. The first goal is to get me a car. My second goal is to go back to work and I'm going through a process of going to do that right now. . . . When you set goals, if you don't make it, fine, start again. And if you do make it, good for you.

attaining goals,

> So I gradually built myself up over the years. . . . They introduced me as having a girlfriend and having a college degree which I completed.

> I guess I feel that I have accomplished my first goal and that was to help other people.

and accepting setbacks.

> I could be whole and have a break and still recover and move on.

> There are varying degrees of illness. . . . And a setback doesn't mean that you're not successful and success has a lot of different meanings.

In summary, SA's community narrative and the beliefs it communicates about schizophrenia reflect a view of recovery based on the experiential knowledge of its members. This community narrative is reflected in the personal stories of SA members. It influences and is reinforced by the presence of role models, the availability of valued roles, and the support of others.

Sharing of Personal Stories

SA assists participants in developing and telling a coherent story of their recovery by providing a community narrative that includes the possibility of recovery and by encouraging them to think about, tell, and retell their own stories around mental illness and recovery. Many opportunities are provided for the telling of these stories, both formally and informally. Members share their verbal stories at meetings, social events, conference presentations, SA leadership meetings, and informally with one another. They have opportunities to contribute written stories to the SA literature. These stories are included in the Blue Book and on the SA Web site.

In an analysis of SA members' stories of recovery (Weaver Randall, 2000), it is noteworthy that participants who had more opportunity to be exposed to the community narrative and to share their personal stories (i.e., had been in SA longer or were leaders in the organization) had more well-developed narratives than members who were new to the organization or participated in groups that were not functioning according to the specified SA format. Both exposure to SA's community narrative, which offers an alternative understanding of recovery, and the act of telling and retelling one's personal story assist members in developing personal narratives around mental illness and recovery that reflect understandings of recovery that are different from those espoused by proponents of the medical model.

Members value the opportunity to share their own stories and hear the stories of others:

> I think just sharing with other schizophrenic people. Yeah, hearing what their lives have been like and the hell they've gone through. That, for me, is the biggest part of it. It draws me to it because I can share my own story with them and they understand. They know what it's like to hear voices that nobody else hears or they know what

it's like to get paranoid and think the whole world's talking about you and be convinced of it and not be able to shake the feeling, even though people reassure you, it doesn't mean a thing. That's touched me the most.

Role Models

SA is unique in its ability to provide role models who are in the process of recovering from schizophrenia. The stigma attached to a diagnosis of schizophrenia is so great that those who are coping successfully with the illness often keep it hidden. Most people with schizophrenia do not have the opportunity to get to know others who are recovering from the same illness. Not only does SA provide access to others who are recovering, it provides a mechanism for learning about their lives, their views of recovery, and their methods of coping.

Through the telling and retelling of stories and the mutual exchange of support, SA provides members the opportunity to get to know people on a more intimate level than is typically available in other types of settings. In traditional, professionally run settings, consumers tend to have few opportunities for sharing their stories. In SA, a number of mechanisms are used to facilitate the process of getting to know role models. First, members have access to potential role models in their SA groups, including group leaders or other members who have experiential knowledge to share. Second, by making the personal stories of SA members and leaders public by publishing them in the Blue Book, putting them on the Web, presenting them on video, or telling stories at organizational-level gatherings and conferences, members have access to potential role models outside of their group. The founder and leader of the SA organization, although not personally known by all members, is looked to as a role model by many. Because she cannot get to know all of the members of SA personally, she has made a video that tells her story. Through this video and through written accounts of her story, she has become an influential role model for many SA members.

In their personal stories members describe how the founder of SA has affected their lives:

> I knew in the very beginning that she was very caring and she was running it herself and she was describing her experience which, you know, was somewhat similar to me. I wasn't holding a full-time job at the time and I haven't since. But she was holding a full-time job. She had been through the hospital thing. She was taking her meds. She was seeing a psychiatrist. The whole, you know, a big portion of the experience that people that have this illness, in a big way she had experience and she was making it.

Members also describe how knowing group leaders and other members provides them with inspiration:

> You know, it still surprises me that she's schizophrenic. I can't believe it. I can't believe it, because she seems so knowledgeable and thoughtful and wears a lot of hats.

They also provide a means of measuring how well they are doing in coping with schizophrenia,

> She was an engineer and she had MS plus schizophrenia really bad. So she had some really interesting views on how to stay healthy. I found somebody who had some common interests with me and someone who . . . also has education like I did, but she got demoted to a different area once she was diagnosed. And so that made me realize that maybe keeping my job at an easy level and the stress off and just trying to live life the way I could get by, would be the best thing to do.

Role models help to reinforce and validate SA's belief that recovery is possible by providing access to people who have had similar experiences, but who are viewed as being in recovery and living successfully. The existence of role models also provides a sense of hope for members around their ability to live successfully with a diagnosis of schizophrenia.

Opportunity Role Structures

SA provides members the opportunity to participate in meaningful social roles that may not be available in other settings or in other areas of their life. At the group level, multiple roles are available to members. Members can be both the recipients and providers of help, may assume the role of group leaders, or may take on other responsibilities that are associated with sustaining the group (e.g., making coffee, calling members, arranging for a meeting space). At the organizational level, members can participate in roles and activities that are needed to sustain the growth of the organization. These include participating in the group consciousness meetings (i.e., the monthly organizational decision-making meeting), developing and revising the organization's literature, contributing to the newsletter, organizing the annual leadership conference, helping with mass mailings to members and leaders, representing SA at conferences or other professional venues, and getting new SA groups up and running. Whether members participate in these roles at the individual, group, or organizational level, these opportunities provide members with a sense of meaning and purpose.

SA members' roles in providing help and assistance to other members is well documented in members' stories of mental illness and recovery:

> I can see if I can help people because I feel like I'm at a good part in the illness, where I've overcome a lot. You know, the voices and the hallucinations, and maybe I can help somebody else out since I'm not having any symptoms right now.

> Not only do I get help, but [Jane] has made it clear that she counts on my point of view at times in order to shore up the others, believe it or not.

Members also reflect on other opportunities they have to make meaningful contributions to the functioning of their group:

> SA really kinda saved my life in a sense, because I didn't have any direction and so very early on, I was beginning to think of ways where I could make a contribution. The first way I could make a contribution was very small, which was making coffee and cleaning up the tables afterwards. Something simple. We need people to put literature out. You know. There's just a million little small things a person can do to build up a sense, you know, with the other people that they can follow through.

At the organizational level, members also described opportunities to participate in valued roles:

> We would go down to Southfield on a Saturday, I believe, and collate letters that were produced to introduce professionals to SA. We would spend a whole afternoon that way and all we would be doing would be putting letters into envelopes and sealing them and stamping them and getting ready to mail. And I felt that that was important to me, because I felt that I was beginning to believe that SA was giving me a profitable direction for my life, which it has.

Finally, SA members express how being able to help others, give back, and participate in other worthwhile ways makes them feel better about themselves and gives them a sense of meaning and purpose:

> Well, when I started leading the groups, then I began feeling better about myself. I think God made me schizophrenic to help people.

> It makes me feel like I've got something to give back to a system that's given to me. And it does definitely give me a purpose.

Social Support, Sense of Belonging, and Connection

SA helps members in many different ways to combat their feelings of loneliness and social isolation and to increase their level of social support and sense of belonging and connection. SA helps members realize that they are not alone with their illnesses; provides a sense of identification with others who really understand their experiences; provides a safe place for members to talk about their illnesses; and it provides support, acceptance, friendship, and fellowship. In this context, members can hear the stories of others, reflect on their own experiences, discuss their experiences with others who understand, and engage in the process of recovery.

Members report that participating in SA decreases their sense of being alone, because they learn that there are many others who share similar experiences:

> Well, the most thing that I like about it was the people have the same illness. . . . That I was not alone. There was [sic] people out there hurting just like I'm hurting.

SA members describe the value of being with others with whom they can identify and who can really understand their experiences:

> Because I can relate to these people. They can relate to me and my psychiatrist and my therapist cannot. You know, no matter how much I try to make them understand, they will never know what it's really like. Just like if I had my arms and legs chopped off and I had to see a therapist about it, I would rather see a therapist that was in the same position than I was than someone who was not, because they wouldn't understand and that's how I feel. I want someone who understands.

> Normally, anything that you say, there's at least one other person who's been there.

SA provides a setting that encourages members to express their feelings and to be open and communicative with other members. For many SA members, this is the first time they have been able to talk openly and freely about their experiences and illness:

> Because I never talked about it before I started SA. I never talked to anybody about delusions or . . . except for maybe my doctor, you know, or the nurses in the hospital. But I didn't feel lonely anymore . . . I think it healed some of that pain. Because now I can speak about it without tearing up or whatever.

This provides an opportunity to interact with others around the process of recovery:

And I started to depend on a dialogue instead of the usual soul search-ing that's done, you know, it's like a self thing. I started to depend on the dialogue with other people.

Participating in SA provides members with feelings of belonging,

I feel like I belong. I don't know. It sounds crazy but I thought I found my niche for now, for now. Maybe a year from now, I don't know. Might be doing your job.

acceptance,

Acceptance, absolute acceptance. I have a problem with tardive dyskinesia, but here, it doesn't matter. . . . In the hospital, in group therapy, everybody tries to outdo everybody else. But here, you're accepted, if you want to speak, you can speak if you want. Nobody's going to jump on your case, nobody's watching you critically. To me, that's wonderful.

support,

What has been the most helpful to me? The people clapped, rewarded me, what I said. What other members had to say. . . . Helped me get stronger, function through other things, to move on. . . . I kept my job for almost two years now and [Anna] says all right. You're working. We're so proud of you. A big clap. That's encouraging, that makes me wanta go further. You get positive feedback from others and yourself.

I have to say that this is one of the most wonderful things that ever came into my life. It definitely is a strong, huge 2 × 4 that holds up my life.

friendship,

The friendship, the friendship that I get out of it. . . . I've never been a person to go out and make friends. I always had trouble making friends. But going here, it seems like I've had an easier time making friends.

and fellowship,

They are kind of a tether for my balloon. It's kinda like you see these hot air balloons all inflated and they've got their tethers down and it's kinda like all the balloons are schizophrenics and the crew is influenced by [a] schizophrenia inflated thing and they all tethered each other down until it's time to be released.

SA Members' Beliefs About Recovery[3]

The examples provided in the preceding section clearly demonstrate that SA members adopt many beliefs about recovery from SA's community narrative. Analysis of members' stories at a meta-level reveals that SA members' personal stories reflect many of the components of recovery identified in published consumer accounts of recovery. Analysis of SA members' views of recovery from schizophrenia indicate that recovery is experienced as an ongoing, iterative process that encompasses many life domains. Cross-case analysis of members' stories of recovery revealed that recovery is a multiphase process, which can be characterized by four identifiable phases (Weaver Randall, 2000). Generally speaking, the phases were related to (a) grief, (b) recognition, (c) redefinition, and (d) enhanced well-being.

Within–case analysis that examined the pattern of each individual's story of recovery revealed the following:

1. Participants move through the different phases of the recovery process in an ongoing or continuous manner with no clear or identifiable end point. All of the participants ($n = 15$) who were identified as reaching Phase 4 (enhanced well-being) also described being in all of the other three phases at some point in their recovery process.

2. Movement between the four phases is iterative, with back-and-forth movement between the phases being common. Participants described moving back and forth between the phases as they faced new challenges or grew and changed in new ways. Even when a person reached Phase 4, at times movement back to earlier phases occurred as the circumstances of their lives unfolded. One example of how participants described moving back to earlier phases is when they developed a new awareness that brought them back to Phase 2 (recognition). Becoming aware of and recognizing new ways that having a diagnosis of schizophrenia had negatively impacted their lives then led them back to Phase 1 (grief).

3. The recovery process encompasses the whole person. Recovery is not described as being solely about addressing the symptoms of the illness, finding the right treatment plan, or taking the right medication. Recovery involves emotions, beliefs,

---

[3]The summary of members' beliefs about recovery that is presented in this section is based on cross-case and within-case qualitative analysis of 46 open-ended semistructured interviews with SA members and leaders that were designed to elicit members' stories of mental illness and recovery (Weaver Randall, 2000).

and attitudes; one's relationship to other people and one's self; participation in valued roles; redefining one's life; and accomplishing valued goals. This means that in the course of one's life, a person may simultaneously experience different phases for different aspects of their life.

The following case summary of Lisa's story of recovery illustrates these points:

Lisa describes how it took her more than 7 years to realize and accept that she had a mental illness. After she would experience successes in school or work she would "still test the waters and go for a second opinion," because she did not believe that someone diagnosed with schizophrenia could achieve the things she was able to [Phase 1]. Next she describes how being in therapy and trying to find out as much information as possible about schizophrenia [Phase 3] eventually brought her to SA. She describes her participation in SA as helpful, because it helped her to realistically assess her situation and understand how schizophrenia had impacted her life [Phase 2]. It also helped her to reassess her goal of being a CEO of a big company and settling for nothing less [Phase 3]. Later in her story she describes her recovery as really progressing when she was able to maintain a full-time job and eventually buy a car with the money she saved [Phase 4]. At the time of the interview Lisa was doing very well by her own evaluation and had achieved many of her goals, including being content at her job, getting married, and owning a home [Phase 4]. In the last year, however, she and her husband have been thinking about having children and this has made her recognize and acknowledge that it may not be possible for her to have a healthy baby [Phase 2]. She had also experienced recent discrimination at work, when co-workers told her that she was the only person who was not supposed to have a key to the office [Phase 2]. In spite of these experiences, Lisa describes herself as "coming around to another phase again" in her recovery. This comment was made in reference to her desire to become involved doing some volunteer work with a mental health advocacy organization, which she saw as providing a renewed sense of meaning and purpose in her life [Phase 4].

Lisa's story of recovery and the stories of other SA members reflect many beliefs about recovery that are consistent with SA's community narrative and with the experiences of recovery reported by other mental health consumers (e.g., Deegan, 1988, 1996; Houghton, 1982; Leete, 1989). Recovery in SA is experienced as a process that does not involve success or failure or a predetermined end point. It is an ongoing process that covers many aspects of individuals' lives. Engaging in recovery means moving back and forth between the different phases or aspects of the process as new issues and life situations arise. This view of recovery is a significant departure from the medical model view of recovery, which entails reaching a desired set of outcomes. SA's reliance on experiential knowledge makes the definition of recovery that is available in this setting distinct from what is found in more traditional, professionally run settings.

SUMMARY

Institutional environments influence the beliefs, structures, and function of settings that exist within that environment. In turn, settings influence the beliefs and actions of their participants. Mutual-help groups have the potential to provide unique environments for understanding and promoting recovery from mental illness, because they function based on experiential, rather than professional, knowledge and expertise (Borkman, 1990). SA provides an example of how mutual-help settings that operate outside of the mental health system function based on their belief in the value of experiential knowledge of their participants. This leads to the development of community narratives that come directly from the experience of participants. SA's community narrative includes beliefs around schizophrenia, recovery, and what an individual's role is in his or her own recovery and in the recovery of others. Specifically, it states that although schizophrenia is a lifelong, no-fault biological illness, recovery is possible and all people can engage in recovery regardless of symptom severity or other circumstances. The community narrative includes the belief that recovery is an ongoing process with ups and downs, which consists of changing one's attitudes, beliefs, and approach to life. It defines people's roles in recovery as recognizing that they have inner strength and resources that can be used in their recovery and understanding that recovery can only be achieved with the help of others.

SA's community narrative both influences the development of and is reinforced by its opportunity role structure, the presence of role models, and the availability of a supportive context in which to grow and change. The availability of truly meaningful and powerful roles and responsibilities, in a sense, "puts SA's money where its mouth is." The organization validates the idea that people have valuable contributions to make by depending on them to do so to sustain the setting. The presence of role models shows members that it can be done—people can recover. Recovery can be achieved by people with whom they feel they have essential things in common, such as experiences with symptoms, stigma, discrimination, and loss. The supportive context provides a safe and validating place to try, fail, and try again. These characteristics of SA act to reinforce its community narrative around schizophrenia and recovery.

The understanding and experience of recovery in SA are different from that which is communicated in professionally controlled settings or even in some other types of consumer-operated settings. Settings that are not based on experiential knowledge may produce different or more limited understandings of recovery. For example, traditional mental health settings often espouse the belief that schizophrenia is a chronic illness with a poor prognosis and little chance of recovery. Not only does this create a sense of hopelessness, but it prevents the development of a community narrative of recovery, which in turn has implications for how the setting is structured and what organizational roles and opportunities are available for setting participants.

Although the public mental health system consists of a wide array of services and settings, few of them have structures or mechanisms for incorporating experiential knowledge in a way that alters how participants think about and experience recovery. Mental health service systems have tried to address this by including consumer-operated services as a legitimate adjunct to traditional treatment. One of the dangers of integrating consumer-operated services, including mutual-help groups, into the mental health sector is that their ideology may be compromised (Antze, 1976), leading them to look and behave more like other services found within the sector. The recently conducted Consumer-Operated Services Program (COSP), a national, multisite research initiative federally funded by SAMHSA, may provide some additional understanding about how alternative service settings influence outcomes and recovery.

Settings based on experiential knowledge have the capacity to develop and communicate understandings of recovery that reflect the lived experiences of their members. These beliefs about recovery help to create settings in which participants can actively and optimistically engage in the process of recovery. In seeking to support and interact with these settings, it is crucial that we understand and respect their underlying belief systems and the impact that these beliefs have on participants' understanding of their mental illness and on their experience of recovery.

REFERENCES

American Psychiatric Association. (1994). *Diagnostic and statistical manual of mental disorders* (4th ed.). Washington, DC: Author.

Antze, P. (1976). The role of ideologies in peer psychotherapy organizations: Some theoretical considerations and three case studies. *Journal of Applied Behavioral Sciences, 12,* 323–346.

Arntson, P., & Droge, D. (1987). Social support in self-help groups: The role of communication in enabling perceptions of control. In T. L. Albrecht & M. B. Adelman (Eds.), *Communicating social support* (pp. 148–171). Beverly Hills, CA: Sage.

Bandura, A. (1986). *Social foundations of thought and action: A social cognitive theory.* Englewood Cliffs, NJ: Prentice Hall.

Borkman, T. J. (1990). Experiential, professional and lay frames of reference. In T. J. Powell (Ed.), *Working with self help.* Silver Spring, MD: NASW Press.

Cain, C. (1991). Personal stories: Identity acquisition and self-understanding in Alcoholics Anonymous. *Ethos, 19,* 210–253.

Chamberlin, J. (1978). *On our own: Patient-controlled alternatives to the mental health system.* New York: McGraw-Hill.

Chamberlin, J. (1990). The ex-patient's movement: Where we've been and where we're going. *The Journal of Mind and Behavior, 11,* 323–336.

Chamberlin, J., & Rogers, J. A. (1990). Planning a community-based mental health system. *American Psychologist, 45,* 1241–1244.

Corin, E. E., & Lauzon, G. (1992). Positive withdrawal and the quest for meaning: The reconstruction of experience among schizophrenics. *Psychiatry, 55,* 266–278.

Corin, E. E., & Lauzon, G. (1994). From symptoms to phenomenon: The articulation of experience in schizophrenia. *Journal of Phenomenological Psychology, 25*(1), 3–50.

Corrigan, P. W., Calabrese, J. D., Diwan, S. E., Keogh, C. B., Keck, L., & Mussey, C. (2002). Some recovery processes in mutual-help groups for persons with mental illness; I: Qualitative analysis of program materials and testimonies. *Community Mental Health Journal, 38,* 287–301.

Davidson, L., Chinman, M., Kloos, B., Weingarten, R., Stayner, D., & Tebes, J. K. (1999). Peer support among individuals with severe mental illness: A review of the evidence. *Clinical Psychology: Science and Practice, 6,* 165–187.

Deegan, P. E. (1988). Recovery: The lived experience of rehabilitation. *Psychosocial Rehabilitation Journal, 11*(4), 11–19.

Deegan, P. E. (1993). Recovering our sense of value after being labeled. *Journal of Psychosocial Nursing, 31*(4), 7–11.

Deegan, P. E. (1996). Recovery as a journey of the heart. *Psychiatric Rehabilitation Journal, 19*(3), 91–97.

DiMaggio, P. J., & Powell, W. W. (1983). The iron cage revisited: Institutional isomorphism and collective rationality in organizational fields. *American Sociology Review, 48,* 147–160.

Emerick, R. E. (1991). The politics of psychiatric self-help: Political factions, interactional support, and group longevity in a social movement. *Social Science Medicine, 32,* 1121–1128.

Emotions Anonymous. (1973). St. Paul, MN: Emotions Anonymous International.

Festinger, L. A. (1954). A theory of social comparison processes. *Human Relations, 7,* 117–140.

Fisher, D. (1994). Hope, humanity, and value in recovery from psychiatric disability. *The Journal, 5*(3), 13–15.

Fraser, M. E. (1994). Educating the public about mental illness: What will it take to get the job done? *Innovations and Research, 3*(3), 29–31.

GROW Inc. (1982). *GROW World Community Mental Health Movement: The program of growth to maturity.* Sidney, Australia: Grow Publications.

Hooper, M. (1982). Explorations in the structure of psychological identifications with social groups and roles. *Multivariate Behavioral Research, 17,* 515–523.

Houghton, J. F. (1982). First person account: Maintaining mental health in a turbulent world. *Schizophrenia Bulletin, 8,* 548–553.

Humphreys, K. (1993). *Worldview transformation in adult children of alcoholics mutual-help groups.* Unpublished doctoral dissertation, University of Illinois, Urbana-Champaign.

Humphreys, K. (1997, Spring). Individual and social benefits of mutual aid self-help groups. *Social Policy,* 12–19.

Humphreys, K., & Rappaport, J. (1994). Researching self-help/mutual aid groups and organizations: Many roads, one journey. *Applied and Preventative Psychology, 3,* 217–231.

Katz, A. H. (1993). *Self help in America. A social movement perspective.* New York: Twayne.

Katz, A. H., & Bender, E. I. (1990). *Helping one another: Self-help groups in a changing world.* Oakland, CA: Third Party Publishing.

Kessler, R. C., Mickelson, K. D., & Zhao, S. (1997, Spring). Patterns and correlates of self-help group membership in the United States. *Social Policy,* pp. 27–46.

Kurtz, L. (1997). *Self help and support groups: A handbook for practitioners.* Thousand Oaks, CA: Sage.

Leete, E. (1987). The treatment of schizophrenia: A patient's perspective. *Hospital and Community Psychiatry, 38,* 486–491.

Leete, E. (1989). How I perceive and manage my mental illness. *Schizophrenia Bulletin, 15,* 197–200.

Levine, M. (1988). An analysis of mutual assistance. *American Journal of Community Psychology, 16*(2), 167–183.

Lovejoy, M. (1984). Recovery from schizophrenia a personal odyssey. *Hospital and Community Psychiatry, 35,* 809–812.

Maton, K. I. (1988). Social support, organizational characteristics, psychological well-being, and group appraisal in three self-help group populations. *American Journal of Community Psychology, 16*(1), 53–77.

Maton, K. I., & Salem, D. A. (1995). Organizational characteristics of empowering community settings: A multiple case study approach. *American Journal of Community Psychology, 23,* 631–657.

Mead, S., Hilton, D., & Curtis, L. (2001). Peer support: A theoretical perspective. *Psychiatric Rehabilitation Journal, 25*(2), 134–141.

Meyer, J. W., & Rowan, B. (1977). Institutional organizations: Formal structures as myth and ceremony. *American Journal of Sociology, 83,* 340–363.

John, P. (1997). Schizophrenics Anonymous and psychiatric rehabilitation. In C. T. Mowbray, D. P. Moxley, C. A. Jasper, & L. L. Howell (Eds.), *Consumers as providers* (pp. 95–105). Columbia, MD: IAPSRS.

Pfeffer, J., & Salancik, G. R. (1978). *The external control of organizations.* New York: Harper & Row.

Powell, T. J. (1975). The use of self-help groups as supportive reference communities. *American Journal of Orthopsychiatry, 45,* 756–764.

Rappaport, J. (1993). Narrative studies, personal stories, and identity transformation in the mutual help context. *The Journal of Applied Behavioral Science, 29*(2), 239–256.

Rappaport, J., Reischl, T. M., & Zimmerman, M. A (1992). Mutual help mechanisms in the empowerment of former mental patients. In D. Saleebey (Ed.), *The strengths perspective in social work* (pp. 84–97). New York: Longman.

Rappaport, J., Seidman, E., Toro, P. A., MacFadden, L. S., Reischl, T. M., Roberts, L. J., et al. (1985, Winter). Collaborative research with a mutual-help organization. *Social Policy,* pp. 12–24.

Rappaport, J., & Simkins, R. (1991). Healing and empowering through community narrative. *Prevention in Human Services, 10,* 29–50.

Recovery, Inc. (1985). *1985 Directory of group meeting information.* Chicago: Author.

Riessman, F. (1965). The "helper" therapy principle. *Social Work, 10,* 27–32.

Roberts, L. J., Luke, D. A., Rappaport, J., Seidman, E., Toro, P. A., & Reischl, T. M. (1991). Charting uncharted terrain: A behavioral observation system for mutual help groups. *American Journal of Community Psychology, 19*(5), 715–737.

Roberts, L. J., Salem, D. A., Rappaport, J., Toro, P. A., Luke, D. A., & Seidman, E. (1999). Giving and receiving help: Interpersonal transactions in mutual-help meetings and psychosocial adjustment of members. *American Journal of Community Psychology, 27,* 841–868.

Salem, D. A., Bogat, G. A., & Reid, C. (1997). Mutual help goes on-line. *Journal of Community Psychology, 25*(2), 189–207.

Salem, D. A., Reischl, T. M., Gallacher, F., & Randall, K.W. (2000). The role of referent and expert power in mutual help. *American Journal of Community Psychology, 28,* 303–324.

Schizophrenics Anonymous. (1999). *Schizophrenics Anonymous: A self-help support group.* Leasing, MI: National Schizophrenia Foundation.

Schubert, M. A., & Borkman, T. A. (1994). Identifying the experiential knowledge developed within a self-help group. In T. J. Powell (Ed.), *Understanding the self-help organization: Frameworks and findings.* Thousand Oaks, CA: Sage.

Scott, W. R. (1995). *Institutions and organizations.* Thousand Oaks, CA: Sage.

Sherif, M. (1962). The self and reference groups: Meeting ground of individual and group approaches. *Annals of the New York Academy of Sciences, 96,* 797–813.

Slack, W. (1995). Just talking and listening. *The Journal, 6*(3), 13.

Solomon, P., & Draine, J. (2001). The state of knowledge of the effectiveness of consumer provided services. *Psychiatric Rehabilitation Journal, 25,* 20–27.

Spaniol, L., & Koehler, M. (1998). *The experience of recovery.* Boston: Boston University, Center for Psychiatric Rehabilitation.

Steinman, R., & Traunstein, D. M. (1976). Redefining deviance: The self-help challenge to the human services. *The Journal of Applied Behavioral Science, 12,* 347–361.

Unzicker, R. (1989). On my own: A personal journey through madness and re-emergence. *Psychosocial Rehabilitation Journal, 13*(1), 71–77.

Wahl, O. (1998). *Consumer experience with stigma: Results of a national survey.* Retrieved (n.d.) from http://www.nami.org/research/970913201441.htm

Walker-Davis, W. (1995). Promoting the values of the self-help movement. *The Journal, 6*(3), 40–41.

Walsh, J. (1994). Schizophrenics Anonymous: The Franklin county, Ohio experience. *Psychosocial Rehabilitation Journal, 18*(1), 61–74.

Weaver Randall, K. (2000). *Understanding recovery from schizophrenia in a mutual-help setting.* Unpublished master's thesis, Michigan State University, East Lansing, MI.

Weingarten, R. (1994). The ongoing processes of recovery. *Psychiatry, 57,* 369–375.

Zimmerman, M., Reischl, T. M., Seidman, E., Rappaport, J., Toro, P., & Salem, D. A. (1991). Expansion strategies of a mutual help organization. *American Journal of Community Psychology, 19,* 251–278.

Zinman, S. (1987). Definition of self-help groups. In S. Zinman, Howie the Harp, & S. Budd (Eds.), *Reaching across: Mental health clients helping each other* (pp. 19–24). Sacramento: California Network of Mental Health Clients.

9

DARING TO PICK UP THE PIECES IN THE PUZZLE: A CONSUMER–SURVIVOR MODEL OF HEALING FROM CHILDHOOD SEXUAL ABUSE

MARY JANE ALEXANDER, KRISTINA MUENZENMAIER, JEANNE DUMONT, AND MARY AUSLANDER

This chapter describes a collaboration among consumer–survivors, clinicians, and researchers to map the important dimensions of recovery from physical and sexual abuse trauma. People who have severe mental illness diagnoses have very high rates of exposure to physical and sexual abuse trauma, and symptoms of post-traumatic stress disorder (PTSD). The mental health community is becoming aware of the far-reaching and complicated

This work was supported by The Center for the Study of Issues in Public Mental Health, NIMH Grant 2P50 MH51359-06A1. The authors wish to give special thanks to the courageous women and men who participated in the concept mapping groups and dared to pick up the pieces in the puzzle. We also thank Janet Chassman, director, Trauma Unit, and New York State Office of Mental Health for her participation in the design of the project, and for her continuous help and commitment; Donna Brophy, Susanna Sussman, and Alix Teleki for their graphic and editorial assistance in preparing the manuscript; and Donald E. Sampson, PhD, and Joseph Battaglia, MD, for their support and understanding.

difficulties experienced by people who have histories of childhood sexual abuse, and helpful approaches are emerging. But there are no survivor-generated models of healing from early abuse that would help people validate their experiences, identify the connection between their abuse and their current symptoms and coping strategies, move beyond disability, and help restructure the larger systems among which they move as they reconstruct their lives.

We put forth here two conceptual models of healing from childhood sexual abuse. The models were developed separately by men and women mental health service consumers who are abuse survivors, but the models are remarkably similar in content, with different focal points of importance. Survivors will want a guide as they pick up the arduous work of releasing the trauma's hold on their lives. As approaches to address the complications that abuse histories add to the lives of people using public mental health services continue to emerge, we need to understand whether and how they are helpful.

This framework of healing developed by abuse survivors can be used both to conceptualize the important issues for therapeutic work and to frame the evaluation of its success. Existing measures of symptoms, problems, and behaviors rarely directly reflect the perspective and experience of consumer–survivors. The healing model described in this chapter will be used to develop a measure of healing from childhood sexual abuse that can be used as an evaluation tool and as a road map for healing from childhood trauma. Because so many people who use mental health services are trauma survivors, the model described in this chapter will be widely applicable to people with severe mental illness diagnoses. It will also overlap with other models that conceptualize recovery from mental illness (Fisher, 1994; Ralph, 2004).

During the past decade, largely due to advocacy from survivors as well as clinical and policy advocates, mental health service systems have begun to acknowledge the extent and consequences of childhood sexual abuse among their service recipients. Beginning with a forum of trauma survivors held in New York state (Chassman, 1995), and continuing with the unanimous position statement of the National Association of State Mental Health Program Directors (1998) and trauma initiatives in at least 11 states, some inroads have been made to train staff, to institute procedures that identify trauma histories, to develop helpful and effective clinical approaches, and to develop policies that make institutional environments safer.

In the *Diagnostic and Statistical Manual of Mental Disorders* (DSM–IV; American Psychiatric Association, 1994), early abuse figures as a traumatic event that can lead to symptoms of PTSD: intrusive reexperiencing of the event, numbing, and hyperarousal. Although people in the general population experience high rates of trauma—56% of respondents in a representative national household sample reported that they had been exposed to a traumatic event during their lives (Kessler, Sonnega, Bromet, Hughes, &

Nelson, 1995), as did 39% of a sample of 1,007 young adults in Michigan (Breslau & Davis, 1992)—exposure is higher and more severe for people with severe mental illness diagnoses.

In the general population it is relatively uncommon to have been molested, physically attacked, raped, or physically abused. People most frequently report experiencing trauma through witnessing a serious injury or a death, being in a fire, flood or natural disaster, or being in a life-threatening accident (Kessler et al., 1995). Mueser and his colleagues (1998) report that among people with severe mental illness diagnoses using mental health outpatient services, the most frequently reported traumatic events were sexual assault as an adult or as a child, a car or work accident, and being attacked with a weapon. Childhood sexual assault was the event most frequently reported by the women in their multisite study. The strongest predictors of co-occurring PTSD symptoms and another Axis 1 severe psychiatric diagnosis were childhood sexual abuse and the number of traumatic events reported. In studies of people with severe mental illness in inpatient and outpatient psychiatric treatment settings, 34% to 53% of the people sampled reported histories of childhood sexual abuse or physical abuse (Beck & van der Kolk, 1987; Bryer, Nelson, Miller, & Krol, 1987; Carmen, Rieker, & Mills, 1984; Cole, 1988; Craine, Henson, Colliver, & MacLean, 1988; Herman, 1992; Jacobson, 1989; Jacobson & Herald, 1990; Jacobson & Richardson, 1987; Muenzenmaier, Meyer, Struening, & Ferber, 1993; Rose, Peabody, & Stratigeas, 1991; Rosenfeld, 1979), and 43% to 81% reported lifetime exposure to violence (Carmen et al., 1984; Hutchings & Dutton, 1993; Jacobson, 1989; Lipschitz et al., 1996).

In marginal environments such as homeless shelters, these figures are higher, with 77% reporting childhood victimization and 97% reporting victimization in the prior year (Goodman, Dutton, & Harris, 1997). Rates of PTSD among this population range from 26% to 43% (Cascardi, Mueser, DeGiralomo, & Murrin, 1996; Mueser et al., 1998, 2002; Neria, Bromet, Sievers, Lavelle, & Fochtmann, 2002; Switzer et al., 1999).

Other significant mental health problems frequently co-occur with PTSD. In the general population, 59% of men and 44% of women with PTSD meet the criteria for three or more other psychiatric diagnoses (Kessler et al., 1995), most frequently affective disorders such as depression, anxiety disorders, and substance abuse disorders (Davidson, Hughes, Blazer, & George, 1991). PTSD is more likely to be long-term when these other problems are also present, or when the trauma consisted of a personal assault, when it occurred at an early age, or when the perpetrator was known and trusted by the victim (Breslau, Kessler, & Chilcoat, 1998; Ford & Kidd, 1998). In fact, one third of people who have PTSD symptoms continue to have them 10 or more years following trauma exposure (Kessler et al., 1995).

Regardless of diagnosis, prolonged and pervasive traumatic experiences such as early sexual abuse, because they disrupt the development of basic trust, intimacy, autonomy, and self-concept, profoundly alter a person's belief in the safety and meaning of the world, the trustworthiness of others, and one's own competence (Herman, 1992; van der Kolk, 2002). Trauma survivors struggle with a range of problems related to these developmental disruptions, including alterations in consciousness, experience, and memory; fragmentation of the self; difficulties in attachment, relationships, trust, and emotion regulation; and disturbances of physiological processes. Studies consistently show that people with histories of childhood sexual abuse are likely to have severe psychiatric, substance abuse, and physical symptoms (Alexander & Muenzenmaier, 1998; Ford & Kidd, 1998). Among people with diagnoses of severe mental disorder, those who experience early, ongoing, and intimate abuse are more likely to develop PTSD (Neria et al., 2002).

Early and intimate abuse, then, creates long-lasting and complex difficulties that do not easily fit symptom pictures or diagnostic categories such as PTSD. But abuse survivors do not necessarily make the connection between their long-ago experiences and their current difficulties. People with PTSD who seek help, do so for problems such as depression, anger, self-destructive behavior, and feelings of shame, self-blame, and mistrust. They report that the problems most troubling to them are not necessarily the trauma-reexperiencing flashbacks of PTSD, but rather the difficulties they face as they try to handle strong emotions and impulses in ways that do not harm themselves or others, and as they try to establish and maintain healthy, mutual relationships (van der Kolk, 2002; van der Kolk, MacFarlane, & van der Hart, 1996). These challenges, commonly faced by survivors of terror, captivity, domestic violence, and childhood sexual abuse, led others to suggest a different framework—Complex PTSD, or Disorders of Extreme Stress, Not Otherwise Specified (DES-NOS)—to be included in *DSM–IV* (Herman, 1992; van der Kolk, 2002; van der Kolk et al., 1996). Although DES-NOS was not included in the diagnostic manual, these complicated difficulties persist in the lives of survivors. DES-NOS or "PTSD Plus" (Courtois, 2002) remains a useful framework that incorporates the observed long-term changes in how people handle emotional arousal; perceive the abuse perpetrator(s); relate to other people; and experience bodily symptoms in their attention, consciousness, and self-perception; and, finally, in how they construct meaning and belief (Herman, 1992).

In this context, then, how does it make sense to frame healing—the process of reconciling or becoming whole or sound—from early, persistent, and pervasive abuse? Treatment approaches for individuals who have histories of childhood sexual abuse and these complicated consequences have emerged (Alexander & Muenzenmaier, 1998; Bloom, 1997; Harris, 1997; Harris & Fallot, 2001; Najavits, Weiss, Shaw, & Muenz, 1998; van der Kolk, 2002). Beginning with a forum of trauma survivors held in New York state (Chassman, 1995), through the Maine Trauma Advisory Groups (Jennings

& Ralph, 1997), survivors have given voice to what happened to so many people in childhood homes as well as in institutions. They have also spoken about what hurts and what helps. But there is no systematic model that brings together how survivors construct for themselves the process of healing from early sexual abuse. This chapter describes an effort to do so. Most important, it describes a survivor-generated model of healing from sexual abuse trauma that has been developed through a collaborative effort among mental health consumer–survivors, clinicians, and researchers—from framing the questions to writing this chapter. We plan to test a measure of recovery from sexual abuse trauma based on the healing model described here.

METHOD: DEVELOPING A VISUAL MODEL OF HEALING FROM CHILDHOOD ABUSE

A picture can be worth a thousand words. In this work, we wanted to develop a visual representation of trauma survivors' experience of healing from sexual abuse and its aftermath. The authors developed a conceptual framework, using *concept mapping* (Trochim, 1989a, 1989b) to explore the relationships among ideas generated in focus groups with 24 consumer–survivors.

Concept Mapping

Concept mapping combines group process and structured analysis in a way that enables a group to lay out their ideas, on any topic, in a three-dimensional picture or "map." Typically participants brainstorm as a group to generate statements about a focus question. After the brainstorming session, participants receive a stack of cards with one of these statements on each card. Each participant then sorts the statements into piles on the basis of how similar they seem. Each participant also rates the importance of each statement on a Likert scale from 1 (relatively unimportant) to 5 (extremely important). Multidimensional scaling[1] (Kruskal & Wish, 1978) uses the sorted statements to develop a two-dimensional point map of the statements produced in the brainstorming session. Hierarchical cluster analysis[2]

---

[1]For each person, an n by n (where n = the number of statements) square matrix is constructed from the sort information. Values in the matrix represent the number of joint occurrences between pairs of statements. Any cell of the individual matrices takes integer values between 0 and 1. The values are summed across people to comprise one similarity matrix of integer values between 0 and N (where N = the number of sorters). High values in this matrix indicate pairs of statements that were consistently placed in the same pile. High values imply greater conceptual similarity.

[2]Nonmetric multidimensional scaling is conducted from the sort data compiled in the similarity matrix. The multidimensional scaling algorithm finds a set of coordinate points for which the ratio-scaled interpoint distances best fit the rank order of the interpoint distances or summed sort data where higher values are interpreted as closer in distance.

(Everitt, 1980) is then used on the x-y coordinate data obtained from the multidimensional scaling analysis, and its results are superimposed on the point map[3] (Dumont, 1989). A number of cluster solutions are produced, so an analytic decision can be made that creates a map that preserves the detail of the statements while yielding interpretable clusters. The average of the importance ratings assigned to each statement are then overlaid on the maps, producing a three-dimensional picture in which the clusters with more depth contain statements that were rated as more important than those with less depth. These maps provide a framework for exploring interrelationships among the ideas and concepts generated in the groups.

Key to this process are the "bridging values" for each statement and cluster. The program computes the bridging value using the multidimensional scaling output and sort data. The bridging value is an indicator of whether the statement was sorted with others close to it or with statements further away from it on the map. Low bridging values mean that a statement is more central to the meaning of the cluster, whereas higher bridging values mean that the item "bridges" areas of the map, and is more peripheral to the cluster's meaning.[4] The lower the average bridging value of a cluster, the more coherent the cluster.

To validate these data reduction methods, a second group process is held, with as many of the original participants as possible, to review and interpret the map and name the clusters. To do this, each participant receives the maps that resulted from the multidimensional scaling analysis (point map) and from the cluster analysis (cluster map). They also receive a list of the statements in the order in which they were generated, a list of the statements grouped into the clusters that resulted from the sorting task, the multidimensional scaling and the cluster analysis, the average importance rating for each statement and for each cluster, and the bridging value for each statement and cluster. Because statements with high bridging values

---

[3]In the development of the methodology, the x-y coordinate values for each point from the multidimensional scaling were used as the data input to the cluster analysis rather than applying the cluster algorithm to the original similarity matrix for at least three reasons: (a) Multidimensional scaling has a more reliable mathematical basis for depicting basic interentity conceptual similarity than cluster analysis; (b) results from two separate analyses provided a complicated depiction of interentity conceptual similarity and, in some conceptualizations, results were difficult to interpret; and (c) to support progression of the methodology.

[4]With a large data set (e.g., greater than 60 statements), there are more opportunities for two entities located proximately on a multidimensionally scaled map to be in that position for reasons other than the highest degree of perceived conceptual similarity. For example, the position represents, in part, a bridge between two entities that were not sorted together but are indirectly connected to one another through being sorted with a third entity or statement, the bridging entity. The concept mapping computer program uses the standardized straight-line Euclidean distance from the x-y coordinate to compute the bridging value. In computing this value, only the distances between points or statements that had been piled together by at least one person are considered. Thus the value represents a reliance on the multidimensional scaling output and the sort data.

are more peripheral to a cluster, they should receive less consideration in naming the cluster. The interpretation group uses all of this information, with a focus on the statements grouped into clusters and the bridging values, as they work to achieve group consensus in the naming of each cluster.

In the study reported here, men and women with histories of sexual abuse and mental illness diagnoses were invited to participate in the study focus groups through letters and flyers sent to support and advocacy groups, mental health clinics, and state-operated hospitals in different parts of New York State. Our goal was to convene groups that were diverse with respect to gender, race, mental health treatment histories, use of self-help, and geography. Interested people who called a study phone number were sent an information sheet describing the groups as well as a short series of questions requesting demographic information, history of psychiatric diagnosis and hospitalization, and experiences of sexual abuse. Thirty-seven women responded to the flyer, 30% ($n = 11$) of whom were able to participate in the concept mapping. Twenty-three men responded to the flyer, and 57% ($n = 13$) of these were able to participate in the concept mapping. A group of male and female participants met by teleconference to develop the statement that would guide the brainstorming sessions. They agreed that the focus group should concentrate on healing rather than recovery. Because abuse pervaded their developmental years, many survivors of childhood sexual abuse feel there is little to return to. The group agreed that "healing" better expressed the idea of a process toward wellness. They developed the following focus statement: "Generate statements that describe the patterns or signs that someone is coping with or is on a path toward healing or recovering from sexual abuse." Separate groups were held for men and women because we felt participants might feel safer talking about these painful and possibly intimate topics in same-gender groups.

In the brainstorming session, participants were encouraged to generate as many statements as possible, up to 100, that would ". . . describe the patterns or signs of . . . healing . . . from sexual abuse." During the session, statements could be discussed to clarify meaning, but criticism of others' statements was not permitted. Participation from all group members was encouraged. The women generated 84 statements in a 1-hour session; the men generated 79 statements in a 1.5-hour session. After the brainstorming session, participants sorted and rated the importance of each statement. They were encouraged to develop from 10 to 25 groupings of statements with the following rules: (a) All statements had to be sorted into groups, (b) there could be no "miscellaneous" group, and (c) there could not be as many groups as there were statements.

These procedures yielded a composite picture—literally a picture, or a map—depicting the dimensions of healing from early abuse as conceptualized by the participants. A 10-cluster solution was chosen for the interpretive maps as the solution that allowed for abstraction, yet preserved the detail of the statements. Led by the same researcher who had facilitated the brainstorming groups, five women and five men who had participated in the brainstorming sessions also participated in multiple teleconference meetings to interpret the maps and develop the model. This chapter sets forth a model of healing from sexual abuse that is based on all of these pieces.

Concept Mapping Participants

Table 9.1 shows the characteristics of those attending the groups. Men and women were not statistically different in their ages, ethnicity, nor in their histories of education, employment, psychiatric hospitalization, or the age at which they remember being first abused. All participants had experienced childhood sexual abuse, including abuse perpetrated by close and distant male and female relatives, teachers, friends, and strangers. Three quarters of the participants had been abused by family members. Twenty-one percent of the participants had received diagnoses of PTSD as part of their most recent diagnosis; two women had received a diagnosis of dissociative identity disorder.

TABLE 9.1
Comparisons of Characteristics of Men and Women Study Participants

		Women %	Men %
Ethnicity[1]	White	82	69
	Person of color	18	31
Education[2]	Less than high school	18	23
	High school/ some college	46	31
	College graduate or more	36	46
Ever employed? (Yes)		100	100
Currently employed?[3] (Yes)		18	23
Ever had a psychiatric hospitalization?[4] (Yes)		100	83
Mean (SD) number of psychiatric hospitalizations[5]		14 (12.4)	6 (3.8)
Mean (SD) age abuse began (SD)[6]		5.2 years (3.5)	2.8 (2.2)
Mean age (range)[7]		46 years (36–58)	41 years (23–57)

Note. [1]$t(22) = 1.65$ ns; [2]$X^2_{(1, 24)} = 0.88$ ns, Fisher's exact; [3]$X^2_{(1, 24)} = 0.54$ ns; [4]$X^2_{(1, 24)} = 0.77$ ns, Fisher's exact; [5]Not applicable; [6]$t_{(1, 20)} = 2.18$; $p < .05$; [7]$t_{(1, 20)} = 1.86$ ns.

The Concept Maps

The healing maps presented here for women (Figure 9.1) and for men (Figure 9.2) provide two pictures of how participants grouped their statements about healing, and how they interpreted, or named, each of those groups. The maps also show a third dimension for each cluster—its importance, which gives the cluster visual depth. It is the computed average of the importance score assigned to each item in the cluster by the participants.

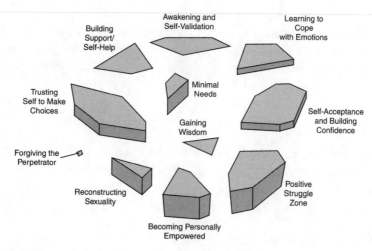

Figure 9.1. Women's concept map depicting grouped statements about healing.

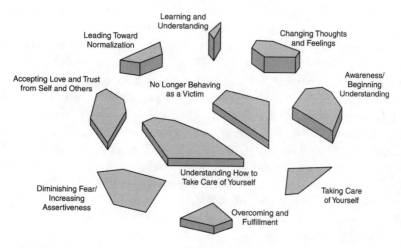

Figure 9.2. Men's concept map depicting grouped statements about healing.

Tables 9.2 and 9.3 list the concepts developed in the second teleconference, ranked by the average importance of the statements in the cluster. For each concept, the average importance and average bridging values for the statements in the cluster are listed, as well as the number and percent of all brainstormed statements that were grouped in that concept for the women's and the men's maps. The names given to the groups of statements describe how the participants conceptualize healing from abuse at a second, more abstract level than the brainstorming and sorting of items level. The number of items in a cluster reflects the amount of discussion generated by an idea, but not its importance. For each cluster, the statement rated as most important (I) and the statement rated as most central (C) to the cluster is listed. Some very large clusters or very important clusters contained more than one of the top 15 statements with the highest importance ratings. These additional statements are included as well. One of the women's statements stands alone, grouped with no cluster, on the basis of the consensus of the group in the second, interpretive meeting.

RESULTS: MAPS OF HEALING FROM CHILDHOOD TRAUMA

We now take a more detailed look at the concept maps that evolved from the women's and men's studies.

The Women's Healing Map

The women's map is presented in Figure 9.1. The most important ideas about healing from sexual abuse trauma in this map are located in the south and west parts of the map, as well as at the map's center. The cluster at the center of the map is named *Minimal Needs*. It is compact and coherent and is rated as a very important cluster. Also at the core of the map and very cohesive, but less important, is *Gaining Wisdom*. *Minimal Needs* and *Gaining Wisdom* each accounted for 5% of all of the statements generated in the women's brainstorming session. The statements grouped into *Minimal Needs* indicated that, at the very least, healing rests on allowing one's self to succeed, having compassion for oneself, filling in gaps in time and events, and identifying boundaries. The whole range of the women's feelings, "even at times, the joy" was central to *Gaining Wisdom*. This concept also focused on having confidence in their own judgment, and in their ability to turn away despair in the face of failure. Both concepts suggest that wholeness, that is, owning all of one's time, history, and feelings, as well as self-compassion and hope, are central to healing from sexual abuse.

The women named the groups moving from south to west on the map, *Positive Struggle Zone*, *Becoming Personally Empowered*, *Reconstructing Sexuality*, and *Trusting Self to Make Choices*. *Becoming Personally Empowered*, which

TABLE 9.2
Women's Map of Healing From Childhood Sexual Abuse

Clusters and Statements	Importance	Bridging	Items (n = 84) N	%
Becoming Personally Empowered Having the power and control to say no and be effective (I) Recognizing revictimization and stopping it	4.52	0.16	7	8
Positive Struggle Zone Accepting yourself the way you are (I) Having confidence to say what you really feel (I) Separating yourself from others' "stuff"	4.43	0.07	13	5
Reconstructing Sexuality Being aware of what hurts your child physically, emotionally, and sexually (I) Not feeling guilty when you enjoy sex (C)	4.38	0.35	6	7
Trusting Myself to Make Choices Not physically hurting your own child, intentionally (I) Knowing what your triggers are (C)	4.31	0.38	9	11
Minimal Needs Giving yourself permission to succeed (I) Having compassion for yourself (I) Starting to fill in the gaps of time and events (C)	4.42	0.14	4	5
Self-Acceptance and Building Confidence Not blaming myself anymore (I) Being able to tell the difference between nightmares and what really happened (I) I am who I am because of what I've been through (C) Not dissociating and splitting off (C)	4.22	0.09	16	19
Learning to Cope with Emotions Acknowledging that the abuse happened (I) Not feeling abandoned when therapist is away (C)	4.18	0.15	8	9
Awakening and Self-Validation Believing that sexual abuse happened (I) Being able to identify with literature on abuse (C) I feel like a puzzle and I am daring to pick up the pieces and put them where they belong	4.11	0.15	10	12
Building Support/Self-Help Being aware that you are a whole person (I) Choosing your own family (C)	4.10	0.28	7	8
Gaining Wisdom Believing I can make good judgments (I) Acknowledging my feelings, even at times of joy (C)	4.08	0.10	4	5
Forgiving the Perpetrators	2.00	—	—	—

Note. Importance, cohesion, N, and % items in clusters are in order of importance. For each cluster, the statement rated as most important (I) and the statement rated as most central (C) is listed.

TABLE 9.3
Men's Map of Healing From Childhood Sexual Abuse

Clusters and Statements	Importance	Bridging	Items (n = 79) N	%
Changing Thoughts and Feelings Be able to cry and experience feelings—don't run (I) No longer having suicidal thoughts (C) You stop blaming yourself for what happened	4.08	0.33	8	10
Awareness/Beginning Understanding Become a survivor, not a victim (I) Be aware of your own angry retribution tendencies (C)	4.02	0.30	12	15
Learning and Understanding About Sexual Abuse Learn more about sexual abuse (I) Attend groups and get different viewpoints (C)	3.93	0.38	4	5
Leading Toward Normalization as a Process Be able to disclose abuse to professionals (I) Work through negative thoughts (C)	3.73	0.53	5	6
Overcoming and Fulfillment Empower yourself (I) Be assertive and stop being manipulated (C)	3.58	0.20	8	10
Taking Care of Yourself Be aware of setbacks (I) Be kind to yourself (I) Look to the future rather than the past (C)	3.55	0.10	11	14
Understanding How to Take Care of Yourself Have someone to support you (I) Take one day at a time, or less, if necessary (C)	3.53	0.13	8	10
No Longer Behaving as Victim Watch for signs of relapse, or triggers (I) Understand how to develop healthy relationships with boundaries (I) Learn to say no about anything (C)	3.53	0.28	6	8
Accepting Love and Trust From Self and Others Be able to accept love and trust from others when it's genuinely offered (I) Explore the abuse as soon as possible	3.49	0.84	8	10
Diminishing Fear/Increasing Assertiveness Not being passive to the abuser (I) Speak out and let people know you are not alone Have someone to support you (I) Take one day at a time, or less as necessary (C)	2.96	0.57	9	11

Note. Importance, cohesion, *N*, and % items in clusters are in order of importance. For each cluster, the statement rated as most important (I) and the statement rated as most central (C) to the cluster is listed.

is located due south, is rated as the most important cluster, and contains 8% of the brainstormed statements. This idea encompasses personal and public awareness, control, courage, and effectiveness. Brainstorming statements included "Having the power and control to say no and be effective," "Challenging (in thought or action) the mental health system," and "Being able to stand up for what you believe in, even if alone." The cluster also included "Recognizing revictimization and putting a stop to it" and "Taking those who abused you to task." "Being an advocate" was also included in this idea cluster, but had a high bridging value, indicating that it was not central to this idea.

Positive Struggle Zone, the adjacent cluster to the east, reflects confidence in one's own internal cues, including questioning diagnostic labels, and a willingness to take risks and make mistakes. It contains 15% of the brainstormed statements and is the second largest cluster on the map. The most central items were "Having much love for myself," "Separating my stuff from others' stuff," "Having the confidence to say what I really feel and it doesn't matter what someone else says," "Learning to rely on my instincts," and "Not questioning myself based on someone else's reactions." The most important statement was "Accepting yourself the way you are." In this cluster, women also included statements such as "Giving myself permission to make mistakes" and "Taking a minute to think and not act impulsively." Here, the women also indicated that the effects of abuse are different for different people, even in the same family. "Part of me never bought into the mental illness diagnosis" was included here, but was not central to the cluster. Taken as a whole, these statements provide a transition from the strength of personal empowerment and positive struggle, to *Self-Acceptance and Building Confidence* at the map's east point, which contains more tentative and complex statements.

Self-Acceptance and Building Confidence, the largest cluster on the women's map, contains 19% of the brainstormed statements. The statements rated as very important in this cluster were "Not blaming myself anymore," "Being able to interpret the difference between nightmares and what really happened," and "Knowing I have choices." Self-acceptance includes, besides moving past self-blame, accepting all of one's feelings—good or bad—and the bittersweet understanding that "I am who I am because of what I've been through." This last statement was most central to this cluster, as were "Not dissociating and splitting off," "Not feeling guilty about my feelings—good and bad," "Not confusing authority with perpetrators," and "Not being so frightened." Many statements in this cluster reflect the complexity of a whole life: knowing that healing is painful, that not all authority figures are perpetrators, and that one's own reactions are human, and not necessarily reflections of a diagnosis.

In this model, confidence is built on a whole and cohesive self. The second most central item in *Self-Acceptance and Building Confidence* is "Not dissociating to go off the memory, and splitting off." Many other statements in this cluster reflect this concern with difficulties self-grounding in the present: "Not being fearful of sleep because you might wake up as another person," "Distinguishing real physical symptoms from body memories," and "Knowing when feelings of shame are connected to past history versus what is happening in the present." Trusting self and time connects to additional statements: "Not being so frightened anymore" and not needing "To sleep or sleep it away."

At the map's west point is *Trusting Self to Make Choices*, another of the four clusters rated as most important. This cluster is about awareness, competence, and choice. It contains 11% of the statements brainstormed, and most central to it are awareness of one's triggers, the ability to distinguish what is real from what is not, and having hope. Less central, but rated as highly important, are statements about being a competent, nonabusive parent and making choices about sex and sexuality. These border on the cluster slightly to the south named *Reconstructing Sexuality*.

Reconstructing Sexuality contains 7% of the brainstormed statements. Its central ideas concern not feeling guilty about sexual activity, choosing sexual activity, and separating love from sex. "Awareness of one's child's sexuality" is located at the periphery of this cluster, with a high bridging value, indicating that it is not central to the idea. The cluster has an odd appearance on the map because survivors in the interpretive meetings came to a consensus that forgiving the perpetrator, the statement with the lowest importance rating of any of the 84 statements, should remain separate from the others. It is depicted as a lone statement in the map and in Table 9.2.

At the map's north end are three idea clusters that ranked in the middle of the importance scale. The most important of this group, adjacent to *Self-Acceptance and Building Confidence*, is the idea of *Learning to Cope with Emotions*, which contains 9% of the brainstormed items. Central to this idea cluster is the struggle with feeling abandoned and alone. Most important is acknowledging that sexual abuse happened. It includes "Not feeling so abandoned when my therapist is away," "Not needing to separate yourself from others all the time," "Feeling helpless, with no control over the abuse," " Learning not to drink and drug about problems," and "Turning 'I can't' into 'I can.'" The statement that healing requires a person to acknowledge that abuse happened transitions us into the northernmost cluster of *Awakening and Self-Validation*.

Awakening and Self-Validation contains 12% of the statements, including belief and awareness that sexual abuse happened, the ability to talk about abuse, to identify with the literature, and to write about one's feelings. Besides these connections to others (the metaphorical images are less central to the idea being expressed in the cluster), people saw awakening as "Being able to visualize a more whole self." One person likened the experience to "Feeling like a puzzle and ... daring to pick up the pieces and put them where they belong." The ideas of access to the broad and public community of survivors who write and speak about their experiences also provides a transition to the adjacent cluster to the west, *Building Support/Self-Help*.

Building Support/Self-Help contains 8% of the brainstormed statements. It is one of the less cohesive clusters, on the basis of its average bridging value. The statements most central to this idea reflect reconnection with a community of positive, nurturing people whom one can choose as family, as well as with the larger community of those who write and talk about abuse. Here, the survivor herself also talks about abuse. Strong images convey the support and hope of the statements in this cluster: "No hole anymore in my heart or in my body" and "I can see light at the end of the tunnel." The bridging values of these imagined statements indicate that they are not central to the cluster. Their metaphoric nature may have made it difficult for the women to consistently place them with similar statements.

The Men's Healing Map

The men's map is presented in Figure 9.2. Look at the men's map going from east, counterclockwise to north. There are three clusters that move from early awareness of the abuse (*Awareness/Beginning Understanding*) through *Changing Thoughts and Feelings, Learning and Understanding*, and *Leading Toward Normalization* to *Accepting Love and Trust from Self and Others*. The men rated these statements and ideas, on average, as very important, and tended to frame their statements as recommendations.

The most important idea for the men is *Changing Thoughts and Feelings*. Most importantly, to heal, a person needs to "Be able to cry and experience feelings—don't run" and to "Learn to accept your anger and decrease your guilt." Most central to *Changing Thoughts and Feelings* were "No longer having suicidal thoughts" and "Develop positive ways to ventilate anger, like pursuing a desired goal." The men saw that it is key to "Learn to recognize feelings" to deal with and change them, and that "Decreased self-abuse" is a landmark in healing. This cluster contained 10% of the brainstormed statements.

The adjacent and still highly important idea, *Awareness/Beginning Understanding* contains 15% of the statements. Here, the strongest theme is the men's understanding that they were not to blame for what happened: "Become a survivor, not a victim," "Forgive yourself because you're not to blame." The most central statements to this idea dealt with anger and negative feelings: "It's ok to be angry," "Be aware of your own angry retribution tendencies," and the less central "Don't be afraid of negative feelings." In this dimension of healing the men suggest that healing requires a person to "Look at your strengths instead of weaknesses," "Take care of your physical and mental health" and "Start working on the problem as soon as it happens." The men were also optimistic: "Have faith that compulsions can be overcome."

The next cluster, *Learning and Understanding About Sexual Abuse* is compact, containing 5% of the men's statements. Most important to this concept is a statement reiterated in the cluster's name: "Learn more about sexual abuse." Most central is to "Attend groups and get different points of view." Part of understanding is to "Recognize that abnormal reactions to abnormal situations are normal" and to "Be able to mourn the loss of childhood."

In the next idea cluster, which contains 6% of their statements, the men continue to focus on normalizing their experience. Most central to *Leading Toward Normalization as a Process* is minimizing shame, anger, and the negative thoughts associated with the abuse. Most important to this idea is to "Be able to disclose abuse to professionals." The men also include in this cluster a connection that diminishes the isolation and stigma of a psychiatric diagnosis: "Many times abuse leads to mental illness."

Overcoming and Fulfillment, at the base of the men's map, contained 10% of the brainstormed statements. Most important to this idea was "Empower yourself"; most central was to "Look for equality in relationships." Also central to overcoming is to "Be assertive and stop being manipulated" and to be assertive about the privacy of one's sexual orientation. The men also talked about the "Desire to help others," "Reaching out," "Having a vocation and/or avocation," and being able to "Resist manipulating others."

A set of ideas moves down the center of the map and this set was rated medium in importance. These were *No Longer Behaving as a Victim, Understanding How to Take Care of Yourself, Taking Care of Yourself,* and *Overcoming and Fulfillment*. The first of these, *No Longer Behaving as a Victim*, contains 8% of the brainstormed statements. Here, men suggest that it is important to "Watch for signs of relapse or triggers" and to "Understand how to develop healthy relationships with boundaries." Most central to not being a victim is "Learn to say no about anything." Healing in this dimension also includes not having self-pity, incorporating old and new selves into one integrated self, and "Learning how to accept nurturing."

Understanding How to Take Care of Yourself (10% of the items) and *Taking Care of Yourself* (14% of the items) both describe a point of view needed for recovery. Most important is, "Have someone to support you." Most centrally is, "Take one day at a time, or less if necessary," and "Know that your emotions and feelings are normal, even though you are a man." Other points in this idea cluster include the following advice: "Don't sabotage your achievements," "Don't dwell on the past," "Be kind to yourself," "Participate in activities," "Cultivate positive thoughts," and "Look to the future rather than the past." This dimension of *Understanding How to Take Care of Yourself* links quite naturally to the most central notion in *Taking Care of Yourself*: "Look to the future." This cluster also includes the conviction that sexual abuse can be overcome, with awareness of setbacks and kindness for oneself as most important. More specifically, the men advised others to "Beware the dangers of substance use" and "Do reality checks and get a second opinion." Taking care of yourself also includes enjoying activities and life in general. One person suggested "Making yourself look and feel rich for a day." Here the men talked about self-protection and about the struggles that male abuse survivors have with social gender norms that do not allow men to easily access and accept their feelings.

In *Accepting Love and Trust from Self and Others*, which contains 10% of the statements, the men discussed reconnection in terms of family ties, their own sexuality and parenting, and accepting genuinely offered love and trust from others. Most important to this idea is to "Be able to accept love and trust from others when it's genuinely offered." Most central is to "Explore the abuse as soon as possible." "I know that I am not alone" is also a key statement in this cluster.

Finally, there is a cluster in the southwest corner of the men's map called *Diminishing Fear/Increasing Assertiveness*. This cluster, containing 11% of the brainstormed items, had the lowest importance rating for the men. Here men discussed how they deal with the pervasive presence of the abuser: "Knowing that not everyone is an abuser," "Reaching out to the abuser," "Fighting the abuser," "Not being passive to the abuser," and "Repairing relationships that were damaged because of the abuse." The theme of reaching out and helping others from the adjacent idea cluster continues here with statements about engaging in personal and political advocacy activities: "Speak out and let people know you are not alone."

SUMMARY

These maps are visual and dynamic representations of frameworks generated by men and women survivors for healing from sexual abuse trauma. During the past 15 years, astute and compassionate clinicians and clinician/survivors, having identified a connection between childhood sexual abuse and the diffuse and debilitating problems of adults, have developed safe environments and techniques to help survivors recognize and grapple with the consequences of childhood sexual abuse (Alexander & Muenzenmaier, 1998; Bloom, 1997; Harris & Fallot, 2001; Herman, 1992; Miller, 1994; Najavits et al., 1998; van der Kolk, 2002; van der Kolk et al., 1996). These environments and techniques are all built on careful listening to their patients. But the direct and systematic expression by survivors of the dimensions they perceive as key to alleviating their suffering is rare and invaluable. It is risky and difficult for a group of both survivors and witnesses to engage their minds and emotions intensely over a prolonged period, in the struggle, uncertainty, power, and joy of overcoming abuse. These maps were developed at a time when psychiatric consumers were finding the voice to speak about the impact of childhood sexual abuse on their lives. A small group of survivors who had received major psychiatric diagnoses and who had frequent and intense contact with the mental health system were able to participate. They represent a small piece in a larger effort to overcome suffering that occurs when the integral relationships between self and self and between self and others become unraveled.

Both maps depict movement toward becoming a whole person that begins by validating that what happened was sexual abuse for which the survivor is not to blame. Access to the shared experiences of the larger community of survivors who have written or talked about their experiences, and to the more personal fellowship of support groups, helps people move past self-blame and the identity of victim. These varied perspectives on a similar experience of abuse allow survivors to place their own histories in a context, and to see how they have devised or could devise strategies for resilience in response to them. Survivors found it important to frame the abuse as atypical and themselves as human in their responses to it. As they mourn the loss of childhood and honor the people they have become because and in spite of their experiences, they come to forgive, accept, and love themselves. Their assumptions about the benevolence of the world are tempered, but not shattered, by the betrayal of trust they experienced (Janoff-Bulman, 1992).

In this model, survivors grouped together their awareness that they were, indeed, sexually abused, that the responsibility for those acts lay not with them, but with the perpetrator, and other ideas that expressed their personal autonomy: the ability to effectively disagree with and challenge authority and to stand up for their own beliefs. The men in particular felt that they needed to discard the role of victim and focus on their strengths. Survivors connected their ability to acknowledge that they were abused to their ability to challenge dominant structures, to say no, and to be effective. The major organizing concepts in mental health systems stress biological etiologies of brain disorders, and do not easily accommodate the difficulties of sexual abuse survivors that appear to result from a complex interaction between environment and physiological and psychological responses to long-term stress (MacFarlane, Golier, & Yehuda, 2002; Yehuda, 2001). The maps show that for survivors, seeing this relationship is essential to their healing. Going yet another step, both men and women stressed their need to see their own humanity, rather than a diagnostic label, in their behavior and reactions.

To build confidence in their own experiences into their lives, survivors must at a minimum be able to rely on the enduring integrity, or cohesion, of time and self. Studies consistently show that childhood abuse and neglect impair individuals' capacities to monitor and modulate their emotions (Cicchetti & Toth, 1995; Rodriguez, Ryan, van der Kamp, & Foy, 1997). As they move toward healing, survivors of childhood sexual abuse tell us that their connection to all of their emotions, including anger and negative feelings, and even the joy is enhanced. In these models, survivors identified new or reestablished trust in their bodies and minds as signs of healing, including the self-awareness and control to diminish the power of triggers. Because survivors of early and long-term abuse were victimized in familiar, everyday environments, by people they knew well, they continue to be surrounded by everyday, familiar sounds, smells, sights, and interactions that can reinduce their repeated physical experiences of terror and the strong emotions and coping strategies that followed. As children, they lived with the perpetrator's construction of their relationship, and frequently their emotional and even physical survival depended on their ability to take their minds away, or to suppress overwhelming rage. In this model, when survivors can trust that they can remain grounded in reality, they find that their fears diminish.

Men and women identified many similar elements in the healing process: They needed to validate their experience of abuse; to trust their own sense of self; to accept and control strong feelings like anger, sadness, shame, and guilt; to stay in the present; to accept the support of others; and to provide help and support to others. But men and women named and rated groups of ideas differently, reflecting differences in their thinking about how the elements fit together in the healing process.

The most pronounced difference was the importance men placed on learning to cope with strong emotions compared to the importance women placed on personal empowerment and self-trust. Besides this, women focused on gaining control over splitting off from the present. As they healed they were not fearful of waking up as another person; they could distinguish real, physical symptoms from body memories, or shame about the past from discomfort in the present. They reported that they need to move past the numbing and self-fragmenting aspects of a trauma response, including excessive sleep, and dissociation. The men did not bring up dissociation. Instead, they identified reality checks, which call on sources of social support, as helpful, and they stressed awareness of the dangers of using alcohol, drugs, or sleep to escape. The men stressed their need to learn how to recognize and cope with their anger and desire for retribution as well as their self-directed rage and despair The women were more attuned to learning to trust their experience of anger and to become assertive Men and women also constructed their statements differently as well. Many of the women's statements were process oriented (e.g. "Turning I can't into I can"), while many of the men's statements were directive (e.g. "Be kind to yourself").

It is both empowering and fulfilling for a person to meet the challenge of moving past victimization to experience vulnerability with a sense of safety. Through individual and group trauma work, survivors can learn to identify and disrupt the cycles of trigger–fear–dissociation, trigger–rage–outburst, trigger–shame–despair by using words, images, and other cognitive associations to locate the trauma at its true distance: in the past rather than the present (van der Kolk, 2002). These symptom- and behavior-focused skills are necessary, even critical, and need to be developed for people with severe mental illness diagnoses who use public sector services (Mueser, Rosenberg, Goodman, & Trumbetta, 2002; Mueser & Taylor, 1997; Rosenberg et al., 2001). But the healing models described here, as well as models of trauma-informed services (Harris & Fallot, 2001) show that symptoms and behaviors are not the whole story.

Trauma survivors in these models are keenly aware of how damaging isolation and secrecy are and how they perpetuate victimhood. Trauma-sensitive providers are clear, too, that treatment is not just about addressing symptoms, but for different people at different times involves the quality of a person's life—their family relationships, their employment and vocational aspirations or frustrations, their friendships, and the meaning of their lives (MacFarlane et al., 2002). Healing, then, from sexual abuse does not just involve the person-centered work of self-knowledge and self-management. Personal struggles toward courage, compassion, separation, and self-reliance, rated as very important, form the foundation for the healing process. Environments, communities of peers, support groups, and therapeutic groups need to provide the space for learning about and sharing the effects of sexual abuse on people's concepts of self and others. These environments can promote the basic elements of healing identified by survivors in these maps: moving past the victim identity, self-blame isolation, and fragmentation.

The recently completed SAMHSA project to create trauma-informed and trauma-specific service models for women with co-occurring mental illness and substance abuse problems has identified several approaches that may be helpful (Moses, Reed, Mazelis, & D'Ambrosio, 2003) The maps indicate that community and relationship are essential to taking care of oneself in moving toward the sense of overcoming and empowerment. Becoming a whole person and moving into relationship with others is as central to healing from childhood sexual abuse as it is to recovery from mental illness (Ralph, Kidder, & Lambric, 2000; Ridgeway, 1999) and, indeed, to dealing with the suffering that attends many forms of medical disability. People may need to rely on the strength of others until his or her own personhood is intact (Cassell, 1991). But those who take these supportive roles, including the survivor, must strike a balance between a survivor's fragility and his or her emerging self-reliance and separation, which are central to the healing models described here. Genuine relationship in the endeavor of recovery requires such risk (Mead, personal communication, December 2002).

Survivors agree that they must look at where they stand in relationship to the perpetrator of their abuse and to those who allowed it to happen. This includes, certainly, avoiding revictimization, and goes on to holding accountable the perpetrator and those who kept silent or who did not believe them responsible. It moves from the past to the future, as survivors themselves take care not to allow abuse to be perpetuated across generations and in other situations. People are most competent in key adult social roles, like mature friendship, parenting, and freely chosen sexuality when they have confidence in their own perceptions and judgments of world, self, and others. In the maps, these aspects of healing are closely aligned with awareness and self-regulation—knowing one's triggers and being grounded in reality—and with the desire to turn from the past to the future. The model moves, then, past despair at failure and toward pleasure in success and achievement. Across both maps, survivors stressed that they need to experience the entire range of their feelings, including a sense of surprise, joy, and pleasure. The women cite the overcoming of guilt at experiencing sexual pleasure as they reconstruct their sexuality. There is playfulness in the men's suggestion that taking care of yourself might include making yourself look and feel rich for a day.

As people look ahead, they define themselves in new ways—seeing, for instance, that they can trust the choices they make. This is built on understanding and owning that the adults who abandon, with astonishing frequency, their charge to protect and care for children are responsible for the abuse they perpetrated. Survivors look for new ways to take care of themselves and to connect with others. Connection is most frequently and assuredly a personal and sometimes a private enterprise. But beside this individual re-creation of community, some survivors of sexual abuse are clear that they need to represent the interests of other survivors as well as their own in a public way. They feel that they can and should shape the future by directly building connection for others, or by working to change the assumptions and directions of the systems consumers negotiate as they construct their lives.

The impact of trauma on people's experience of their own vulnerability is profound. Survivors of childhood sexual abuse do not return to the place where they began. In some instances, when abuse pervaded their entire childhood, there is no beginning that does not include betrayal. But these initial models of healing underscore the human capacity to go beyond self-preservation. Survivors face their demons, master skills that enable them to manage the overwhelming emotions that once accompanied terror, develop sustainable relationships with themselves and with others, become competent and contributing adults, take pleasure as one does, and move beyond themselves to stand against personal and systemic violence. These efforts all take personal courage, but survivors cannot pick up the pieces in the puzzle that is the traumatized self by themselves. They rely on the strength, hope, and compassion of close and caring people. Every encounter that dares to share in this endeavor is a commitment to healing.

The work begun in partnership with survivors in this project continues with the development, pilot testing, and validation of a measure of healing from sexual abuse trauma that is based on the dimensions and statements developed in these concept maps.

REFERENCES

Alexander, M. J., & Muenzenmaier, K. (1998). Trauma, addiction and recovery: Addressing public health epidemics among women with severe mental illness. In B. L. Levin, A. Jennings, & A. Blanche (Eds.), *Women's mental health services: A public health perspective* (pp. 215–239). Thousand Oaks, CA: Sage.

American Psychiatric Association. (1994). *Diagnostic and statistical manual of mental disorders* (4th ed.). Washington, DC: Author.

Beck, J. C., & van der Kolk B. (1987). Reports of childhood incest and current behavior of chronically hospitalized psychotic women. *American Journal of Psychiatry, 144,* 1474–1476.

Bloom, S. L. (1997). *Creating Sanctuary: Toward the evolution of sane societies.* New York: Routledge.

Breslau, N., & Davis, G. C. (1992). Posttraumatic stress disorder in an urban population of young adults: Risk factors for chronicity. *American Journal of Psychiatry, 149,* 671–675.

Breslau, N., Kessler, R. C., & Chilcoat, H. D. (1998). Trauma & PTSD in the community: The 1996 Detroit Area Survey of Trauma. *Archives of General Psychiatry, 55,* 626–632.

Bryer, J. B., Nelson, B. A., Miller, J. B., & Krol, P. A. (1987). Childhood sexual and physical abuse as factors in adult psychiatric illness [Comment]. *American Journal of Psychiatry, 144,* 1426–1430.

Carmen, E., Rieker, P. P., & Mills, T. (1984). Victims of violence and psychiatric illness. *American Journal of Psychiatry, 141,* 373–383.

Cascardi, M., Mueser, K. T., DeGiralomo, J., & Murrin, M. (1996). Physical aggression against psychiatric inpatients by family members and partners. *Psychiatric Services, 47,* 531–533.

Cassell, E. J. (1991). *The nature of suffering and the goals of medicine.* New York: Oxford University Press.

Chassman, J. (1995). *Proceedings from a forum on individuals diagnosed with serious mental illness who are sexual abuse survivors. January, 1994.* Albany: New York State Office of Mental Health.

Cicchetti, D., & Toth, S. L. (1995). Developmental psychopathology and disorders of affect. In D. Cicchetti & D. J. Cohen (Eds.), *Developmental psychopathology, Vol. 2. Risk, disorder, & adaptation* (pp. 369–420). New York: Wiley.

Cole, C. (1988). Routine comprehensive inquiry for abuse: A justifiable clinical assessment procedure. *Clinical Social Work Journal, 16,* 33–42.

Courtois, C. (2002). *Advances in the treatment of complex, dissociative PTSD.* Paper presented at Nineteenth International Fall Conference of the International Society for the Study of Dissociation, Baltimore, MD.

Craine, L. S., Henson, C. E., Colliver, J. A., & MacLean, D. G. (1988). Prevalence of a history of sexual abuse among female psychiatric patients in a state hospital system. *Hospital and Community Psychiatry, 39,* 300–304.

Davidson, J. R., Hughes, D., Blazer, D. G., & George, L. K. (1991). PTSD in the community: An epidemiological study. *Psychological Medicine, 21*, 713–721.

Dumont, J. (1989). Validity of multidimensional scaling in the context of structured conceptualization. *Evaluation and Program Planning, 12*, 81.

Everitt, B. (1980). *Cluster analysis*. New York: Halsted Press.

Fisher, D. (1994). The empowerment model of recovery: Finding our voice and having a say. *National Empowerment Center Newsletter*. Retrieved (n.d.) from http://www.power2u.org

Ford, J. D., & Kidd, P. (1998). Early childhood trauma and disorders of extreme stress as predictors of treatment outcome with chronic posttraumatic stress disorder. *Journal of Traumatic Stress, 11*, 743–761.

Goodman, L. A., Dutton, M. A., & Harris, M. (1997). The relationship between violence dimensions and symptom severity among homeless, mentally ill women. *Journal of Traumatic Stress, 10*, 51–70.

Harris, M. (1997). *Sexual abuse trauma among women diagnosed with severe mental illness*. Newark, NJ: Gordon and Breach.

Harris, M., & Fallot, R. D. (2001). Evisioning a trauma-informed service system. In M. Harris & R. Fallot (Eds.), *New directions for mental health services using trauma theory to design service* (Vol. 89, pp. 3–22). San Francisco: Jossey-Bass.

Herman, J. L. (1992). *Trauma & Recovery*. New York: Basic Books.

Hutchings, P. S., & Dutton, M. A. (1993). Sexual assault history in a community mental health center clinical population. *Community Mental Health Journal, 29*, 59–63.

Jacobson, A. (1989). Physical and sexual assault histories among psychiatric outpatients. *American Journal of Psychiatry, 146*, 758.

Jacobson, A., & Herald, C. (1990). The relevance of childhood sexual abuse to adult psychiatric inpatient care. *Hospital and Community Psychiatry, 41*, 154–158.

Jacobson, A., & Richardson, B. (1987). Assault experiences of 100 psychiatric inpatients: Evidence of the need for routine inquiry. *American Journal of Psychiatry, 144*, 508–513.

Janoff-Bulman, R. (1992). *Shattered assumptions: Toward a new psychology of trauma*. New York: Free Press.

Jennings, A., & Ralph, R. O. (1997). *In their own words: Maine Trauma Advisory Groups Report*. Augusta, ME: Department of Mental Health, Mental Retardation, & Substance Abuse Services.

Kessler, R. C., Sonnega, A., Bromet, E., Hughes, M., & Nelson, C. B. (1995). PTSD in the National Comorbidity Survey. *Archives of General Psychiatry, 52*, 1048–1060.

Kruskal, J. B., & Wish, M. (1978). *Multidimensional scaling*. Beverly Hills, CA: Sage.

Lipschitz, D. S., Kaplan, M. L., Sorkenn, J. B., Faedda, G. L., Chorney, P., & Asnis, G. M. (1996). Prevalence and characteristics of physical and sexual abuse among psychiatric outpatients. *Psychiatric Services, 47*, 189–191.

MacFarlane, A. C., Golier, J., & Yehuda, R. (2002). Treatment planning for trauma survivors with PTSD: What does a clinician need to know before implementing

PTSD treatments? In R. Yehuda (Ed.), *Treating trauma survivors with PTSD* (pp. 1–20). Washington, DC: American Psychiatric Association.

Miller, D. (1994). *Women who hurt themselves: A book of hope and understanding.* New York: Basic Books.

Moses, D. J., Reed, B. G., Mazelis, R., & D'Ambrosio, B. (2003). *Creating trauma services for women with co-occurring disorder.* Washington, DC: Substance Abuse and Mental Health Services Administration.

Muenzenmaier, K., Meyer, I., Struening, E., & Ferber, J. (1993). Childhood abuse and neglect among women outpatients with chronic mental illness. *Hospital and Community Psychiatry, 44,* 666–670.

Mueser, K. T., Goodman, L. B., Trumbetta, S. L., Rosenberg, S. D., Osher, F. C., Vidaver, R., et al. (1998). Trauma and posttraumatic disorder in severe mental illness. *Journal of Consulting and Clinical Psychiatry, 66,* 493–499.

Mueser, K. T., Rosenberg, S. D., Goodman, L. A., & Trumbetta, S. L. (2002). Trauma, PTSD, and the course of severe mental illness: An interactive model. *Schizophrenia Research, 53,* 123–143.

Mueser, K. T., Salyers, M. P., Rosenberg, S. D., Ford, J. D., Fox, L., & Carty, P. (2001). A psychometric evaluation of trauma and PTSD: Assessments in persons with severe mental illness. *Psychological Assessment, 13,* 110–117.

Mueser, K. T., & Taylor, K. L. (1997). A cognitive-behavioral approach. In M. Harris & C. L. Landis (Eds.), *Sexual abuse in the lives of women diagnosed with severe mental illness* (pp. 67–90). Amsterdam: Harwood Academic Publishers.

Najavits, L. M., Weiss, R. D., Shaw, S. R., & Muenz, L. R. (1998). "Seeking Safety": Outcome of a new cognitive-behavioral psychotherapy for women with posttraumatic stress disorder and substance dependence. *Journal of Traumatic Stress, 11,* 437–456.

National Association of State Mental Health Directors. (1998). *Position statement on services and supports to trauma survivors.* Retrieved (n.d.) from http://www.nasmhpd.org/posstmb.htm

Neria, Y., Bromet, E. J., Sievers, S., Lavelle, J., & Fochtmann, L. J. (2002). Trauma exposure and posttraumatic stress disorder in psychosis: findings from a first-admission cohort. *Journal of Consulting and Clinical Psychiatry, 70,* 246–251.

Ralph, R. O., & the Recovery Advisory Group. (1999). *The recovery advisory group recovery model.* Washington, DC: National Conference on Mental Health Statistics.

Ralph, R. O. (2004). Verbal definitions and visual models of recovery: Focus on Recovery Advisory Group Recovery Model. In R. O. Ralph & P. Corrigan (Eds.), *Recovery and mental illness: Broadening our understanding of wellness.* Washington, DC: American Psychological Association.

Ralph, R. O., Kidder, K., & Lambric, P. (2000). *Can we measure recovery? A compendium of recovery & recovery related measures.* Cambridge, MA: Human Services Research Institute.

Ridgeway, P. (2001). Re-storying psychiatric disability: Learning from first person narrative accounts of recovery. *Psychiatric Rehabilitation Journal 24,* 335–343.

Rodriguez, N., Ryan, S. W., van der Kamp, H., & Foy, D. W. (1997). Posttraumatic stress disorder in adult female survivors of childhood sexual abuse: A comparison study. *Journal of Consulting and Clinical Psychiatry, 65*, 53–59.

Rose, S. M., Peabody, C. G., & Stratigeas, B. (1991). Undetected abuse among intensive case management clients. *Hospital and Community Psychiatry, 42*, 499–503.

Rosenberg, S. D., Mueser, K. T., Friedman, M. J., Gorman, P. G., Drake, R. E., Vidaver, R. M., et al. (2001). Developing effective treatments for posttraumatic disorders among people with severe mental illness. *Psychiatric Services, 52*, 1453–1461.

Rosenfeld, A. A. (1979). The clinical management of incest and sexual abuse of children. *Journal of the American Medical Association, 242*, 1761–1764.

Switzer, G. E., Dew, M. A., Thompson, K., Goycoolea, J. M., Derricott, T., & Mullins, S. D. (1999). Posttraumatic stress disorder and service utilization among urban mental health center clients. *Journal of Traumatic Stress, 12*, 25–39.

Trochim, W. M. (1989a). An introduction to concept mapping for planning and evaluation. *Evaluation, & Program Planning, 12*, 1–16.

Trochim, W. M. (1989b). Concept mapping: Soft science or hard art? *Evaluation & Program Planning*, 87–110.

van der Kolk, B. A. (2002). Assessment & treatment of complex PTSD. In R. Yehuda (Ed.), *Treating trauma survivors with PTSD* (pp. 127–156). Washington, DC: American Psychiatric Association.

van der Kolk, B. A., MacFarlane, A. C., & van der Hart, O. (1996). A general approach to treatment of posttraumatic stress disorder. In B. A. van der Kolk, A. C. MacFarlane, & L. Weisaeth (Eds.), *Traumatic stress: The effects of overwhelming experience on mind, body, & society* (pp. 417–440). New York: Guilford Press.

Yehuda, R. (2001). Biology of posttraumatic stress disorder. *Journal of Clinical Psychiatry, 62*(Suppl. 17), 41–46.

10

RECOVERY FROM ADDICTION AND FROM MENTAL ILLNESS: SHARED AND CONTRASTING LESSONS

WILLIAM WHITE, MICHAEL BOYLE, AND DAVID LOVELAND

A qualitative shift is occurring in the conceptual foundation and design of behavioral health services. Grassroots advocacy movements and a growing body of longitudinal research are challenging mental health and addiction treatment service providers to refocus their services toward the goals and processes of long-term recovery. In the mental health field, the "ex-patients' survivor" movement of the 1970s (Chamberlin, 1978) was followed by new "consumer" voices in the 1980s (Deegan, 1988; Unzicker, 1989) and the christening of the 1990s as the "decade of recovery" (Anthony, 1993). Dramatic changes in the conceptual underpinnings of mental health treatment

Work on this chapter was supported by the Behavioral Health Recovery Management project, a joint venture of Fayette Companies, Chestnut Health Systems, and the University of Chicago Center for Psychiatric Rehabilitation funded by the Illinois Department of Human Services' Office of Alcoholism and Substance Abuse.

were spurred by research studies confirming that between half and two thirds of people with serious mental illness achieve substantial recovery (Harding, 1989; Harding, Brooks, Ashikaga, Strauss, & Breier, 1987; Harding, Zubin, & Strauss, 1992; Strauss, Hafez, Lieberman, & Harding, 1985). Today, well-organized consumer/survivor/ex-patient (C/S/X) groups and visionary professionals are moving beyond the call for "recovery-oriented" systems of care to actually create such systems (Anthony, 2000).

The addiction treatment field is being similarly challenged by a "New Recovery Advocacy Movement" led by recovering people and their families (White, 2000b, 2001a). These recovery advocates and their professional allies are demanding that addiction treatment be reconnected to the larger and more enduring process of recovery, and that treatment shift from serial episodes of unconnected acute interventions to a model of sustained recovery management (McLellan, Lewis, O'Brien, & Kleber, 2000; White, Boyle, & Loveland, 2002). The consumer and professional renewal movements within the mental health and addiction treatment fields have much that they can learn from one another. Both movements are trying to shift the focus of services from symptom suppression to global health and development. Both are trying to balance the preoccupation with managing social costs with more qualitative measures of service outcomes, for example, post-treatment meaningfulness and quality of life. Yet, each field brings areas of marked contrast. Such similarities and differences suggest the potential for positive synergy between the two fields.

In this chapter, we attempt to do three things. First, we compare and contrast the experiences and processes of recovery from addiction with recovery from psychiatric disability. Second, we explore lessons learned within the addictions field about recovery mutual-aid groups and their potential role in long-term recovery. Third, we explore what has been learned within recovery advocacy movements in the addictions field that may have relevance to parallel movements within the mental health field. Our focus is on lessons learned within the addictions field that may have relevance to personal recovery from psychiatric disability and to mutual-aid and political advocacy movements organized by and on behalf of people who have experienced psychiatric disability. Before drawing on the addictions literature, we begin by exploring the emerging concept of recovery in the mental health field.

THE RECOVERY EXPERIENCE

A common theme noted throughout this book, and a theme that is central to the C/S/X movement, is that recovery from mental illness must be defined as a complex, dynamic, and enduring process rather than a biological end state described by an absence of symptoms. Recovery is, in its essence, a lived experience of moving through and beyond the limitations of one's disorder. Viewing recovery in terms of an ongoing and highly personalized experience, rather than a biomedical disease, is a new and radical concept in the mental health field and one that requires a paradigm shift in how we think, how we design service systems, and how we conduct clinical research.

A Process of Healing: Treatment Versus Recovery

Recovery from mental illness is the process of healing the effects of (a) one's illness and its consequences, (b) the social stigma attached to the illness, and (c) the iatrogenic effects of treatment interventions (Spaniol, Gagne & Koehler, 2003). Recovery implies a process of retrieval (regaining what was lost because of one's illness and its treatment) and a process of discovery (moving beyond the illness and its limitations).

Treatment of mental illness and recovery from mental illness are not the same. Treatment encompasses the way professionals intervene to stabilize or alter the course of an illness; recovery is the personal experience of the individual as he or she moves out of illness into health and wholeness (Onken, Dumont, Ridgway, Dornan, & Ralph, 2002). Recovery is the experiential shift from despair to hope, alienation to purpose, isolation to relationship, withdrawal to involvement, and from passive adjustment to active coping (Ridgway, 2001). Recovery can occur within or outside the context of professionally directed treatment, and where professional treatment is involved, it may, depending on its orientation and methods, play a facilitative, insignificant, or inhibiting role in the recovery process (Onken et al., 2002). Recovery can be claimed only by the person in recovery, and that ownership includes the right to take risks, make mistakes, and learn from one's experiences (Deegan, 1992).

Recovery Is a Continuum

Recovery exists on a continuum of improved health and functioning. The mental health field is just now developing a multidimensional concept of recovery. It has long embraced a concept of partial recovery (some residual disability with reduced social costs and improved health and functioning), but has lacked a vision of full recovery from severe mental illness (minimal residual disability and resumption of preillness levels of health and functioning) (Anthony, 1993; Ralph, 2000). In contrast, the addiction treatment field has for more than 150 years had a clear concept of full recovery (sustained abstinence and increased emotional and relational health), but has lacked an operational concept of partial recovery (reduced frequency and intensity of alcohol and other drug use and related problems and increased quality of life). Both fields are struggling to correct this imbalance. It may also be time for both fields to recognize within the growing body of recovery narratives the existence of what might be called *transcendent recovery* (minimal residual disability and the achievement of health, functioning, and quality of life superior to that which existed before the onset of illness). The concept of transcendent recovery acknowledges the existence of people who, following the experience of addiction or mental illness, get "better than well," not in spite of the illness but because of the experiences and insight that emerged within their recovery processes (Young & Ensing, 1999).

Recovery Debts and Capital

The potential for recovery and the quality of recovery are determined by the synergy between recovery debits (personal and environmental factors that inhibit and limit recovery) and recovery capital (internal and external resources that serve to initiate, sustain, and expand recovery) (Granfield & Cloud, 1999). This is a lesson from the addictions field that is now being rediscovered in the mental health field. In what is likely to be a milestone study, Onken and colleagues (2002) explore the interaction of recovery facilitating and inhibiting factors that are drawn from the experiences of individuals in recovery from mental illness. They conclude that such factors exist at multiple, interacting levels: characteristics of the individual (e.g., the presence or lack of hope, resourcefulness, self-reliance, recovery self-management skills), characteristics of the environment (e.g., the presence or lack of safety-enhancing material resources—housing, transportation, health care, and a means of communication), and characteristics of the interaction between the individual and the environment (e.g., the presence or lack of meaningful relationships and activities, choices, empowering service, and peer relationships).

Varieties of Recovery Paths

The addictions field has begun to document the many pathways to, and varieties of, recovery experience (Humphreys, Moos, & Finney, 1995; Vaillant, 1983). The course and outcome of alcohol and other drug problems vary across transient and persistent patterns. The former are amenable to self-resolution or brief professional intervention, whereas the latter often require sustained professional- and peer-based supports (Kandel & Raveis, 1989). Those with a more prolonged course are often marked by greater personal vulnerability (e.g., family history, lower age of onset), greater problem severity, interlocked co-occurring problems, and low family and social supports. Recovery styles span natural recovery (without the aid of professional or peer support), peer-assisted recovery (mutual-aid involvement), and professionally assisted recovery (professional treatment). Although the body of research on natural recovery from addiction is growing (Granfield & Cloud, 1999), the absence of comparable data in the mental health field raises two important questions: (a) What is the prevalence of natural recovery among people with different types of mental illness? (b) How do those who experience natural recovery differ from those treated by mental health agencies?

Diversity of Recovery Styles

There are variations in recovery style based on the extent to which one's disorder becomes a central part of one's identity and one's degree of affiliation with a larger community of recovering people. In the addiction recovery arena, there are acultural styles of recovery (no affiliation with other recovering people), bicultural styles of recovery (affiliation with recovering people and people without addiction–recovery backgrounds), and culturally enmeshed styles of recovery (immersion in a culture of recovery; White, 1996). People in recovery display highly variable but viable styles of relationship to professionally directed treatment, peer-driven support services, and mutual-aid societies. The addictions field is slowly (and painfully) learning to work within this variability of styles rather than attempting to program all recovery experiences through a narrow vision of how recovery must be achieved and sustained. A cartography of pathways and styles of recovery from mental illness has yet to be drawn.

Self as Agent of Recovery

The role of self is essential to understanding the process of recovering from mental illness; the self, not the service professional, is the "agent of recovery" (Davidson & Strauss, 1992; Spaniol et al., 2003). Recovering people are more than passive recipients of recovery. Although they may draw on the clinical technologies of professional helpers and the experience, strength, and hope of others in recovery, each recovering person must ultimately become the architect and engineer of his or her own recovery. Recovery involves a reconstruction of personal identity, a reformulation of the relationship between self and illness, and a reconstruction of one's relationship with the world. These dimensions are often evident in the three-part story style of people in recovery: (a) the way it was (depiction of the onset and course of the illness), (b) what happened (the experience of recovery initiation), and (c) what it is like now (depiction of life in recovery; White, 1996).

Transformational Versus Incremental Change

The initiation of recovery may be marked by processes of transformational or incremental change. The former, which has been christened "quantum change," involves sudden, recovery-inducing experiences that are dramatic, unplanned, positive, and enduring (Miller & C' de Baca, 2001). Whereas quantum change has long been noted within the history of addiction recovery (White, 1998), the authors are aware of no studies exploring the role of quantum change experiences in initiating recovery from severe mental illness. In contrast, several studies have explored the developmental stages of long-term recovery from addiction (Brown, 1985; Prochaska, DiClimente, & Norcross, 1992) and from mental illness (Davidson & Strauss, 1992; Jacobson, 2001; Morse, 1997; Ridgway, 2001; Strauss & Carpenter, 1981; Weaver Randall, 2000; Young & Ensing, 1999). These stage models of recovery depict a process of recovery initiation (acceptance of one's illness, hope and resolution for change, first steps toward self-management), a process of stabilization (ownership and active management of one's own recovery), a mastery of rituals of daily living (increased comfort and confidence), self-monitoring and active efforts to prevent relapse (deepened insight about self in relationship to illness), and a sustained movement toward health and wholeness (increased quality of life via greater independence, self-acceptance, a safe and pleasant living environment, satisfying relationships, and meaningful activities). Studies of addiction have revealed that those factors required to initiate recovery are often quite different than the factors that later serve to maintain and enrich recovery (Humphreys et al., 1995). This suggests that interventions helpful at one stage of recovery may be ineffective or even harmful at other stages. For example, continuing to provide caretaker functions within an assertive community treatment model could well have iatrogenic effects on individuals who are developmentally ready to take ownership of their own recovery. The extent to which these developmental stages of recovery differ by type, severity, and duration of illness and across developmental age, gender, and culture is an important research agenda.

Developmental Stages of Recovery

Critical developmental opportunities arise within the course of mental illness that constitute doorways of entry into recovery or opportunities to move from one stage of recovery to another (Young & Ensing, 1999). These milestones can mark a shift either toward greater problem severity or the initiation or qualitative strengthening of recovery. When such transitional experiences initiate or deepen recovery, they are nearly always characterized by a synergy of pain and hope. This birth of hope that is such a central theme in recovery narratives almost always occurs in the context of relationships and resources beyond the self, and often occurs through encounters with the experience, strength, and hope of others in recovery. Historically, the addiction field believed that recovery initiation was grounded in the experience of pain ("hitting bottom"), but there is growing recognition that the deepest despair incites recovery only in the presence of hope. It is often at the point of this synergy of pain and hope that people experiencing addiction or mental illness, like the mythical phoenix, rise from the ashes of their own self-destruction (Johnson, 1993; White, 1996).

Zones of Recovery

Recovery occurs at a different pace across a number of zones: physical, intellectual, emotional, relational, personal (rituals of daily living), and spiritual. Progress in one zone can help prime and sustain additional positive change within and across other zones. For example, addictions research has confirmed that successfully quitting smoking can bolster one's confidence in achieving abstinence from other addictive drugs (Burman, 1997) and that those in remission from problem drinking are more than three times as likely to quit smoking as those continuing to drink (Breslau, Peterson, Schultz, Anderski, & Chilcoat, 1996). This represents a form of solution synergy through which accumulating successes deepen and expand the range of recovery effects.

Spirituality

Spirituality is a potentially important but often ill-understood ingredient of the recovery process (Sullivan, 1994). The role of spirituality to provide hope, to neutralize stigma and shame, and to bolster strength and courage is frequently noted in recovery narratives (White, 1996; Young & Ensing, 1999). The addictions field has a long history of emphasizing the role of spirituality in the recovery process—so much so that purely secular frameworks of recovery are lauded as innovations. Mental health professionals are just beginning to explore the role of spirituality in recovery (e.g., see Liberman & Kopelowicz, 2002; Lindgren & Coursey, 1995; Noordsy et al., 2002). What the addictions field is slowly learning is that, like many aspects of recovery, spirituality is a highly personal experience and a choice, not something to be codified within a "program."

Dual and Serial Recovery

People recovering from two or more co-occurring problems may address these interacting processes simultaneously (dual recovery) or sequentially (serial recovery). People may be at different stages or levels of motivation for addressing various problems that they are experiencing (Prochaska, Norcross, & DiClemente, 1994). The same person can experience differential rates of recovery from multiple disorders/experiences, for example, mental illness, addiction, traumatic victimization, and loss.

Medication-Assisted Recovery

The relationship between medication and recovery is a complex and potentially stage-dependent one. The addiction and mental health fields have histories that underscore the value as well as the potential iatrogenic effects of medications on the recovery process. The mental health field has had a bias toward medication, including medications with severe and debilitating side effects (e.g., Cohen, 1994; Cohen & McCubbin, 1990; Valenstein, 1998). The addictions field has had a bias against medication, even when those medications, such as methadone, have had overwhelming research support for their safety and efficacy. The narratives of recovering people emphasize that medication can facilitate or hinder recovery and that symptom elimination or minimization via medication, in and of itself, does not constitute recovery. The future promises more effective medications and a widening menu of alternatives and adjuncts to medication.

Family Context of Recovery

Both illness and recovery require substantial adaptational energy of one's family and social network (Brown, 1994; Brown & Lewis, 1999). The responses of family members to illness and disability and to stages of recovery represent normal rather than pathological reactions. Family recovery is the process of finding the best ways to adapt to the presence and then the absence of illness as an organizing motif within the family system. Developmental stages of family recovery may parallel the stages of personal recovery. It has been suggested that family members make these adaptations in their own style and at their own pace (Spaniol & Zipple, 1994). There is a marked absence of research on how family members of people with severe mental illness and the family as a whole recover from the impact of mental illness and its associated stigma. In the addictions field, interest in this area evolved from the concept of co-alcoholism, into offering "family programs," to the emergence, corruption (by overextension), and commercialization of the concept of codependence. The latter stage created an ideological backlash that has diminished interest in this area by clinicians and researchers.

Transcending Stigma

Recovery involves transcending the stigma that has been attached to addiction or mental illness. Stigma within the larger culture creates conceptual (how one sees oneself) and concrete (discrimination resulting from how one is seen by others) barriers to recovery. Stigma-shaped practices within treatment systems have also served to depersonalize and dehumanize. Deegan (1990) has collectively christened such practices as "spirit-breaking." Confronting and exorcising stigma within oneself (self-healing) and within one's environment (political advocacy) are parallel dimensions of the recovery process.

The Language of Recovery

Language is important to personal recovery (Spaniol & Cattaneo, 1997; White, 2001c). Words are the conceptual building blocks of recovery. The ability of recovering people to coin or select words that accurately and respectfully portray their experiences and aspirations is a crucial dimension of the personal recovery experience. Words have long been used to objectify and demonize people experiencing mental illness and substance use disorders. In recovery, alternative words become instruments of personal and collective liberation. Crafting language is about personal and social change, not political correctness.

Recovery Experts

Recovering people have served as "wounded healers" for more than two centuries within the addictions field, with such service work providing a boon to others and a source of strength within their own recovery processes (White, 2000a). Although the mental health field has acknowledged that recovering people can become their own recovery experts (Deegan, 1992), until recently, the field excluded consumers from service provider roles. Indications, however, seem to point to a growing appreciation for consumer-providers or ex-consumer-providers in all levels of service provision (e.g., see Basto, Pratt, Gill, & Barrett, 2000; Carlson, Rapp, & McDiarmid, 2001; Mowbray, Moxley, Jasper, & Howell, 1997; Salzar & Shear, 2002). A few important lessons from this tradition within the addictions field may be important for the rising "prosumer" movement (the inclusion of individuals who are former service consumers in paid service delivery roles) in the mental health field:

- Paid service work, in and of itself, is not a program of personal recovery and, for some individuals, can pose a significant obstacle to recovery. (The potential for relapse of recovering alcoholics working in the field of alcoholism treatment has been well-documented; see White, 1979, and White, 2000a.)
- People in recovery can work as prosumers in circumstances that are empowering to their recoveries (e.g., treated with respect, held accountable, and provided salaries commensurate with their work) or work in circumstances that are disempowering (e.g., treated as "senior clients," hired as token consumers via minimal or lack of comparable performance expectations, exploited financially via low pay and excessive and undesirable hours, and abandoned and discarded in the face of relapse).

- People in recovery can become so professionalized that assets drawn from their own recovery experiences are lost.
- There is a danger that recruiting people from recovery networks into paid service jobs could undermine the service ethic within those networks. It is very important that distinctions be made between services for which one is paid and service work that is done as part of one's personal recovery process.
- Although those who hold dual roles as consumers and service providers may serve as "translators" (interpreting and synthesizing the multiple voices within the mental health recovery advocacy movement; Frese, 1998), the experiences of consumer-providers may not be representative of the larger community of recovering people, and the consumer-provider must avoid the problem of "double agentry"—representing themselves as the voice of consumers, yet consciously or unconsciously representing their own financial interests or the institutional interests of service providers.
- People in recovery hired into service roles can benefit from special training and supervision on managing issues related to this duality of roles (see expanded discussion later in this chapter).

RECOVERY MUTUAL-AID GROUPS: A BRIEF HISTORY

Peer-based systems of mutual support for addiction recovery predate the professionalized field of addiction treatment, and their continued importance in long-term recovery support is a unique aspect of the addictions field. Such systems of mutual aid (reciprocal support as a solution to a shared problem) are distinguished from "self-help" approaches (efforts made by individuals to solve their own problems) (Ogborne, 1996). What addiction recovery mutual-aid societies have provided is an esteem-salvaging framework for understanding illness, a cognitive and emotional road map of recovery, a strategy for reframing and countering stigma, and social support and fellowship. In this section, we explore what the mental health field can learn from the addiction recovery mutual-aid societies.

Addiction recovery mutual-aid societies in America have a long and rich history. Eighteenth-century Native American recovery "circles" and other abstinence-based cultural and religious revitalization movements mark the beginning of peer-based models of alcoholism recovery (White, 1998). These were followed in the 19th century by mutual-aid societies that emerged as part of the "rescue work" of the American temperance movement (White, 2001b). The largest and most geographically dispersed of such societies included the Washingtonian Temperance Societies (1840s), the fraternal temperance societies (1840s–1870s), and the Ribbon Reform

Clubs (1870s). Mutual-aid societies also sprouted within inebriate asylums (Ollapod Club), inebriate homes (Godwin Association), the addiction cure institutes (Keeley Leagues), urban rescue missions (United Order of Ex-Boozers, Drunkard's Club), and early 20th-century alcoholism clinics (Jacoby Club) (White, 2001b).

The founding of Alcoholics Anonymous (AA) in 1935 marks the beginning of modern addiction recovery mutual-aid societies. AA has become the standard by which all mutual-aid groups are measured because of its size (2.2 million members and more than 100,000 groups worldwide; 1.1 million members in the United States alone), its geographical dispersion (more than 175 countries), and its longevity (more than 65 years) (http://www.alcoholics-anonymous.org). As AA grew, its 12-step program was adapted for family members (Al-Anon, founded in 1951), for people addicted to drugs other than alcohol (Narcotics Anonymous, founded in 1947–1953, and Cocaine Anonymous, founded in 1982), and for people experiencing addiction and other problems (Dual Disorders Anonymous, founded in 1982, and Dual Recovery Anonymous, founded in 1989). There were also a growing number of religious adjuncts to AA (Alcoholics Victorious, founded in 1948; the Calix Society, founded in 1949; Jewish Alcoholics, Chemically Dependent People and Significant Others, founded in 1979) and alternatives to AA (Women for Sobriety, founded in 1975; Secular Organization for Sobriety, founded in 1985; Rational Recovery, founded in 1986; LifeRing Secular Recovery, founded in 1999; Teen-Anon, founded in 1999; and Moderation Management, founded in 1994) (White, 2003). All of this offers testimony to the growing varieties of recovery experience within and outside of Alcoholics Anonymous.

Addiction recovery mutual-aid societies constitute an important historical backdrop to modern mutual-aid societies in the mental health field, for example, consider Recovery, Inc. (founded in 1937), GROW, Inc. (1957), Emotions Anonymous (1971), National Alliance for the Mentally Ill (NAMI; 1979), Anxiety Disorders Association of America (1980), Schizophrenics Anonymous (1985), National Depressive and Manic-Depressive Association (1986), and Obsessive-Compulsive Foundation, Inc. (1986).[1] Because of the longer history, larger membership, and greater geographical dissemination of addiction recovery mutual-aid groups, we thought that some of what has been learned in these groups might be helpful to existing and new recovery mutual-aid groups in the mental health field. Seen as a whole, the addiction recovery mutual-aid societies offer 10 lessons about the promises and perils of peer-based models of recovery

---

[1]The functions of mutual aid and advocacy are much more likely to be blended within the same organization within the mental health field.

support. These 10 lessons are discussed next and are from White (2001a) unless otherwise noted.

Recovery for Disempowered People

Addiction recovery for historically disempowered peoples (groups that have experienced physical or cultural assault, enslavement, economic exploitation, and oppression) must be offered within a framework of hope for a community as well as the individual and family. Such frameworks have been particularly evident with Native American and African American communities, which still experience the effects of such oppression. For example, African Americans represent 15% of illicit drug users, but more than 60% of drug offenders entering prison; 1 in 20 African American men older than age 18 is under the control of the criminal justice system (U.S. Department of Justice, 2000). Substance-involved African American women are 10 times more likely to be reported to child welfare agencies for prenatal drug exposure than their Caucasian counterparts (Neuspeil, 1996). In such communities, abstinence-based cultural and religious revitalization movements have long provided a shared pathway of addiction recovery and community survival and renewal (Coyhis & White, 2002; Williams & Laird, 1992). When Native American leaders proclaim that "the community is the treatment center," they point out the inextricable link between personal recovery and the broader health of the community in which that recovery is nested (*The Red Road to Wellbriety*, 2002). Such proclamations simultaneously provide hope to individuals and hope for the future of a people.

Vulnerability for Colonization

Recovery mutual-aid societies are vulnerable to colonization by more powerful forces within their operating environments, particularly domination by larger social or professional movements. AA, for example, was deluged with groups wanting to join and use AA to address a wide variety of problems other than alcoholism. AA took the position that other groups could adapt the 12 steps and traditions for their own use but could not become a member of AA unless they met AA membership criteria ("a desire to stop drinking"). The most resilient of the recovery mutual-aid societies are ones that maintain their indigenous leadership and "closed" meeting structure.

Successful recovery mutual-aid societies must also carefully construct their relationship with professionally directed treatment agencies. The historical relationship between mutual-aid societies and treatment institutions is a complex one. Treatment institutions have emerged from mutual-aid organizations, for example, the 19th-century Washingtonian Homes. Treatment institutions have co-opted and corrupted mutual-aid organizations; consider, for example, the attempt to manipulate the Keeley Leagues to market the proprietary services of the Keeley Institutes. Treatment institutions have also created partnerships with mutual-aid societies in which boundaries were clear and respected, as seen in the relationship between AA and local hospitals in the 1940s and 1950s.

The long history of strain between mutual-aid societies and professional treatment agencies has centered on (a) poorly defined boundaries between mutual aid and professional treatment, particularly when people in recovery are hired to do the latter; (b) differences in philosophies and helping practices; and (c) the near universal attempt by professional agencies to colonize or at least control mutual-aid movements. This tension has pervaded the history of mutual-aid movements in the United States as well as the Alcoholic Treatment Clubs in Italy (Patussi, Tumino, & Poldrugo, 1996) and the Abstainer Clubs in Poland (Swiatkiewicz, 1992). Professionals have played important roles in the birth of many mutual-aid societies, but have also played a role in conflict that has led to the demise of such groups.

Forces of Dissension

Professionalism, money, property, publicity, and religious/political conflict are potential forces of dissension that can threaten the survival of local mutual-aid societies. Money and professionalism are particularly problematic. Addiction mutual-aid programs—from the Washingtonians in the United States (White, 1998) to the Links Societies in Sweden (Kurube, 1992)—have experienced strife when their members assumed paid helping roles. In Germany, for example, recovery activists condemn paid service work on the grounds that it creates status hierarchies within the recovery community (Appel, 1996). Guidelines governing how such dual roles can be maintained have helped manage these potential problems (A.A. *Guidelines*, 1993). Maintaining ideological and financial autonomy seems to be crucial to the survival and health of mutual-aid societies. Outside funding has often turned out to be a mechanism of control and co-optation, and mutual-aid groups have a long history of death via ideological (political and religious) schisms. Conflict over money, religion, and politics within the early history of AA led AA to pledge itself to corporate poverty, self-sufficiency, and neutrality on all outside issues. On the basis of AA's example, American mutual-aid societies have, until recently, tended to be financially self-supporting and neutral on questions of political or religious doctrine, whereas such societies in Europe are much more likely to be financially supported by the state (e.g., the Abstainer Clubs in Poland) and to be linked to particular political movements (e.g., the New Left influence on mutual-aid groups in Germany; Room, 1998). The recent growth of faith-based recovery ministries, church-based mutual-aid recovery groups, and the funding of these ministries by federal, state, and local governments marks a new chapter in the history of mutual aid in America; these groups constitute a living experiment whose processes and fate warrant close examination.

Sharing Experience, Strength. and Hope

The centerpiece of all successful recovery mutual-aid groups is the process of sharing experience, strength, and hope. The glue of such societies is mutual identification and mentorship within relationships that are time sustained, nonhierarchical, and noncommercialized. Recovery mutual-aid groups constitute a community of shared vulnerability whose members draw resilience and power from the safety of this sanctuary to do things within their lives in consort that they could not do alone. These communities of recovery also constitute cultures of resilience and recovery (with their own language, values, rituals, and symbols) that for many constitutes an alternative to the cultures of pathology and dependence within which they have been enmeshed. It is here that the most personal and intimate experiences of healing are wed to an intuitive understanding of the social ecology of recovery.

Transcending Charismatic Founders

A major challenge of mutual-aid societies is transcending the foibles and deaths of their founding, charismatic leaders. The Ribbon Reform Clubs that thrived across America in the 1870s and 1880s as local sobriety-based support fellowships collapsed as their charismatic leaders aged, became infirm, and died. Successful mutual-aid societies emphasize leadership development and rotation. For example, in AA groups, there are no elected officers and the meetings are chaired by a variety of members rather than by a single leader.

Decentralized Organization

The most resilient of the mutual-aid societies use a highly decentralized cell structure; the essential organizational unit is the small, local group that provides its members a venue for mutual identification and support. Such decentralization allows forces of potential disruption (e.g., explosive growth, personality conflicts, ideological schisms) to serve as mechanisms of growth via the spawning of new groups rather than member attrition.

Responding to Social Stigma

All addiction recovery mutual-aid societies have had to decide how their members should respond to social stigma, from encouraging bold visibility (public declarations of one's addiction and recovery) to hiding one's stigmatized status via assurances of secrecy and anonymity. In cultures in which addiction or mental illness is highly stigmatized, mutual-aid societies have provided a variety of vehicles through which their members can salvage their "spoiled identities." The Keeley Leagues of the 1890s defined recovery as a sign of manhood. Members were boldly challenged to write letters to local newspapers proclaiming their recoveries, and they proudly wore the Keeley League pin on their clothing. In contrast, other societies have promised their members confidentiality and have discouraged or prohibited public disclosures of their affiliation. Where some societies integrate recovery and advocacy, others become secret societies. An interesting question is the extent to which such secrecy actually serves to perpetuate stigma. One is forced to wonder: What would the effect have been on public attitudes and public policies if hundreds of thousands of people in recovery from addiction or mental illness had publicly proclaimed their recovery during the past decades? Strategies that protect members from stigma at an individual level may inadvertently help perpetuate that very stigma at a societal level. Some recovery advocates argue that living in silence and secrecy in terms of one's recovery status perpetuates stigma by withholding faces and voices of successful recovery and placing in the national consciousness images only of those who fail to recover.

The Need for a Framework of Core Values

Successful recovery mutual-aid societies must have both a "program" or operational framework of recovery (e.g., AA's 12 steps) and a set of core values (e.g., AA's 12 traditions) to manage forces that can threaten the life of the organization. These forces include those earlier noted (ideology, professionalism, publicity, and money) as well as personality conflicts and sexual attraction or behavior among members. Successful mutual-aid societies develop values ("group conscience") and rituals to minimize interpersonal conflict (e.g., AA's emphasis on "principles before personalities") and protect vulnerable members from potential exploitation by other members (e.g., the sexual exploitation of new members pejoratively referred to in AA as "thirteenth stepping").

Membership and the Society's Life Span

The length of expected member involvement in a mutual-aid society must reflect both the time span of needed recovery support of its members and what will be required to maintain the life of the organization. Lifelong mutual-aid participation may not be a requirement for effective self-management of recovery, but a core of individuals committed to such participation may be crucial to the survival of any recovery mutual-aid society.

Coexisting Mutual-Aid Societies

Recovery mutual-aid societies can peacefully coexist, collectively offering a menu of pathways of recovery, or they can enter into competition and conflict in an effort to define the "right" pathway of recovery. The former is illustrated by the coexistence of many recovery support societies in Germany (Appel, 1996); the latter is illustrated by the acrimony that has sometimes characterized the relationship between members of AA and members of secular and religious alternatives to AA (White, 1998). Recovery pluralism is evident in the number of people who simultaneously participate in more than one mutual-aid society or who move from one society to another during different stages of their recovery careers (Appel, 1996; Humphreys & Klaw, 2001).

Although the preceding lessons are deeply imbedded within the history of addiction recovery mutual-aid societies, they may not apply universally to the organizational processes of shared recovery from mental illness. In applying these lessons to the mental health field, the following question seems apt: What is qualitatively different about mental illness and recovery from mental illness that would influence the ideal structure and process of mutual-aid groups? A definitive history of such groups that answers that question has yet to be written. (See chap. 6, this volume, for a related discussion of mutual-aid groups for people with schizophrenia.)

RECOVERY ADVOCACY MOVEMENTS

Substantial differences exist between peer-based recovery movements and recovery advocacy movements. The former focus on the needs of the individual for mutual support of long-term recovery; the latter focus on promoting pro-recovery attitudes, social policies, and recovery-oriented systems of care. Although advocacy movements provide a voice to the experiences and needs of people in recovery that may have therapeutic effects, their target is primarily the social and political environment rather than the individual. Recovery advocacy provides a means through which people in recovery can confront stigma and its resulting social and institutional obstacles to recovery and shape service systems that reflect their own aspirations and needs. In this section, we explore the history of recovery advocacy in the addictions field with a particular eye on what this history may offer regarding recovery advocacy within the mental health field.

There is a long history of recovery advocacy in both the addiction and mental health fields. The former range from 19th-century patient clubs to the local alcoholism councils of the mid-20th century (White, 1998); the latter span early patient advocates (Elizabeth Packard, Elizabeth Stone, and Clifford Beers) to the rise of an ex-patients' movement in the 1970s (Chamberlin, 1984, 1990, 1995; Frese, 1998; Kaufmann, 1999; McLean, 1995). The restigmatization and recriminalization of the status of addiction in the United States in the 1980s and 1990s has spurred the rise of a New Recovery Advocacy Movement (White, 2000b). In this section, we describe this movement and compare it to the C/S/X movement within the mental health field.

Representative Organizations

Organizationally, the New Recovery Advocacy Movement is made up of (a) local affiliates of the National Council of Alcoholism and Drug Dependence who are trying to recapture their advocacy roots, (b) grantees of the Center for Substance Abuse Treatment's Recovery Community Support Program (RCSP, 2004), (c) faith-based recovery ministries, (d) abstinence-based cultural revitalization movements in communities of color, and (e) survivor organizations (family members who have lost a loved one to addiction). These organizations are loosely linked through their involvement in various recovery advocacy conferences and the National Faces and Voices of Recovery Campaign (http://www.facesandvoicesofrecovery.org). These organizations are the historical counterparts to the National Association of Mental Patients (later the National Association of Psychiatric Survivors), the National Mental Health Consumers' Union, and the earlier noted mutual-aid societies (e.g., NAMI) that also function as advocacy organizations.

Membership Constituency

Although membership in mental health advocacy organizations such as NAMI and local mental health associations has until recently been dominated by family members and professionals, the addiction recovery advocacy movement has been dominated by people in recovery from addiction. As each of these respective movements matures, its constituencies expand, with people in recovery from mental illness now emerging as a powerful force within the mental health advocacy movement and family members becoming increasingly involved in the New (Addiction) Recovery Advocacy Movement.

Membership Recruitment

The greatest barrier to recruitment in both the addiction and mental health recovery advocacy movements is fear of the stigma associated with public disclosure of one's recovery status. The addictions field has an added concern about clarifying the potential conflict between the requirement for anonymity within AA and Narcotics Anonymous (NA) and encouragement by advocacy groups to step forward to put a face and a voice on recovery (White, 2000b). Those RCSP grantees working to organize the (addiction) recovery community during the past 5 years have found that considerable groundwork must be laid before significant numbers of people in recovery join or participate in recovery advocacy activities.

Movement Goals

The goals of the New Recovery Advocacy Movement are to (a) portray alcoholism and addictions as problems for which there are viable and varied recovery solutions; (b) provide role models that illustrate the diversity of those recovery solutions; (c) counter attempts to dehumanize, objectify, and demonize people with alcohol- and other drug-related problems; (d) enhance the variety, availability, and quality of local/regional treatment and recovery support services; (e) remove environmental barriers to recovery; and (f) promote pro-recovery laws and social policies.

Core Values

The values of recovery advocacy organizations are reflected in the core values adopted by the board of Recovery Communities United in Chicago:

1. Primacy of personal recovery (reminding ourselves that service work alone is not a viable program of addiction recovery),
2. Authenticity of voice and representation (empowering recovering people and their family members to express their own needs and aspirations),
3. Varieties of recovery experience (respecting varied pathways, styles, and stages of recovery),
4. Diversity and inclusion (representation of all people in recovery across the boundaries of age, gender, ethnicity, sexual orientation, and problem severity),
5. Hope-based interventions (providing "living proof" of the reality of long-term recovery to those in need of recovery, to service professionals, and to the larger community),
6. Resilience and recovery (focusing on the strengths of individuals, families, and communities),
7. Collaboration (community-building between recovering people/families, treatment providers, indigenous healers/institutions, and researchers),
8. Recovery community development (building the service and leadership capacity of the recovery community rather than competing, replacing, or otherwise undermining the natural leadership and service ethic of that community), and
9. Ethics of mutual support (elevating our ethical sensitivities and decision-making skills within the arena of recovery support services).

Kinetic Ideas

In 1942, Dwight Anderson coined a set of "kinetic" ideas (ideas capable of shifting people's attitudes and actions) that were later integrated into the campaign of the National Committee for Education on Alcoholism, the precursor to today's National Council on Alcoholism and Drug Dependence (Anderson, 1942; Mann, 1944). These ideas were intended to reframe the nature of the problem ("Alcoholism is a disease"), change the perception of those with the problem ("the alcoholic is a sick person"), and posit hope for the problem ("the alcoholic can be helped and is worthy of being helped"). These ideas became the ideological foundation for modern addiction treatment.

A reformulated set of kinetic ideas is emerging within the New Recovery Advocacy Movement (NRAM). Each idea is designed as an antidote to a prevailing idea within the culture. In response to renewed cultural pessimism about the prospects of recovery, the NRAM is declaring that recovery is a living reality in the lives of hundreds of thousands of individuals, families, and communities. Internally, this movement is calling for a vanguard of recovering people to step forward publicly to offer "living proof" of the transformative power of recovery. In response to the idea that there is only one way to recover, the NRAM is declaring that there are many pathways of recovery. In response to a treatment system that has become increasingly coercive, the NRAM is declaring that recovery is a voluntary process. In response to the restigmatization and recriminalization of the status of addiction, the NRAM is declaring that recovery flourishes in supportive communities (White, 2000b). Local recovery advocates across the country are enlisting the support of local policy makers to help create the physical, psychological, and social space where the seeds of recovery can be sown and nurtured into maturity. The NRAM is offering its members as evidence that recovery gives back what addiction has taken from individuals, families, and communities and that recovering and recovered people are part of the solution (to alcohol and other drug problems).

Core Strategies

Eight strategies make up the action agenda of (addiction) recovery advocacy organizations:

1. *Recovery organization.* Develop leadership within communities of recovery so that these groups can declare their existence, express their collective voice, and provide a venue for community service.
2. *Recovery representation.* Ensure that the voices of recovering people and their families are included in all venues that address severe and persistent alcohol and other drug problems.
3. *Recovery needs assessment.* Identify obstacles to recovery, evaluate existing service structures, and prioritize needed recovery support services.

4. *Recovery education*. Educate lay and professional audiences on the varieties, stages, and styles of addiction recovery.
5. *Resource development*. Cultivate volunteerism within the recovery community and expand philanthropic and public support for recovery support resources.
6. *Policy advocacy*. Champion (through negotiation and social action) stigma-reduction and pro-recovery policies at federal, state, and local levels.
7. *Recovery celebration*. Enhance the identity and cohesion of local recovery communities, make recovery visible within the larger community, and put faces and voices on recovery via major media outlets.
8. *Recovery research*. Support studies to illuminate the strategies, structures, and processes associated with long-term recovery.

The experiences of the local organizations that make up the New Recovery Advocacy Movement offer some lessons for their counterparts within the mental health field. First, the specialization and fragmentation of recovery advocacy movements is almost inevitable given the diversity of experiences and varying needs of recovering people and their families, the competition for public attention and limited financial resources, and the threats such movements pose to established mutual-aid groups, service professions, and service institutions (Kaufmann, 1999). Schisms within advocacy movements reflect different views of addiction and mental illness, different languages used to characterize these conditions, and sometimes radically different visions about the desired alternative to the existing service system. Battles between various advocacy factions may also reflect internalized stigma and the avoidance of confrontation with more powerful forces outside the movement. Such displacement has a long history among the social movements of disempowered peoples.

The problems of organizational leadership and structure that have long plagued recovery mutual-aid societies also pose a threat to recovery advocacy organizations. Charismatic leadership and hierarchical structures can undermine the egalitarian, democratic values of these movements and alienate leaders from grassroots constituencies (McLean, 1995). Minimalist approaches to organization and rotating leadership constitute viable antidotes to such tendencies.

Advocacy organizations that evolve into alternative service organizations are vulnerable to losing their advocacy focus as they get caught up with funding requirements and the demands of running a service organization. This happened to many local councils on alcoholism in the 1960s and 1970s when funding became available for community-based alcoholism treatment. Advocacy groups that pose a threat to the status and financial interests of service professionals and treatment institutions are often colonized by these institutions via recruitment of leaders into paid roles, by pitting moderate groups against more radical groups, and by the theft, dilution, and distortion of the language and core concepts of advocacy groups (McLean, 1995).

The trend in both the mental health and the addictions field is to hire consumers within mainstream service agencies or to develop consumer-controlled and -operated agencies that provide a wide spectrum of recovery support services. These agencies vary in their philosophies, with some serving as adjuncts to professional treatment and others competing as alternatives to professional treatment. These roles and agencies constitute the emerging service frontier of the mental health and addictions fields and will force a rethinking of many areas of service philosophy, design, and delivery. No area within this reevaluation is likely to be more difficult than the issue of appropriate, ethical boundaries in the relationship between service providers, whether paid or volunteer, and service consumers. Both fields need to invest substantial energy in redefining such standards as the relationship hierarchies collapse and as the line between service provider and service consumer becomes less distinguishable.

SUMMARY

In this chapter, we have tried to explore what has been learned within the addictions and mental health fields about the recovery experience, the lessons learned within the addiction field about recovery mutual aid, and recovery advocacy. Many shared characteristics and themes are seen in recovery from addiction and from mental illness: definitional controversies; the role of self as the "agent of recovery"; levels of recovery (partial, full, and transcendent); the variability of pathways, styles, and stages of recovery; the roles of recovery debits and recovery capital; the sequencing of change across multiple zones of recovery (physical, intellectual, emotional, relational, rituals of daily life, and spiritual); and the adaptation demands on the family to both illness and recovery. Service work has a distinguished role within the history of recovery, but there are pitfalls as well as promises in the professionalization of such service activities. Such professionalization must be actively managed to reduce potential harm to the "prosumer," other service consumers, the service organization, and local recovery mutual-aid and recovery advocacy organizations.

Lessons from the history of addiction recovery mutual-aid societies that have salience for other mutual-aid groups include the potentially destructive influences of colonization, professionalization, money, property, publicity, and religious/political conflict. The most successful and enduring mutual-aid societies maintain their singularity of purpose and closed meeting structure; use a flattened, decentralized organizational structure; regularly rotate leadership at the national and local levels; craft a preferred style of responding to social stigma; and create both a framework (program) of personal recovery and a set of core values to protect the organization and enhance its future viability.

Recovery advocacy organizations in the addictions and mental health fields share many characteristics (and some subtle differences) in the evolving areas of their membership, organizational goals, core values, central ideas, and core strategies. As the addictions and mental health fields are again being pushed toward greater collaboration and integration, the recovery concept seems to be a bridge of shared experience and a vision through which these fields can reach out to one another. Particularly promising are states such as Connecticut where human service policy leaders are reshaping both the addiction and mental health service systems around this recovery vision. We close this investigation believing that there is great potential for positive synergy between these two fields whose histories have been so closely related for more than two centuries, and that the recovery concept may provide a framework for such synergy.

REFERENCES

A.A. guidelines for A.A. members employed in the alcoholism field. (1993). New York: General Service Office, Alcoholics Anonymous.

Anderson, D. (1942). Alcohol and public opinion. Quarterly Journal of Studies on Alcohol, 3, 376–392.

Anthony, W. A. (1993). Recovery from mental illness: The guiding vision of the mental health service system in the 1990s. Psychosocial Rehabilitation Journal, 16, 11–23.

Anthony, W. A. (2000). A recovery-oriented system: Setting some system level standards. Psychiatric Rehabilitation Journal, 24(2), 159–168.

Appel, C. (1996). Different stories: Self-help groups for alcoholics and illicit drug users in Germany. Contemporary Drug Problems, 23, 57–75.

Basto, M., Pratt, C. W., Gill, K. J., & Barrett, N. M. (2000). The organizational assimilation of consumer providers: A quantitative examination. Psychiatric Rehabilitation Skills, 4, 105–119.

Breslau, N., Peterson, N., Schultz, L., Anderski, P., & Chilcoat, H. (1996). Are smokers with alcohol disorders less likely to quit? American Journal of Public Health, 86, 985–990.

Brown, S. (1985). Treating the alcoholic: A developmental model of recovery. New York: Wiley.

Brown, S. (1994). What is the family recovery process? The Addiction Letter, 10(10), 1–2.

Brown, S., & Lewis, B. (1999). The alcoholic family in recovery: A developmental model. New York: Guilford Press.

Burman, S. (1997). The challenge of sobriety: Natural recovery without treatment and self-help programs. *Journal of Substance Abuse, 9*, 41–61.

Carlson, L. S., Rapp, C. A., & McDiarmid, D. (2001). Hiring consumer-providers: Barriers and alternative solutions. *Community Mental Health Journal, 37*, 199–213.

Chamberlin, J. (1978). *On our own: Patient controlled alternatives to the mental health system.* New York: McGraw-Hill.

Chamberlin, J. (1984). Speaking for ourselves: An overview of the ex-psychiatric inmates movement. *Psychosocial Rehabilitation Journal, 8*(2), 56–64.

Chamberlin, J. (1990). The ex-patients' movement: Where we've been and where we're going. *Journal of Mind and Behavior, 11*, 323–336.

Chamberlin, J. (1995). Rehabilitating ourselves: The psychiatric survivor movement. *International Journal of Mental Health, 24*(1), 39–46.

Cohen, D. (1994). Neuroleptic drug treatment of schizophrenia: The state of the confusion. *The Journal of Mind and Behavior, 15*, 139–156.

Cohen, D., & McCubbin, M. (1990). The political economy of tardive dyskinesia: Asymmetries in power and responsibility. *The Journal of Mind and Behavior, 11*, 465–488.

Coyhis, D., & White, W. (2002). Addiction and recovery in Native America: Lost history, enduring lessons. *Counselor, 3*(5), 16–20.

Davidson, L., & Strauss, J. S. (1992). Sense of self in recovery from severe mental illness. *British Journal of Medical Psychology, 65*, 131–145.

Deegan, P. (1988). Recovery: The lived experience of rehabilitation. *Psychosocial Rehabilitation Journal, 11*(4), 11–19.

Deegan, P. (1990). Spirit breaking: When the helping professions hurt. *Humanistic Psychologist, 18*(3), 301–313.

Deegan, P. (1992). The independent living movement and people with psychiatric disabilities: Taking back control over our own lives. *Psychosocial Rehabilitation Journal, 15*(3), 3–19.

Frese, F. (1998). Advocacy, recovery, and the challenges of consumerism for schizophrenia. *Psychiatric Clinics of North America, 21*(1), 233–249.

Granfield, R., & Cloud, W. (1999). *Coming clean: Overcoming addiction without treatment.* New York: New York University Press.

Harding, C. M. (1989). Long-term follow-up studies of schizophrenia: Recent findings and surprising implications. *Yale Psychiatric Quarterly, 11*(3), 3–5.

Harding, C. M., Brooks, G., Ashikaga, T., Strauss, J., & Breier, A. (1987). The Vermont longitudinal study of persons with severe mental illness, I: Methodology, study sample, and overall status 32 years later. *American Journal of Psychiatry, 144*(6), 718–726.

Harding, C. M., Zubin, J., & Strauss, J. S. (1992). Chronicity in schizophrenia: Revisited. *British Journal of Psychiatry, 161*, 27–37.

Humphreys, K., & Klaw, E. (2001). Can targeting nondependent problem drinkers and providing Internet-based services expand access to assistance for alcohol problems? A study of moderation management self-help/mutual aid organization. *Journal of Studies on Alcohol, 62*, 528–532.

Humphreys, K., Moos, R. H., & Finney, J. W. (1995). Two pathways out of drinking problems without professional treatment. *Addictive Behaviors, 20*, 427–441.

Jacobson, N. (2001). Experiencing recovery: A dimensional analysis of recovery narratives. *Psychiatric Rehabilitation Journal, 24*, 248–256.

Johnson, J. R. (1993). J. Rock Johnson. *NAMI Advocate, 14*(5), 5–6.

Kandel, D. B., & Raveis, V. H. (1989). Cessation of drug use in young adulthood. *Archives of General Psychiatry, 46*, 109–116.

Kaufmann, C. (1999). An introduction to the mental health consumer movement. In A. Horwitz & T. Scheid (Eds.), *A handbook for the study of mental health: Social contexts, theories, and systems* (pp. 493–507). Edinburgh, Scotland: Cambridge University Press.

Kurube, N. (1992). The ideological and organizational development of the Swedish Links movement. *Contemporary Drug Problems, 19*, 649–676.

Liberman, R. P., & Kopelowicz, A. (2002). Recovery from schizophrenia: A challenge for the 21st century. *International Review of Psychiatry, 14*, 245–255.

Lindgren, K. N., & Coursey, R. D. (1995). Spirituality and serious mental illness: A two-part study. *Psychosocial Rehabilitation Journal, 18*, 93–111.

Mann, M. (1944). Formation of a national committee for education on alcoholism. *Quarterly Journal of Studies on Alcohol, 5*(2), 354.

McLean, A. (1995). Empowerment and the psychiatric consumer/ex-patient movement in the United States: Contradictions, crisis and change. *Social Science Medicine, 40*(8), 1053–1971.

McLellan, A. T., Lewis, D. C., O'Brien, C. P., & Kleber, H. D. (2000). Drug dependence, a chronic medical illness: Implications for treatment, insurance, and outcomes evaluation. *Journal of the American Medical Association, 284*, 1689–1695.

Miller, W., & C' de Baca, J. (2001). *Quantum change: When epiphanies and sudden insights transform ordinary lives.* New York: Guilford Press.

Morse, J. (1997). Responding to threats to integrity of self. *Advances in Nursing Science, 19*(4), 21–36.

Mowbray, C. T., Moxley, D. P., Jasper, C. A., & Howell, L. L. (Eds.). (1997). *Consumers as providers in psychiatric rehabilitation.* Columbia, MD: International Association of Psychosocial Rehabilitation Services.

Neuspeil, D. R. (1996). Racism and perinatal addiction. *Ethnicity and Disease, 6*, 47–55.

Noordsy, D., Torrey, E. Mueser, K., Mead, S., O'Keefe, & Fox, L. (2002). Recovery from severe mental illness: An intrapersonal and functional outcome definition. *International Review of Psychiatry, 14*, 318–326.

Ogborne, A. (1996). Addiction mutual-help movements in comparative perspective. *Contemporary Drug Problems, 23*, 1–8.

Onken, S. J., Dumont, J. M., Ridgway, P., Dornan, D. H., & Ralph, R. (2002). *Mental health recovery: What helps and what hinders?* Retrieved September 10, 2003, from National Technical Assistance Center for State Mental Health Planning, National Association of State Mental Health Program Directors Web site: http://www.nasmhpd.org/ntac/reports/MHSIPReport.pdf

Patussi, V., Tumino, E., & Poldrugo, F. (1996). The development of the alcoholic treatment club system in Italy: Fifteen years of experience. *Contemporary Drug Problems, 23,* 29–42.

Prochaska, J., DiClimente, C., & Norcross, J. (1992). In search of how people change. *American Psychologist, 47,* 1102–1114.

Prochaska, J. O., Norcross, J. C., & DiClemente, C. O. (1994). *Changing for good.* New York: Avon Books.

Ralph, R. O. (2000). Recovery. *Psychiatric Rehabilitation Skills, 4*(3), 480-517.

Recovery community support program. (2004). Retrieved March 29, 2004, from Treatment Improvement Exchange Web site: http://www.treatment.org and http://www.ncaddillinois.org

The red road to wellbriety: In the Native American way. (2002). Colorado Springs, CO: White Bison, Inc.

Ridgway, P. (2001). Restorying psychiatric disability: Learning from first person recovery narratives. *Psychiatric Rehabilitation Journal, 24,* 335–343.

Room, R. (1998). Mutual help movement for alcohol problems in an international perspective. *Addiction Research, 6,* 131–145.

Salzer, M. S., & Shear, S. L. (2002). Identifying consumer-provider benefits in evaluations of consumer-delivered services. *Psychiatric Rehabilitation Journal, 25,* 281–288.

Spaniol, L., & Zipple, A. M. (1994). The family recovery process. *The Journal of the California Alliance for the Mentally Ill, 5*(2), 57–59.

Spaniol, S., & Cattaneo, M. (1997). The power of language in the helping relationship. In L. Spaniol, C. Gagne, & M. Koehler (Eds.), *Psychological and social aspects of psychiatric disability* (pp. 477–484). Boston: Center for Psychiatric Rehabilitation.

Spaniol, S., Gagne, C., & Koehler, M. (2003). The recovery framework in rehabilitation and mental health. In D. Moxley (Ed.), *Sourcebook of mental health and rehabilitation* (pp. 37–50). Boston: Kluwer Academic Publishing.

Strauss, J. S., Hafez, H., Lieberman, P., & Harding, C. M. (1985). The course of psychiatric disorder, III: Longitudinal principles. *American Journal of Psychiatry, 42,* 289–296.

Sullivan, W. (1994). A long and winding road: The process of recovery from severe mental illness. *Innovations in Research, 3*(3), 19–27.

Swiatkiewicz, G. (1992). Self-help abstainer clubs in Poland. *Contemporary Drug Problems, 19,* 677–687.

Unzicker, R. (1989). On my own: A personal journey through madness and re-emergence. *Psychosocial Rehabilitation Journal, 13*(1), 71–77.

U.S. Department of Justice, Bureau of Justice Statistics. (2000, April). *Prisoners and jail inmates at midyear 1999*. Washington, DC: Author.

Vaillant, G. (1983). *The natural history of alcoholism: Causes, patterns, and paths to recovery*. Cambridge, MA: Harvard University Press.

Valenstein, E. S. (1998). *Blaming the brain: The truth about drugs and mental health*. New York: Free Press.

Weaver Randall, K. (2000). *Understanding recovery from schizophrenia in a mutual-help setting*. Unpublished master's thesis, Michigan State University, East Lansing.

White, W. (1979). *Relapse as a phenomenon of staff burnout in recovering substance abusers*. Rockville, MD: HCS, Inc.

White, W. (1996). *Pathways from the culture of addiction to the culture of recovery*. Center City, MN: Hazelden.

White, W. (1998). *Slaying the dragon: The history of addiction treatment and recovery in America*. Bloomington, IL: Chestnut Health Systems.

White, W. (2000a). The history of recovered people as wounded healers: I. From Native America to the rise of the modern alcoholism movement. *Alcoholism Treatment Quarterly, 18*(1), 1–23.

White, W. (2000b, April). *Toward a new recovery movement: Historical reflections on recovery, treatment and advocacy*. Paper presented at the Recovery Community Support Program Conference, Washington, DC. Retrieved March 29, 2004, from http://www.facesandvoicesofrecovery.org

White, W. (2001a). The New Recovery Advocacy Movement: A call to service. *Counselor, 2*(6), 64–67.

White, W. (2001b). Pre-A.A. alcoholic mutual aid societies. *Alcoholism Treatment Quarterly, 19*(1), 1–21.

White, W. (2001c). *The rhetoric of recovery advocacy: An essay on the power of language*. Retrieved March 29, 2004, from http://www.facesandvoicesofrecovery.org

White, W. (2003). Alcoholic mutual aid societies. In J. Blocker & I. Tyrell (Eds.), *Alcohol and Temperance in Modern History* (pp. 24-27). Santa Barbara, CA: ABC-CLIO.

White, W., Boyle, M., & Loveland, D. (2002). Addiction as a chronic disease: From rhetoric to clinical reality. *Alcoholism Treatment Quarterly, 20*(3–4), 107–130.

Williams, C., & Laird, R. (1992). *No hiding place: Empowerment and recovery for troubled communities*. New York: Harper San Francisco.

Young, S., & Ensing, D. (1999). Exploring recovery from the perspective of people with psychiatric disabilities. *Psychiatric Rehabilitation Journal, 22*(3), 219–239.

AUTHOR INDEX

Numbers in italics refer to listings in the reference sections.

Matt, A., 86, 91, *98*
Matt, G., *55*
Mattoo, S. K., *55*
Maude, D., 103, *124*
May, P. R., 113, *127*
Mayerhoff, D. I., *127*
Mays, V., 42, *52*
Mazelis, R., 226, *230*
Mazure, C. M., 111, *123*
McCarthy, E., 42, *56*
McCormick, R. V., 29, *51*, 65, 80, 102, *124*
McCubbin, M., 239, *255*
McDiarmid, D., 241, *255*
McFarlane, W. R., *15*
McGlashan, T. H., 30, 32, *51*, 67–68, 72–73, *82*, 112–114, 117, *123–124*
McGlashan, T. K., *127*
McGonagle, K. A., *97*
McGorry, P. D., 103, 113, *124*, *127*
McGovern, M. P., 111, *127*
McGowen, M., 119, *123*
McGrew, J., 46, *55*
McKenzie, J., 118, *127*
McLean, A., 248, 253, *256*
McLellan, A. T., 234, *256*
Mead, S., 35, *55–56*, *128*, 151, 153, *169*, 175, 203, *256*
Mechanic, D., 86, 91, *99*
Medley, I., 29, 53, *55*
Meiser, J., 119, *123*
Meisler, N., *15*, *123*
Mellman, T. A., 8, *16*
Menaghan, E. G., 88, *98*
Meyer, I., 209, *230*
Meyer, J. W., 175, 178, *203*
Michael, S. T., *99*
Michael, T., *58*
Mickelson, K. D., 179, *203*
Miele, L., 113, *126*
Mihalopoulos, C., 103, *127*
Miller, A. L., *16*
Miller, D. H., 92, *98*, 223, *230*
Miller, J. B., 209, *228*
Miller, W., 237, *256*
Mills, T., 209, *228*
Minkoff, K., *15*
Mintz, J., 77, *81–82*, 104, 117–118, *124*, *126–128*
Mintz, L. I., 104, *127*
Mirabi, M., 78, *83*
Mirotznik, J., 86, *97*
Mirowsky, J., 86–88, 92, *98*

Misra, A. K., *55*
Miya, M., *83*, *128*
Mojtabai, R., 29, *55*
Moller, H. J., 30, *55*
Monck, E., 149, *170*
Moorhead, S., 42, *52*
Moos, R. H., 46, *55*, 236, *256*
Mordel, C., *81*
Morgan, O., *16*
Moriss, R., 42, *56*
Morris, D. L., 117, *127*
Morris, L. L., 46, *54*
Morse, J., 19, 27, 37, *56*, 238, *256*
Moses, D. J., 226, *230*
Mowbray, C. T., 241, *256*
Moxley, D. P., 241, *256*
Mueller, C., 67, *80*
Muenz, L. R., 210, *230*
Muenzenmaier, K., 209–210, 223, 228, *230*
Mueser, K. T., 8–9, *16–17*, 42, *52*, *56–57*, 114, *128*, 209, 226, 228, *230–231*, *256*
Mullan, J. T, 88, *98*
Mullins, S. D., *231*
Munetz, M., 152, *169*
Munoz, R., *81*
Murphy, C., 78, *80*
Murrin, M., 209, *228*
Mussey, C., *202*

Najavits, L. M., 210, 223, *230*
Nakazawa, M., *83*, *128*
Narrow, W. E., 7, *16*
Naveh, G., *96*
Nelson, B. A., 209, *228*
Nelson, C. B., 91, *97*, 208, *230*
Nelson, G., 48, *56*, 86, *98*
Nelson, J. C., 111, *123*
Nelson, K., 77, *82*
Nelson, S. D., 20, *50*
Neria, Y., 209–210, *231*
Neuspeil, D. R., *256*
Nicassio, P. M., 26, *57*
Nickou, C., *168*
Noordsy, D., 47, *56*, 106, *128*, 239, *256*
Norcross, J. C., 136, *145*, 237, *257*
Nuechterlein, K. H., *81*, 110, 115, *124*, *128*
Nugter, M. A., 117, *129*
Nunally, J. C., *56*

Oakley, J., 86, *96*

SUBJECT INDEX

Family environment
    addiction recovery affected by, 240
    recovery affected by, 110–111
    schizophrenia affected by, 76–77,
        110–111
    stress in, 111
    support of, 134
Feedback, 39
Fidelity assessments of recovery models, 46
First-person accounts of recovery
    citizenship renewal, 153
    commitment, 151
    description of, 149–150
    hope, 151
    meaningful activities, 152
    redefining of self, 151–152
    self-acceptance, 151–152
    self-control, 153
    self-responsibility, 153
    social roles, 152
    stigmatization, 153
    support of others, 151

Global Assessment Scale, 43–44
Grounded theory analysis, 36
GROW, 180, 182

Hebephrenic schizophrenia, 76
Helper-therapy principle, 182
Hope
    definition of, 6
    recovery and, 5, 133, 151
    renewal of, 238
Hope Scale, 43
Hospitalization, 45

"I am" position, 164–165
"I have" position, 164–165
Incremental change, 237–238
Industrialized societies, 77–78
Inspiration, 11
Institutionalization, 166
Intent-to-treat, 42
Internalization, 153, 157
International Pilot Study of
    Schizophrenia, 65
Iowa 500 study, 66, 71t
Isolation, 133–134, 182–183

Japanese long-term study, 68, 72t

Kinetic ideas, 250–251

Kraepelin, Emil, 63–65

Labeling, 89, 155–156
Lausanne study, 67, 72t
Life satisfaction
    self-esteem effects on, 93
    self-perception and, 92
Longitudinal studies
    components of, 28–29
    cross-study comparison difficulties for,
        30
    description of, 28
    duration of, 30–31
    historical time frame, 30–31
    methodologic variations in, 29–30
    patient exclusions, 31–32
    patient selection, 31–32
    purpose of, 28
    sample attrition, 31
    self-concept, 93
    social causation, 91
    stress-process perspectives, 91
    structure of, 29

Maine–Vermont Comparison Study, 69,
    72t
Medication
    addiction recovery assisted by,
        239–240
    antipsychotic, for schizophrenia,
        74–75, 113–115
Medicine Wheel, 136–137
Mental health services
    changes in, 233–234
    consumer-operated, 9
    evidence-based approach to, 9
    recovery after participation in, 8
    settings for, 174–176
    types of, 8
Mental Health Statistics Improvement
    Project, 46
Mental illness. *See also* Schizophrenia
    adverse consequences of, 90–91
    biomedical model of, 25, 26
    biopsychosocial model of, 26
    consumer/survivor/ex-patient model
        of, 26–27
    despair associated with, 133
    identification of, 155–156
    isolation secondary to, 133–134
    life-altering changes associated with,
        150

Mental illness (*continued*)
posttraumatic stress disorder and, 209
reactions to diagnosis of, 133
refuge from, 159
self-acceptance, 151–152
self-labeling of, 155–156
self-recovery from, 7
socioeconomic status and, 87–88
somatic interventions for, 25–26
stigma associated with, 78, 89, 152
substance use disorder and,
concomitant presentation of,
32
Mutual-help groups. *See also* Self-help
groups
Alcoholics Anonymous, 180
assumptions of, 182
background of, 174–177
beliefs of, 179
colonization vulnerabilities for,
244–245
community narratives from, 179–181
definition of, 179
description of, 173–174
dissension in, 245
experiential knowledge as foundation
of, 177, 183, 201
functioning of, 176–177
GROW, 180, 182
opportunity role structures provided
by, 181–182
participation in, 179
peers in, 180
personal frameworks established by,
178
personal stories in, 179–181
professional treatment agencies and,
244–245
role models in, 181
roles offered in, 181–182
Schizophrenics Anonymous. *See*
Schizophrenics Anonymous
sense of belonging offered by,
182–183
social support gained from, 182–183
statistics regarding, 179
summary of, 200–201
unique characteristics of, 178

Narrative
community
description of, 179–181

Schizophrenics Anonymous
example, 185–192
personal, 176
Narrative interviews
adaptation, 162–165
coping, 162–165
description of, 154
loss of self, 154–158
reconstruction of self, 160–162
supported socialization, 158–160
National New Freedom Commission on
Mental Health, 13
Naturalistic-longitudinal studies
components of, 28–29
cross-study comparison difficulties for,
30
description of, 28
duration of, 30–31
historical time frame, 30–31
methodologic variations in, 29–30
patient exclusions, 31–32
patient selection, 31–32
purpose of, 28
sample attrition, 31
structure of, 29
Neuroleptics, 113
New Recovery Advocacy Movement
advocacy groups, 252
core strategies, 251–252
core values of, 250
description of, 243
dissension in, 252
goals, 249–250
kinetic ideas of, 250–251
leadership in, 252
membership constituency and
recruitment, 249
organizational structure of,
248–249
NRAM. *See* New Recovery Advocacy
Movement

Opportunity role structures
definition of, 175
in mutual-help groups, 181–182
Schizophrenics Anonymous example
of, 194–195
Outpatient treatment, 12

Paranoid schizophrenia, 76
Participatory action research,
148–149

Social causation and selection, 86–88, 91
Social comparison theory, 181
Social life
    negotiation of contact with, 163–164
    stigma effects on, 156–157
Societal indicators of recovery, 45
Socioeconomic status
    historical studies of, 86–87
    mental illness and, 87–88
Spirit-breaking, 157
Spirituality, 6, 162, 239
Stigma
    addiction-related, 240
    mental illness-related, 89, 152
    mutual-help groups response to,
        245–246
    overcoming of, 153
    recovery and, 89
    of schizophrenia, 78–79
    self-concept effects, 89
    self-esteem effects, 89
    social effects of, 156–157
Stress, family-related, 111
Stress-process model, 88–89, 91
Substance abuse
    psychiatric illness and, concomitant
        presentation of, 32
    schizophrenia recovery affected by,
        111–112
Substance Abuse and Mental Health
        Services Administration, 177
Suicide rates, 86–87
Sullivan, Harry Stack, 166
Support
    of others, 134, 151, 158–160
    social, 182–183, 195–197
Supported socialization, 158–160
Supportive therapy, for schizophrenia,
    114–115
Surveys, 43–44
Symptoms
    management of, 152–153
    negative, 116–117
    remission of, 104
    self-concept effects on, 92
    self-esteem effects on, 93

social factors related to, 91

Theory-driven program evaluations,
    40–41
Tracking, 28
Transcendent recovery, 235–236
Transferability, of qualitative methods, 37
Transformational change, 237–238
Treatment
    capitation model of, 119
    changes in, 233–234
    contextual factors that affect, 41
    dropout rates, 41
    evidence-based approaches to, 9
    historical investigations of, 25–27
    recovery vs., 235
    recovery-oriented, 93
    settings for, 174–176
    types of, 8
Triangulation, 37–39

Verbal recovery models
    description of, 132–134
    Recovery Advisory Group Recovery
        Model, 136–137
    summary of, 143–144
Vermont Longitudinal Research Project,
    68–69, 72t, 103–104
Visual recovery models
    childhood sexual abuse, 211–223
    description of, 131–132, 135
    Empowerment Vision of Recovery
        from Mental Illness, 135
    Medicine Wheel, 136–137
    Public Health Model for the Recovery
        of Adult Mental Health
        Consumers, 135–136
    Recovery Advisory Group Recovery
        Model, 136–137
    summary of, 143–144

World Health Organization
    Determinants of Outcome of Severe
        Mental Disorder study, 76
    schizophrenia studies, 33, 65–66, 70,
        72t

ABOUT THE EDITORS

Ruth O. Ralph, PhD, senior research associate at the Edmund S. Muskie School of Public Service at the University of Southern Maine, is a consumer researcher who has conducted mental health research and evaluation for more than 25 years in both Ohio and Maine. Dr. Ralph was the principal investigator of the Maine site—one of seven sites across the country—for the federally funded Cooperative Agreement for the Evaluation of Consumer Operated Services. She has assisted consumer groups in the development of concepts of recovery and has written articles and presented several papers on recovery concepts and dimensions at national conferences. She coordinated a group of consumer leaders, the Recovery Advisory Group, in a series of teleconferences to discuss and define recovery, the result of which has been the development of *The Recovery Model*. Dr. Ralph and colleagues have developed a *Compendium of Recovery and Related Measures*, which includes instruments and information about their development. She was a consumer representative on the Planning Board of the Surgeon General's Report on Mental Health (1999), for which she has written a review of recovery literature. Dr. Ralph has also coordinated a group of consumer writers to develop four other papers as contributions to this important report, which were published in a special issue of *Psychiatric Rehabilitation Skills*.

Patrick W. Corrigan, PsyD, is professor of psychiatry at the University of Chicago where he directs the Center for Psychiatric Rehabilitation, a research and training program dedicated to the needs of people with serious mental illness and their families. Dr. Corrigan has been principal investigator of federally funded studies on rehabilitation, team leadership, and consumer operated services. Two years ago, he became principal investigator of the Chicago Consortium for Stigma Research (CCSR), the only National

Institute of Mental Health funded research center examining the stigma of mental illness. The CCSR comprises more than two dozen basic behavioral and mental health services researchers from nine Chicago area universities and currently has more than 20 active investigations in this area. Dr. Corrigan is a prolific researcher, having published more than 150 papers and 7 books including *Don't Call Me Nuts! Coping With the Stigma of Mental Illness*, coauthored with Bob Lundin.